"This book has two considerable virtues. On the one hand, it counterbalances the negative view of kingship that is often prevalent in biblical scholarship with a more balanced picture. On the other hand, it rightly insists that Kings, no less than Chronicles, is a stylized theological account. There is no direct access to the underlying history."

> —John J. Collins
> Holmes Professor of Old Testament
> Yale Divinity School

"Garrett Galvin provides a case study of five successo... ..... legendary King David—Jeroboam, Ahab, Hezekiah, Manasseh, and Josiah. Each of these controversial kings is remembered chiefly by what the deuteronomistic history says about them. But Galvin helpfully reminds us that twentieth-century thinking often misunderstands ancient kingship and neglects sources more sympathetic to kingship, such as Chronicles and the Psalms. A stimulating and accessible reexamination of a central biblical topic."

> —Richard Clifford, SJ
> Professor Emeritus of Old Testament
> Boston College School of Theology and Ministry

"Garrett Galvin invites us to view the kings of Israel and Judah within the perspectives of biblical and ancient Near Eastern understandings of monarchy. He uses the lenses of the Historical Books of the Bible as well as Psalms, Ruth, Song of Songs, Ecclesiastes, Lamentations, and Esther along with findings from storytelling, archaeology, political science, and cultural studies of ancient Near Eastern kingship to present a nuanced, multifaceted picture of the biblical kings. They were created in the image of God, with human strengths and weaknesses. Galvin's holistic approach is a refreshing contribution to biblical study in today's environment of suspicion and polarization with regard to power and authority, leaders and leadership."

> —Joan E. Cook, SC
> President, Sisters of Charity of Cincinnati

"Galvin's study of the kings, *David's Successors*, backs away from many of the typical notions of kingship in the Bible found in standard histories of Israel and Judah or introductions to the Old Testament. This 'narrative' relies heavily on the books of Samuel through Kings, the deuteronomistic history, with its highly negative view of the kings, read through the critical lens of corrupt and brutal regimes of the twentieth century (including Stalin, Hitler, and Mao). Galvin proposes a 'more nuanced vision of kingship' based on newer approaches to the question: social science analyses, interdisciplinary studies, and intertextual biblical interpretation. His introduction of these different methodologies demonstrates the impact of recent decades of Old Testament scholarship offering new vistas for our imagination."

—John Endres, SJ
Professor of Sacred Scripture, Old Testament
Jesuit School of Theology of Santa Clara University

David's Successors
Kingship in the Old Testament

Garrett Galvin, OFM

A Michael Glazier Book

LITURGICAL PRESS
Collegeville, Minnesota

www.litpress.org

A Michael Glazier Book published by Liturgical Press

Cover design by Ann Blattner. Illustrations courtesy of Wikimedia Commons. Used with permission.

Unless otherwise indicated, Scripture texts in this work are taken from the *New American Bible with Revised New Testament and Revised Psalms*, © 1991, 1986, 1970 Confraternity of Christian Doctrine, Washington, DC, and are used by permission of the copyright owner. All rights reserved. No part of the *New American Bible* may be reproduced in any form without permission in writing from the copyright owner.

© 2016 by Order of Saint Benedict, Collegeville, Minnesota. All rights reserved. No part of this book may be reproduced in any form, by print, microfilm, microfiche, mechanical recording, photocopying, translation, or by any other means, known or yet unknown, for any purpose except brief quotations in reviews, without the previous written permission of Liturgical Press, Saint John's Abbey, PO Box 7500, Collegeville, Minnesota 56321-7500. Printed in the United States of America.

Library of Congress Cataloging-in-Publication Data

Names: Galvin, Garrett, 1968– author.
Title: David's successors : kingship in the Old Testament / Garrett Galvin, OFM.
Description: Collegeville, Minnesota : Liturgical Press, 2016. | "A Michael Glazier book." | Includes bibliographical references.
Identifiers: LCCN 2016009625 (print) | LCCN 2016031827 (ebook) | ISBN 9780814682517 | ISBN 9780814682760
Subjects: LCSH: Kings and rulers—Biblical teaching. | Bible. Old Testament—Criticism, interpretation, etc.
Classification: LCC BS579.K5 G35 2016 (print) | LCC BS579.K5 (ebook) | DDC 221.6/7--dc23
LC record available at https://lccn.loc.gov/2016009625

For Michael Joseph Galvin

Contents

Preface   ix

1. New Insights: An Introduction to an Interdisciplinary Analysis   1

2. Kingship: An Institution Rather than an Individual   19

3. Jeroboam: Heretic or Hero?   40

4. Ahab: Omri's Son or Jezebel's Husband?   62

5. Hezekiah: Religious Reformer and Realist   83

6. Manasseh: Evil Incarnate?   103

7. Josiah: A Perfect King?   122

Conclusion   143

Bibliography   152

Scripture Index   161

Author and Subject Index   166

Preface

There is a partially apocryphal story told about Joseph Stalin by Aleksandr Solzhenitsyn.[1] If it is not completely true, it should be. He was rolling out one of his many five-year plans. He would go around the then–Soviet Union, speaking to local district conferences in the various Soviet republics. These speeches were highly orchestrated affairs. It seems like a bizarre understatement to say that he was an egoist, but there were elaborate rituals before these speeches. The various groups of party members at these congresses were forced by convention to applaud for fifteen or twenty minutes before he ever said a word. Many of these party members were well-intentioned individuals who were in the wrong place at the wrong time in terms of living in the Soviet Union. There were many communists who were just good people trying to survive in a system run amok. At a district conference, one of these well-intentioned individuals decided that Stalin must have something important to say and all this endless applause was unnecessary because there was significant work to be done. He was the leader of this district conference and he decided to sit down after ten minutes. The rest of the bureaucrats followed suit. After the speech, he was promptly arrested for lack of respect to Premier Stalin.

This piece of history tells us something very important about the course of twentieth-century history. Between Stalin, Hitler, and Mao, the world has never seen political cruelty and mass murder on such a scale. This has rightfully influenced Old Testament scholarship. It is easy to read examples of autocracy and political cruelty in the Old Testament, but I think we must ask the question whether biblical studies have been too influenced by the twentieth century. Is the twentieth century really all that similar to biblical Israel and Judah? One scholar

---

[1] "On Violence: Russian Facts Behaving Badly," http://onviolence.com/?e=815.

has claimed that Solomon's advisers would have been perfectly compatible in the Germany of the late thirties of the last century. Is this going too far? Rather than a vision of monsters with a few angelic kings, this study seeks a more nuanced version of kingship.

I will argue for a new reading of kingship in the Old Testament. Rather than take our lead from the worst excesses of the twentieth century, I would like to understand kingship from all the books of the Bible and the understanding of it in the countries around biblical Israel and Judah. Many of the excesses of biblical kingship are only available to us from one source or another, such as 2 Samuel or 2 Kings, yet these are frequently the best known stories about a king. When the Psalms or Chronicles or Sirach do not validate this story, they are dismissed as royal propaganda. I would like to consider all these sources as we reflect on kingship. Rather than focusing on the most negative and pessimistic sources, I think it is important to ponder all the sources. The Bible in Genesis 1 invites us into a hermeneutic in which we view all humans as being made in the image and likeness of God—this includes even kings. So rather than viewing kingship through the lens of the mass murderers of the twentieth century, I believe the Bible fundamentally leads us to understand kings, like the rest of us, as being made in the image of God. The Old Testament preserves many stories of royal atonement, redemption, and conversion. While this is far from the entire story, we must consider this as part of the royal story. I do not desire to whitewash the kings, but I think we have gone too far in the other direction of equating the kings with the worst excesses of the twentieth century.

I will proceed to consider the original concept and context of kingship before concentrating on five kings in particular: Jeroboam, Ahab, Hezekiah, Manasseh, and Josiah. Before looking at these individuals, a brief study of the Royal Psalms and the idea of kingship in other countries of the ancient Near East will be made. While Kings and Chronicles will be the primary sources for most of this book, the Royal Psalms will always have to be in the back of our minds. The Royal Psalms may contain the greatest influence from outside Israel. I will argue that there is nothing wrong with outside influence if we take Genesis 1:26-28 seriously. God's influence is not found in Israel alone, and we have much to learn from exploring the countries around Israel and considering their influence on Israel.

This study is ultimately rooted in a hopeful view of humanity. While one never has to go far to find sin, the divine presence also permeates this world and can be found in kings and politicians alike, no matter how unpopular this view may be. Genesis 1:26-28 is not conditional. I am arguing for a more balanced view of both the nations around Israel and kingship itself. This does not mean there are not great problems with kings and that it is not an outdated institution today, but it does mean there is a need for a reappraisal of biblical kingship and both its potential and successes.

Chapter One
ॐ

New Insights
An Introduction to an Interdisciplinary Analysis

I will use this chapter to present an interdisciplinary methodology. By using intertextual biblical interpretation, social science analysis, and literary criticism, the reader will gain a fresh understanding of the material relevant to kingship. The juxtaposition of methodologies may initially surprise readers, but it will also allow them to frame the text and characters in a new manner. My point will be the need for a new understanding of kingship that resonates with the reality of the Psalms and the books of Chronicles. I will make five case studies.

A. Introduction

Kingship has consumed biblical scholars for centuries. A wide variety of texts confront both scholar and pious reader alike. People have noted the realistic picture of the many failed kings described in books like Samuel, Kings, and Chronicles. The tensions involving kingship have yielded profound literature like the Parable of the Trees in Judges 9. The tensions in biblical times have often translated into our times, as we have shifted in Europe from monarchies and dictatorships over the last 150 years to constitutional democracies. Biblical scholars have been part of this process and influenced by it. Many have seen predecessors of these kings and dictators in the Old Testament as they have imagined societies struggling with the same difficulties.¹ These views may be best represented in Baruch Halpern's *The Constitution of the Monarchy in Israel*.²

Halpern argues legal restrictions controlled the monarchy. This offers a picture of the Israelite and Judean monarchies as very different institutions than their neighbors. As his work was a revised Harvard dissertation, one can easily imagine that Halpern simply reflected the prevailing wisdom of the time. This seems to be a wisdom that in part emanates from George Mendenhall. Mendenhall argues that the "reversion to the old Bronze Age paganism of the United Monarchy is thus a process of rapid erosion of the basic principles of the new religious ethic that stems from Moses."³ Mendenhall understands this process in the inflammatory language of the "paganization of the Jerusalem state."⁴ This viewpoint would seem to stem from an overly literal reading of the Old Testament. Rather than seeing the programmatic nature of elements of the Old Testament like Deuteronomy 17, Joshua 24, and 1 Samuel 8 and 12, Mendenhall and others understand a sharp break from the indigenous culture to Moses and finally to King Solomon.⁵ Halpern will argue: "[T]he Davidic and other Israelite dynasties labored under two laws: the law of Yhwh, and the law of political reality."⁶ This is exactly as Deuteronomy 17 would have it, but I do not think this represents the breadth of the Old Testament, especially the Royal Psalms. We can also read into Halpern's statement similar, if not more subtle, concerns about modern democracies that Mendenhall expressed in more inflammatory language. Devel-

---

¹ George E. Mendenhall, "The Monarchy," *Interpretation* 29, no. 2 (1975): 157: "[I]t has already been argued effectively that a succession of empires imitated their predecessors at least from ancient Assyria to czarist Russia."

² Baruch Halpern, *The Constitution of the Monarchy in Israel*, Harvard Semitic Monographs 25 (Chico, CA: Scholars Press, 1981), 252: "The covenant between king and people served for them to contain theoretical royal authority; and the covenant between king and people on the one hand and god on the other was conservative of inherited practices and vetitive of new ones."

³ Mendenhall, "The Monarchy," 158.

⁴ Ibid., 164.

⁵ Ibid., 159: "Since there can be little doubt that the ideological change derived from the pre-Mosaic pagan tradition of ancient Canaan, there is little ground left for arguing that the changes in social organization stemmed from any but that same ancient pre-Mosaic source."

⁶ Halpern, *The Constitution of the Monarchy in Israel*, 252.

opments since Mendenhall's time display much less assurance about the nature of early Israel. While the book of Joshua will demonstrate big differences with the indigenous culture, the book of Judges will present a more subtle picture. Many will question what society these books are actually portraying and whether they force us to confront a constructed history, especially in the book of Joshua. Rather than blame an "erosion" of Mosaic principles or a "rapid evolution" of kingship, it may be safer to be parsimonious about what we can actually say about early Israel.

This parsimony starts to become evident in Keith Whitelam's *The Just King*.[7] Whitelam describes a process of early restricted monarchical power being replaced by growing monarchical power. David's early forays into judicial power will ultimately develop into "a court of reference in Jerusalem under Jehoshaphat [which] was regarded as an extension of such royal legislative power."[8] Whitelam will go on to argue that while the monarchy was powerful from an early date, "[T]he monarchy gave rise to new categories, e.g., crown officials, the royal estate, etc., which were obviously outside the terms of reference of the already well-established judicial system of the local communities."[9] Contemporary historiography cautions us to be careful about how much access we actually have to past societies through texts such as the Old Testament. I will explore this more fully in the chapter on Hezekiah and will argue that the Deuteronomistic Historian (hereafter DH) worked hard to create this perception of an earlier, pure time, as reflected in Joshua 24, which was replaced by the corrupting influence of kingship (with a few notable exceptions). A growing body of scholarship has focused us on programmatic chapters within the Deuteronomistic History that revise more positive notions of kingship that originally undergirded the whole of the Bible as we find in the Royal Psalms.

Recent studies have stressed just how different biblical times are from our own times. Many have understood the historical books from Joshua to 2 Kings as a narrative of moving from uniquely biblical leaders like Moses and Joshua to many decadent kings in the period

---

[7] Keith W. Whitelam, *The Just King: Monarchical Judicial Authority in Ancient Israel*, Journal for the Study of the Old Testament Supplement Series 12 (Sheffield, UK: JSOT Press, 1979).
[8] Ibid., 218.
[9] Ibid., 220.

of the Divided Kingdom. This view has been challenged by Bernard Levinson, who has argued for the reconceptualization of kingship in Israel: "There is no reason that ancient Israel differed from any other ancient Near Eastern state in its view of the king."[10] This statement forces us to consider kingship in a new light. Rather than paralleling the monarchies and dictatorships that were overthrown in the nineteenth and twentieth centuries, kingship in Israel has evolved from a very different climate. Although kingship in Israel embodies unique elements, it also shares many of the elements from the nations that surrounded it. I will elaborate on this in chapter 2.

Levinson's reconceptualization emanates from the ideological nature of parts of the Old Testament. We can understand the Deuteronomistic History (Deuteronomy–2 Kings) as the subordination of the king to a sovereign legal text,[11] a text which DH has a large part in promulgating. By labeling this as reconceptualization, the dominant notions of Israelite kingship are seen as notions promulgated by scribes rather than representing what the social sciences can help us understand regarding the popular will. Levinson's insights about Deuteronomy 17 are confirmed and carried forth in the book of Samuel. Christophe Nihan argues that 1 Samuel offers a "contrasted image" of kingship that both presents it as a concession to the people and yet allows it to retain something of its sacral status in that both Saul and David are elected by Yahweh.[12] The same reconceptualization found in Deuteronomy 17 occurs in 1 Samuel 8 and 12. First Samuel 12:17b marks the strongest element in this revisionary layer: "Thus you will see and understand how greatly the LORD is displeased that you have asked for a king." Nihan also identifies "the language and ideology of the revisionary layer identified in 8:7b-8 and 10:18-19."[13] Although we see this reconceptualization at work in 1 Samuel, it still is not as marked as Deuteronomy 17, where the powers of the kings are greatly restricted. Joshua 24 discusses the idealized figure of Joshua, but

---

[10] Bernard M. Levinson, "The Reconceptualization of Kingship in Deuteronomy and the Deuteronomistic History's Transformation of Torah," *Vetus Testamentum* 51, no. 4 (October 2001): 511.

[11] Ibid., 532.

[12] Christophe Nihan, "Rewriting Kingship in Samuel: 1 Samuel 8 and 12 and the Law of the King (Deuteronomy 17)," *Hebrew Bible and Ancient Israel* 2, no. 3 (2013): 338.

[13] Ibid., 343.

the book of Samuel must deal with the more human aspects of the figures of Saul and David, who evoke a wide range of emotions. This will become even stronger in the book of Kings, where the authors will promote "more positive"[14] views of the kings. The belief in sacral kingship seems to become stronger the further we move from Deuteronomy 17. It is minimal in 1 Samuel, a little stronger in 1–2 Kings, stronger still in 1–2 Chronicles, and robust in the Psalms.

Recent scholarship has focused more on the popular will. Mark Hamilton asks us: "To pick up the concerns of the late Foucault, in what ways and to what extent do lower-status persons exert power upon the King, limiting (or enhancing) his power? And how does the discipline, display, or exercise of the body play a role?"[15] Hamilton's concerns seem to be quite contrary to the concerns of an older generation thinking about kingship. The social sciences will expose a broader set of interests rather than focusing solely on what the texts allow us to see. As I try to conceive the original conceptualization of the king, I will use the social sciences and biblical texts that offer both DH's perspective and different perspectives on kingship than DH in order to understand kingship.

B. Intertextual Biblical Interpretation

The Old Testament offers us many different views of kingship. We will have a wide range of views—from a very limited array of monarchical power in Deuteronomy to maximal notions of a king and what a king represents in the Psalms. We will find views on kingship becoming more nuanced as we work our way through the Deuteronomistic History, with more diversity at the end of it. The Writing Prophets will also expose a number of different views on kingship, with wide variations from Isaiah to Jeremiah. Finally, we will consider the Megilloth (Ruth, Song, Ecclesiastes, Lamentations, and Esther) and the more compassionate and humanistic views on display there.

1. Deuteronomy 17

Bernard Levinson has already shown us what a central role Deuteronomy 17 has played in setting out the image of the king. The book

---

[14] Ibid., 319.

[15] Mark W. Hamilton, *The Body Royal: The Social Poetics of Kingship in Ancient Israel*, Biblical Interpretation Series (Leiden/Boston: Brill, 2005), 15.

of Deuteronomy treats monarchy in a section concerned with institutions of a secular character, including the judiciary in Deuteronomy 16 and the military in Deuteronomy 20. This has led Moshe Weinfeld to characterize the book of Deuteronomy as having "an absence of sacral institutions."[16] This absence points to Deuteronomy characterizing kingship in a much different way than both the rest of the ancient Near East and much of the Old Testament. For example, we find much more sacral characterizations of kingship in the Psalms. Jeffrey Tigay will tell us that in Deuteronomy 17:14-20, [T]he "role of the king—the official likely to become the most powerful and prestigious—is deemphasized more than that of any other official."[17] Tigay will go on to contrast Israel with Mesopotamia and Egypt, where kingship was absolute, and conclude that these absolute "ideas had few echoes in Israel."[18] While these ideas may not be echoed here in Deuteronomy 17, I will argue that Deuteronomy 17 is responding to echoes of these ideas in other parts of the Old Testament and wonder about how assured we can be of "few echoes in Israel." Was Israel really that different from the rest of the ancient Near East? Do we find few echoes of Mesopotamian prayer forms in the Old Testament? Do we find few echoes of ancient Near Eastern tribal practices in the Old Testament?

Deuteronomy focuses on the ideal rather than the real. Levinson has helped us to understand Deuteronomy 17 as a reconceptualization. The reality of what we find in 1–2 Kings and 1–2 Chronicles has been conformed to the vision of the authors of Deuteronomy. Thomas Mann will argue: "Deuteronomy recognizes the reality, but holds out for the *ideal* ruler."[19] This ideal ruler may finally appear at the end of 2 Kings in Josiah, but the reality from Saul to Manasseh may be very different from what we encounter in the pages of the Bible. Rather than treat Israel as an entity completely foreign to the ancient Near East, political science would suggest that its peoples may have the same desire for kingship as the rest of the ancient Near East. The scribal class has

---

[16] Moshe Weinfeld, *Deuteronomy 1–11: A New Translation with Introduction and Commentary*, Anchor Bible, vol. 5 (New York: Doubleday, 1991), 29.

[17] Jeffrey H. Tigay, *Deuteronomy: The Traditional Hebrew Text with the New JPS Translation*, JPS Torah Commentary (Philadelphia: Jewish Publication Society, 1996), 166.

[18] Ibid.

[19] Thomas W. Mann, *Deuteronomy*, Westminster Bible Companion (Louisville, KY: Westminster John Knox Press, 1995), 126.

constructed an ideal vision here in Deuteronomy, but this is a small class of people with very different interests and influences than the vast majority.

2. 1 Samuel

Christophe Nihan has demonstrated for us how 1 Samuel participates in the reconceptualization of kingship in a more limited manner than Deuteronomy 17. While Deuteronomy 17 treats kingship in a completely secular manner, 1 Samuel still acknowledges some of the sacral nature of Israelite kingship that overflows from the Enthronement Psalms (47; 93; 96–99) and Psalms 74 and 89 as Yahweh asserts to kingship. Critics have noted that 1 Samuel 8–12 seems to combine "a pro- and an antimonarchical source."[20] This section starts with the frank admission of the corrupting influences on the sons of Samuel (1 Sam 8:3). First Samuel 8:11-17 leaves no doubt about the hazards of kingship, as Samuel warns the people that the king will take their sons, daughters, and land for his own needs; yet the chapter concludes with the Lord telling Samuel: "Grant their request and appoint a king to rule them" (1 Sam 8:22a). After noting the relationship between Deuteronomy 17 and 1 Samuel 8, McCarter will acknowledge the sacral nature present here that is not present in Deuteronomy 17: "And in a sense kingship receives a divine sanction here, even if only in a backhanded way, for Yahweh himself consents to the appointment."[21] 1 Samuel 8 may be trying to strike a balance between older notions of the sacral nature of kings and the actual history of having to endure and indulge the excesses of kingship.

If 1 Samuel 8 tries to strike a balance, 1 Samuel 12 moves much more in the direction of Deuteronomy 17. Samuel has granted the wishes of the people and set a king over them (1 Sam 12:1), but he is not about to relinquish all of his power, as he quickly attests to his own virtues of honesty and justice (1 Sam 12:3). Being both a judge and a prophet, Samuel seems willing to cede his powers as judge while maximizing his powers as prophet. "Samuel appears to be claiming an ongoing role before the Lord's anointed. He is far from having been

---

[20] David Jobling, *1 Samuel*, Berit Olam (Collegeville, MN: Liturgical Press, 1998), 71.

[21] P. Kyle McCarter, *I Samuel: A New Translation*, Anchor Bible, vol. 8 (Garden City, NY: Doubleday, 1980), 162.

completely supplanted."[22] The ambiguity found in 1 Samuel 8–12 will play itself out throughout the rest of 1–2 Samuel, but the books will generally have much more positive and sacral accounts of kingship. We will hear of Saul and David as tremendous military leaders remembered for their personal triumphs (1 Sam 18:7). The sacral nature of Saul's kingship manifests itself clearly in the Old Testament as we are told that "God gave him another heart" (1 Sam 10:9), and Saul's peers almost immediately perceive the change (1 Sam 10:11). Samuel discovers David, and we hear that "the LORD rushed upon David" (1 Sam 16:13). We find another maximal presentation of the sacral nature of kingship here. While a prophet remains part of the process, the prophet has become secondary. I believe 1 Samuel 12 can be seen as the last of the maximalist expressions of restrictions on kingly power in the Deuteronomistic History. It shares the spirit of Deuteronomy 17, but the reconceptualization of kingship generally diminishes the further we move from Deuteronomy 17 with the possible exception of Josiah.

3. The Books of Kings

We draw much of the material on the individual kings from the books of Kings. This material comes to us in two basic forms. We have almost standardized reports at the beginning and ending of the life of kings, which many have attributed to some sort of annals. We repeatedly hear about the book of the chronicles of kings of Israel (1 Kgs 16:27) or the book of chronicles of the kings of Judah (2 Kgs 15:31). These reports tend to be summary in nature, connected with the death of the king. In between the reports of the king coming to power or dying, we have much more colorful stories involving the king with his prophets, attendants, and others facing the difficulties and challenges of his time. These stories can be positive about the kings, but they are likely to be quite critical of the king. They have often been used to construct the historiography of the time and used like the annals in a number of histories of Israel. More recent commentators point to the nonhistoriographical nature of the book.[23] This has led to a sea change in how we reconstruct the history of Israel.

---

[22] A. Graeme Auld, *I & II Samuel: A Commentary*, The Old Testament Library (Louisville, KY: Westminster John Knox Press, 2011), 128.

[23] Thomas Römer, "The Case of the Book of Kings," in *Deuteronomy–Kings as Emerging Authoritative Books: A Conversation*, ed. Diana V. Edelman, Ancient Near

4. The Books of Chronicles

The books of Chronicles have been largely overlooked. I will argue for the necessity of thinking about Chronicles as we think about Kings. Many have relegated Chronicles to the status of a tendentious book that cleans up kings like Manasseh. They see the books of Kings as the far more historiographical books. I will argue that both books take theological stances toward the kings rather than objective stances toward the kings. If we see both books as operating out of a powerfully theological hermeneutic, we can see how Chronicles may be a little closer to the original conceptualization of the king. Since it is not part of the Deuteronomistic History like 1–2 Kings, it may allow us a different understanding of kingship that precedes the books of Kings at times. We still need to acknowledge the tremendous influence of the Deuteronomistic History on the books of Chronicles while seeing that there are other influences on Chronicles that do not seem to be as present in the books of Kings.

5. Psalms

While the book of Psalms tells us almost nothing about the individual kings that this book will consider, it will be very helpful in giving us some ideas of the original sacral nature of the king. The psalms represent the fullest expression of the sacral nature of kingship in the Old Testament. Keith Whitelam tells us: "The theme of Yahweh's kingship is given its most explicit treatment in the Psalter."[24] These psalms include Psalms 2, 20, 21, 45, 72, 89, 96–99, 101, 132, and 141. These psalms could not be further from the book of Deuteronomy, which treats the king as a secular institution. These psalms view the king as a wholly transformed being: the anointed of the Lord. "This signifies transformation of his being to that of a man who is fully committed to God's side, as God's representative and heir, as the administrator of God's lordship over Israel."[25] Rather than concerning themselves with the vicissitudes of history, these psalms set out the pure conceptualization

---

East Monographs (Atlanta: Society of Biblical Literature, 2014), 193: "Kings is not much interested in the political achievements of various rulers."

[24] Keith Whitelam, "King and Kingship," in *The Anchor Bible Dictionary*, ed. David Noel Freedman (New York: Doubleday, 1992), 4:43.

[25] Hans-Joachim Kraus, *Theology of the Psalms*, trans. Keith R. Crim (Minneapolis: Augsburg Publishing House, 1986), 115.

of kingship. H.-J. Kraus will tell us the Psalms "present the static world of sacred places and times of worship, while the other books deal with the active dynamic world of the events of history."[26] This book will mostly be considering the other books of dynamic history, but the understanding of Israelite kingship demands that the conceptualization of it from the Psalms not be far from our minds.

Some will say that the Psalms are subjugated to the vision of kingship in Deuteronomy 17:14-20. A common theme emanates from the idea of how different Israel is from the ancient Near East. "The enforcement of law, the source and subject of which was now God and not—in contrast to Egypt and Mesopotamia—the king, also became a *critical institution*, which protected the law from being absorbed by the state or even being turned into its opposite."[27] I believe that we have very little beyond the rhetoric of the Old Testament to differentiate kingship in Israel from the ancient Near East. The Old Testament describes contrasting theological visions, and it is hard to articulate the reality beneath them. It seems safer and more prudent to understand Israel as having many of the same tensions as the other nations of the ancient Near East. This is certainly what we find outside of the idealistic texts concerning the law. I will argue that the fullness of the vision of kingship in the Psalms does not and cannot conform to the texts where kingship is reconceptualized in Deuteronomy 17, 1 Samuel 8, and 1 Samuel 12.

6. Writing Prophets

The so-called Writing Prophets (Isaiah, Jeremiah, and Ezekiel and the Twelve) show an important diversity of opinions toward kingship. We see a figure like Isaiah who works very closely with King Hezekiah. Their relationship is heavily chronicled in both 2 Kings 18–20 and Isaiah 36–39, with a much lighter treatment of it given in Chronicles. Most scholars seem to believe that the Kings text has priority over the Isaiah text as Isaiah seems to be reworking the story.[28] Both sources indicate that Isaiah has important access to him. Second Kings 20:1

---

[26] Ibid., 16.
[27] Bernd Janowski, *Arguing with God: A Theological Anthropology of the Psalms*, trans. Armin Siedlecki (Louisville, KY: Westminster John Knox Press, 2013), 133.
[28] Marvin A. Sweeney, *I & II Kings: A Commentary*, The Old Testament Library (Louisville, KY: Westminster John Knox Press, 2007), 411.

displays a particular closeness between Isaiah and Hezekiah as "the prophet functions as a royal adviser to ensure a proper and orderly succession."[29] Isaiah has bolstered Hezekiah during his standoff with the Assyrians (2 Kgs 19:5-35; Isa 37:21-36), and most commentators see the following episode of Hezekiah's illness (2 Kgs 20:1-3; Isa 38:1-3) as a testament to the strength of their relationship.[30]

Jeremiah is a harder figure to categorize. Parts of his book seem to be quite Deuteronomic, and other parts such as the laments seem to have a theodicy closer to Job. He has even been described as a propagandist on behalf of Josiah.[31] Most of the references to Josiah within Jeremiah are cursory in nature; Josiah is often merely described as the father of Jehoiakim (Jer 35:1) or Zedekiah (Jer 27:1). Jeremiah's only substantive remarks about Josiah are at 22:15, when he is condemning Jehoiakim: "Did not your father eat and drink and do justice and righteousness?"[32]

One can infer from these remarks a certain amount of respect for Josiah, but one does not see the perfect ruler of Judah, as he is described by DH (2 Kgs 23:25). Jeremiah's failure to describe Josiah as a reformer stands in clear contrast to descriptions of Josiah in Kings and Chronicles. This failure to describe Josiah as a reformer is hardly surprising when one considers that Jeremiah condemns the temple in chapter 7, the lack of covenant fidelity in chapter 11, and those who are wise in the Torah in chapter 8. It is notable that Jeremiah does not mention the death of Josiah. Jeremiah had an intense dislike of Israel's political involvement with Egypt, as can be seen from his oracle against Egypt in chapter 46. I wonder why he would fail to mention that Egypt killed this just and righteous king. Jeremiah demonstrates a much more complex relationship with kings than Isaiah. He can see the good in Josiah, but he is implicitly critical of Josiah's successors,

---

[29] T. R. Hobbs, *2 Kings*, Word Biblical Commentary (Waco, TX: Word Books, 1985), 290.

[30] Burke O. Long, *2 Kings*, The Forms of the Old Testament Literature, vol. 10 (Grand Rapids, MI: Eerdmans, 1991), 237.

[31] Norbert Lohfink, "The Cult Reform of Josiah of Judah: 2 Kings 22–23 as a Source for the History of Israel," in *Ancient Israelite Religion: Essays in Honor of Frank Moore Cross*, ed. Patrick D. Miller (Philadelphia: Fortress Press, 1987), 469: "The young Jeremiah also appears to have been active as a propagandist for a pilgrimage to Jerusalem, springing from joy over new salvation to be wrought by Jerusalem."

[32] Scripture translation is by the author.

Jehoiakim (Jer 26:21) and Zedekiah (Jer 29:22). Zedekiah is compared to Ahab, as both were rightfully "roasted" by their adversaries. We end up seeing kingship being far less sacral in Jeremiah than it is in Isaiah.

7. The Megilloth

Finally, we will see different perspectives in the Megilloth (Ruth, Song, Ecclesiastes, Lamentations, Esther). Although these books are found scattered across the Christian Old Testament, they appear in this order in the Hebrew Bible. Kingship comes up in three of the books: Ecclesiastes, Lamentations, and Esther. Solomon is the hero of Ecclesiastes as he dispenses advice and a dissident wisdom to his readers (Eccl 1:1). Solomon will be mentioned six times in Song of Songs, the book that precedes Ecclesiastes. He will also be mentioned three times in a more standard piece of Wisdom literature: Proverbs. I believe all this goes to show a widely held positive attitude toward the king in the popular imagination, as it seems to be important to associate the king with these books. Lamentations concerns the fall of Jerusalem, but it treats kingship respectfully. Lamentations represents a love for even the seemingly disastrous kings that the ideology of DH or Jeremiah does not seem to allow as it mourns "the anointed" (Lam 4:20). The Megilloth closes with the bombastic figure of King Ahasuerus. While he provides mainly comic relief, he is still more part of the solution rather than part of the problem. This figure may highlight a general willingness to forgive the shortcomings of a king and hold his attendants responsible. All these depictions speak in one way or another to the figure of the popular imagination behind the reconceptualization in Deuteronomy 17 and 1 Samuel 8 and 12, which ultimately has diminished in the popular imagination of many contemporary scholars and believers alike.

C. Social Science Analysis

Social science analysis forces us to take seriously the role of the nations around Israel and Judah. Kingship emerges in Israel as the result of the popular demand of the people. Previous generations of scholars have argued for an Israel vastly different from the nations around it, but archeological and historical evidence based on social science argues the opposite. This book will take seriously the needs of the people for an institution that can better serve them. The Bible offers many perspectives on kingship with examples of both good and bad kings. The Bible read as a whole forces the reader to dispatch ideology or theology and try to understand Jeroboam, Ahab, Manasseh, Hezekiah, and Josiah as kings.

Archaeology has demonstrated that the material culture often tells a different story than the Old Testament. While the Old Testament focuses on Jerusalem early and often, the material culture tells us a different story and focuses on the Omrides in the northern kingdom of Israel. "The archaeological evidence also reveals that the Omrides far surpassed any other monarchs in Israel or Judah as builders or administrators."[33] The Omrides refer to the dynasty founded by Omri, who was succeeded by Ahab, Ahaziah, and Joram (ca. 884–842). The Bible gives very little attention to Omri, but I once heard William Dever state at a 2013 conference in San Diego that Omri is the first biblical figure about whom an archaeologist could write a biography. We know the biblical record is very negative about Omri's son Ahab, but Dever claims, "Ahab was one of Israel's most capable rulers, to judge from both the impressive remains that he has left us, as well as the respect accorded to him and his dynasty by his Assyrian enemies."[34] Archaeology tells a different story than the Bible, a story that offers a fresh understanding of kingship that resonates more with a picture of kingship from the Psalms than that of the book of Kings or Deuteronomy.

Political science will force us to consider the realities of the northern kingdom of Israel and Judah as political entities. Israel and Judah are recognized as polities but not on their own terms. Judah is often in an inferior relationship to Israel, although this is not depicted in the Bible. Both states lack the administrative breadth and depth of Assyria, Babylonia, or Egypt. I will frequently offer comparisons to Egypt in order to demonstrate this point. Kingship will also be considered as much more than a king, but rather as a series of relationships with the king at the hub and other important institutions like prophets, priests, and the queen mother playing important roles of legitimation and consultation.

---

[33] Israel Finkelstein and Neil Asher Silberman, *The Bible Unearthed: Archaeology's New Vision of Ancient Israel and the Origin of Its Sacred Texts* (New York/London: Free Press, 2001), 180.

[34] William G. Dever, *What Did the Biblical Writers Know, and When Did They Know It? What Archaeology Can Tell Us about the Reality of Ancient Israel* (Grand Rapids, MI: Eerdmans, 2001), 164.

Although I generally come to the text of the Old Testament with intertestamental and literary concerns, I would also like to think about the cultural memory present in the text. The story of kingship has largely been shaped through the negative lens of the Deuteronomistic History. "All of these set-backs or incidences of suffering can be seen as components of a cultural memory or memories that are themselves based on actual experiences of people or groups within the circle or circles that produced the cultural memory."[35] The Deuteronomistic History is generated from experiences leading to the fall of Jerusalem. Kingship may have been at its weakest at this time. We also must consider other cultural memories than those present in the book of Kings. The Psalms function in a much different way and give us access to different memories and experiences of people that are equally valid.

I will give attention to kingship in Egypt. Although there are considerable differences between kingship in Israel and Egypt, we know a lot more about kingship in Egypt, which will allow us to both confirm some of the expectations of a king in the biblical books and challenge other expectations. While the king was a more exalted position in Egypt than it was throughout the rest of the ancient Near East, I will argue that there are still more similarities than differences between kingship in Egypt and the rest of the ancient Near East.

D. Literary Criticism

As I consider Sacred Scripture, I would also like to focus on the surface meaning of the text. I will use social science analysis to get behind the text or into the world of the text. This is vital for understanding the reconceptualization of kingship that takes place during biblical times. Yet if we pay careful attention through close reading and narratology, it is possible, as Foucault would assert, "to make visible what is invisible only because it's too much on the surface of things."[36] I will try to point to various texts from the Old Testament that show the nature of this reconceptualization of kingship. While we have texts in Deuteronomy 17 and 1 Samuel 8 and 12 that display this reconceptualization, I believe a surface reading of many

---

[35] John W. Rogerson, *A Theology of the Old Testament: Cultural Memory, Communication, and Being Human* (Minneapolis: Fortress Press, 2010), 39.

[36] Stephen Best and Sharon Marcus, "Surface Reading: An Introduction," *Representations* 108, no. 1 (Fall 2009): 13.

other texts will confirm the world behind the text to which the social sciences give us access. The understanding of surface as an intricate verbal structure of literary language "produces close readings that do not seek hidden meanings but focus on unraveling . . . the 'linguistic density' and 'verbal complexity' of literary texts."[37] I will pay careful attention to the Hebrew in which these texts were originally written as surface reading has its limits. Things that are on the surface of a Hebrew text can be hidden in the English text.

Jerome Walsh compares narrative criticism to historical criticism. He argues that the "structure of a narrative text proves to have unexpected complexities comparable to those historical criticism revealed in the author."[38] These complexities become very evident when we compare the book of Kings with the book of Chronicles. Both books are based on a rather parsimonious annalistic source. A close reading of comparable texts reveals different attitudes toward kingship that are right there on the surface of the text. Ultimately, I believe this will lead to a more nuanced reading of the Old Testament, which will "attend to what is present rather than privilege what is absent."[39] Walsh's insights about narrative criticism focus on the "unexpected complexities" of what is present. He will serve as a useful guide to getting the most out of what is present in the text of the Old Testament.

Literary criticism focuses on the importance of simple "storytelling." Rather than constantly mining the pericopes of Kings and Chronicles for historical details, they must be acknowledged first and foremost as stories. "Storytelling—the urge to narrative—is a human universal."[40] Critics will agree that the narratives of Kings and Chronicles act as stories, but they will disagree about the historical content within these stories. Walsh will argue that boundaries between syllables and words are not interesting in terms of narrative, nor are the boundaries between large narrative complexes.[41] "What remains are literary units comparable to the English terms paragraph, episode, scene, and the like—in other words, narrative units that function as subunits of larger,

---

[37] Ibid., 10.

[38] Jerome T. Walsh, *Old Testament Narrative: A Guide to Interpretation* (Louisville, KY: Westminster John Knox Press, 2009), 9.

[39] Best and Marcus, "Surface Reading," 11.

[40] Jerome T. Walsh, *Style and Structure in Biblical Hebrew Narrative* (Collegeville, MN: Liturgical Press, 2001), 1.

[41] Ibid., 117.

connected narratives or closely woven narrative complexes."[42] I will spend a lot of time examining the content of these subunits—how different writers handle similar material but emphasize different things in an episode or a scene. The integrity of these stories, even if they are redactions of an earlier story which we may have seen in the Old Testament, are respected by literary criticism.

Narrative criticism allows different aspects of pericopes to emerge than has traditionally been the case. While they are often mined for history, narratology looks on the historical figures in a different way. Prophets are figures loaded with meaning, but from a narratological perspective, they are often seen within the role of a helper or opponent. The helper or opponent is not the subject of the pericope. They "can give only incidental aid."[43] I believe this perspective helps bring the king to the fore of the text in spite of the theology that might be behind the text. Although the prophets hold a privileged position within the Deuteronomistic History, the very nature of these stories about kings distinguishes between the king as subject and the prophet as helper or opponent. This reinforces the importance of kingship and allows the very nature of the story itself to argue for that importance.

Narrative criticism also points out the artificial nature of oppositions. Kings have often been put in opposition to prophets, but narratology would argue that this is something postbiblical scholars are doing rather than the text itself. Mieke Bal argues: "Oppositions are constructions; it is important not to forget that and 'naturalize' them."[44] We will see kings and prophets play important roles in both Kings and Chronicles. Their roles are often perceived to be different in these books as DH is thought to be less positive toward the king than the Chronicler. If we take Bal's critique seriously, I think we will be forced to take the role of the kings more seriously. Literary criticism seeks to move beyond or behind the constructed oppositions of ideological criticism that has devalued the role of the king at times. As modern readers of the text, it is necessary to confront our biases for governmental forms we would prefer today, but we must allow the past not to be influenced by our current desires. Obviously this is not easy. Bal maintains: "The point is not to notice, confirm, or denounce

---

[42] Ibid.

[43] Mieke Bal, *Narratology: Introduction to the Theory of Narrative*, 3rd ed. (Toronto: University of Toronto Press, 2009), 207.

[44] Ibid., 222.

oppositions but to confront the oppositions we notice with those we hold ourselves, and to use the differences between them as a tool to break their tyranny."[45] We do not want to fall into a "Whig" or progressive view of history where we somehow see ourselves as superior to the biblical peoples.

E. Eclectic Ideas

A number of different scholars have approached kingship in a manner both bridging disciplines and forging new understandings of kingship. These ideas are hard to categorize, but they generally use certain ideas within the social sciences and history that have been underutilized in biblical studies. Mark Hamilton has managed to capture a number of these ideas. He stresses how the royal body is "essential to the well ordering of society, the ramifications of which shape every aspect of social relations in a traditional monarchy."[46] This idea once again stresses the vital importance of a king to society, whether the king is good or bad. The king plays an important role within society that is only partially captured by the stories of good or bad kings. The Psalms help us to capture this role, and we will consider the Psalms' understanding of the king more in a later chapter.

Historiography has been challenged to come to terms with *l'histoire événementielle*. Ever since Braudel's reconceptualization of the ancient Mediterranean, different periods of history have come under investigation through the lens of *l'histoire événementielle's* broader lens of trying to get beyond the events to reconstructing social ideas in general. I will try to place Israel within the ancient Near East, giving attention both to Mesopotamia and Africa. Too often we have focused only on indigenous Egyptian kingdoms, but Israel was influenced by both the Libyan Dynasty in Egypt under Shishak (1 Kgs 11:40; 14:25) and the Nubian Dynasty under Tirhakah (2 Kgs 19:9). While many scholars focus on the exclusivity of Israel, others will point to influences far from Israel that are easily overlooked.

---

[45] Ibid.
[46] Hamilton, *The Body Royal*, 10.

Conclusion

I have argued for a more expansive view of kingship than is generally found in many of the histories of Israel. Rather than limit ourselves to the books of Kings, it is necessary to consider many other factors. The books of Chronicles opens up to us a different perspective on a number of kings. The Royal Psalms militate against the view of kings espoused by Deuteronomy 17:14-20. The social sciences force us to look at other societies of the time and ask whether Israel was really all that different from them. Finally, narrative criticism points to the king as the central figure of these stories. Writers may be positive or negative about the king, but the centrality of the king can never be doubted.

Chapter Two

‿

Kingship
An Institution Rather than an Individual

The institution of kingship in Israel and Judah offers many challenges to those who try to understand it. It emerges from what might be best understood as a "multi-polity decentralized land."[1] The book of Judges is set in a time when we find city-states such as Sidon and territorial kingdoms such as Egypt, but in his unpublished dissertation, Brendan Benz argues that the book of Judges describes a polity that can best be understood as a "multi-polity decentralized land." As we consider the various kings, many of these competing interests flare up. The reader detects many competing interests in the book of Judges. A fundamental question may revolve around just how centralized the leadership of a king is. Benz argues that these interests include origins, lifestyles, and ethnic identities. There was much fluctuation between these interests, but local ethnic identities "were often maintained in the face of political upheaval."[2] Israel and Judah emerge from this background, but I will argue that kingship continues in its struggle to emerge from this background. In some of the key conflicts found in the book of Kings, we see the interests of a "multi-polity decentralized land" striving against the king or, in other words, competing narratives of centralization and decentralization.

---

[1] See Brendan Benz, "The Varieties of Sociopolitical Experience in the Late Bronze Age Levant and the Rise of Early Israel," (PhD diss., New York University, 2012), 6.

[2] Ibid., 422.

A. Polity: Definition

Although Israel and Judah are generally understood as states, I think it will be best to try to be more specific as to what kind of polities they are. In *The Constitution of Society*, Anthony Giddens distinguishes between three types of polities: (1) tribal society, (2) class-divided society, and (3) class society.[3] While Israel and Judah display economic interdependence that is not seen in tribal society, both the importance of tribes[4] and the importance of religion[5] persist as in the "class-divided society" of Giddens. Class-divided societies are characterized by the interaction of multiple social systems.[6] These interactions can be quite competitive, as we often see conflict between the king and these other social systems. Avraham Faust argues that identities and origins are fluid: "People can change their identity and, if necessary, 'reinvent' their origins."[7] This can be a process of centralization and easily morph in response to decentralization. Kingship has often included and been considered to be influenced by fixed hierarchies, but more recent understandings of kingship in Egypt contrast the myth of an enduring and unchanging "eternal" Egypt with the reality of an Egypt decentralized by communication difficulties and deeply

---

[3] Anthony Giddens, *The Constitution of Society: Outline of the Theory of Structuration* (Berkeley: University of California Press, 1984), 181–82.

[4] Ibid., 183: "In class-divided societies traditional practices and kinship relations, even tribal identifications, remain very prominent. The state is unable to penetrate deeply into localized customs, and sheer military power is one of the principal foundations on which government officialdom is able to 'contain' outlying regions where direct administrative control is particularly weak. Class-divided society is marked, however, by some disentangling of the four institutional sphere distinguished above (p. 33). The polity, with its officials, is separated in some part from the procedures of economic activity; formal codes of law and punishment exist; and modes of symbolic co-ordination, based in written texts, make their appearance."

[5] Ibid., 196: "In class-divided societies 'economy' is typically not clearly distinct from 'polity,' and the sense in which the state lodges claims to represent the society as a whole is minimal. State power has not lost its connection with the existential contradiction and is symbolized in persistently religious form. The state may have escaped from tradition in the sense of being able to innovate through the use of consolidated power."

[6] Ibid., 164.

[7] Avraham Faust, *Israel's Ethnogenesis: Settlement, Interaction, Expansion and Resistance* (London: Equinox, 2006), 170.

entrenched local powers who valued personal skills and contacts more than a fixed hierarchy.[8] These same local powers seem to be a part of kingship in Israel and Judah.

B. The Development of a Polity under a King

This competition with the king leads to greater development and complexity of the monarchy. The struggles of Jeroboam and Ahab materialize in a quite different way than those of Hezekiah and Josiah. As polities become centralized, integrative strategies and the implementation of power relations change.[9] A gap exists between what archaeologists describe through material culture and what the books of the Old Testament describe. The Old Testament may have been influenced by a larger historiographical tradition in Mesopotamia that does not correspond to political reality but stresses political unity and integration over differentiation and discord within polities.[10] The fissures of clashing social systems change, but some of the tribal elements are particularly present in the stories of the older kings. These elements dissipate without quite disappearing.

Ann Porter describes kinship as "a set of *social* rules and resources. The state, on the other hand, is a political structure in which different social configurations may pertain."[11] Kinship exists both within the tribal and class-divided society, but the complexity of the class-divided society renders it less powerful. I would like to do a number of case studies in which I examine a king and his competing interests

---

[8] Juan Carlos Moreno Garcia, "The Study of Ancient Egyptian Administration," in *Ancient Egyptian Administration*, ed. Juan Carlos Moreno Garcia, Handbook of Oriental Studies (Leiden/Boston: Brill, 2013), 11.

[9] Gary M. Feinman, "Scale and Social Organization: Perspectives of the Archaic State," in *Archaic States*, ed. Gary M. Feinman and Joyce Marcus (Santa Fe, NM: School of American Research, 1998), 96.

[10] Norman Yoffee, *Myths of the Archaic State: Evolution of the Earliest Cities, States, and Civilizations* (Cambridge/New York: Cambridge University Press, 2005), 55: "The native historiographic tradition in Mesopotamia clearly expresses the importance of city-states in the land and also the ideal of political unity, an ideal that was especially significant in that it was hardly ever fulfilled."

[11] Anne Porter, "From Kin to Class—and Back Again! Changing Paradigms of the Early Polity," in *The Development of Pre-State Communities in the Ancient Near East: Studies in Honour of Edgar Peltenburg*, ed. Diane Bolger and Louise C. Maguire (Oxford/Oakville, CT: Oxbow Books, 2010), 76.

in order to better understand the changes from a tribal or multipolity decentralized land to a class-divided society headed by a king.

1. Jeroboam

Jeroboam has many of the features that we classically associate with a king of Israel or Judah. The writer pays attention to his mother, Zeruah (1 Kgs 11:26), at the beginning of the story. The queen mother appears to be an important part of the polity as she is formulaically described within descriptions of later kings. Her inclusion points to the prominence of Jeroboam since it evokes the special status of the mother of the king within Israel and Judah.

Although we see the beginnings of a monarchical polity here, we also find very strong vested interests that seem to operate outside the king's interests. The cultic practices at Bethel and Dan become an important part of the identity of the northern kingdom of Israel. We see the world of Judges 17–18 and its focus on Levites and Dan returning in 1 Kings 12–13.[12] Jeroboam's appeals to Dan and Bethel (1 Kgs 12:26-33) subscribe to a tribal mentality rather than a class-divided mentality. The clerical leadership in Jerusalem under Solomon was limited to one tribe, but we see Jeroboam able to appeal outside that tribe here, perhaps to entrenched local powers. The problems of popular religiosity continue throughout the monarchy, but they do not seem to revolve around historic shrine sites in the later period; it is a more generalized problem. This tension will continue throughout the monarchical period in one form or another. Here, two sanctuaries represent the interests of geographical locations within Solomon's kingdom. The centralizing motif that has dominated the first ten chapters of 1 Kings is now undercut. This tension will morph in later chapters of 2 Kings into a tension between state-sanctioned religion and popular religiosity. This story, set in the time of Solomon, suggests that popular religiosity may be rooted in other elements that threaten the polity more than simple heterodoxy. Heterodoxy threatens the emerging monarchical polity because the different sanctuaries reach back to the time of a "multi-polity decentralized land."

Finally, the disgruntlement that led to Jeroboam's reign seems to reach back to an earlier time. When we hear, "To your tents, O

---

[12] Walter Dietrich, *The Early Monarchy in Israel: The Tenth Century B.C.E.* (Atlanta: Society of Biblical Literature, 2007), 25.

Israel"[13] in 1 Kings 12:16, we hear decentralizing words. These words represent a rejection of the corvée labor and standardized temples of state religion associated with Solomon.[14] Israel and Judah are just in the initial phase of kingdom building at this stage.

2. Ahab

As we consider the development of a polity, we can think of the complexity of a polity based on the co-occurrence of a number of different institutions.[15] In previous stories of kings, we have seen the interaction of the king with usually one prophet at a time. These interactions are often highly emblematic, involving a symbolic gesture as when the prophet Ahijah rips up his cloak into twelve pieces (1 Kgs 11:30). The stories concerning Ahab introduce another level of complexity to the previous stories we have read about kings. Whether or not these stories date to the time of Ahab is somewhat beyond the point; they represent a complexity that the archaeological record confirms when we consider the Omride (Omri, Ahab, Ahaziah, Joram) kings.

In a recent book on the evolution of complex societies titled *The Creation of Inequality*, Kent Flannery and Joyce Marcus discuss the clues as to the creation of a kingdom. They look for state religion, secular buildings, palaces built by corvée labor, and sumptuary goods appropriate for royalty.[16] Elements of these factors have appeared in earlier stories, as with the corvée labor and Jeroboam or the state religion and David, but all four of these elements come to fruition with the construction of Samaria. We hear in Liverani's history of Israel that

---

[13] Unless otherwise indicated, Scripture translations are taken from the *New American Bible*.

[14] Kent V. Flannery and Joyce Marcus, *The Creation of Inequality: How Our Prehistoric Ancestors Set the Stage for Monarchy, Slavery, and Empire* (Cambridge, MA: Harvard University Press, 2012), 556: "What are the clues that a kingdom has been created? At the regional scale, archaeologists look for signs that the political hierarchy had at least four levels, the upper three of which featured administrators. They look for the standardized temples of state religion, as well as for the secular buildings whose ground plans reflect councils or assemblies. At the capital they look for palaces built by corvée labor and tombs with sumptuary goods appropriate for royalty."

[15] Porter, "From Kin to Class," 76: "[I]t is necessary to think more complexly about what the co-occurrence of king and elders means for ethos, configuration, practice and morphology."

[16] Flannery and Joyce, *Creation of Inequality*, 556.

Samaria "was not merely a simple (and temporary) royal residence, but a real administrative center, a seat of an administration, created by a specific and ambitious building programme."[17] In terms of sumptuary goods, we hear in 1 Kings 22:39 about the famous ivory bed of Ahab, and archaeologists have found about "five hundred ivory inlay pieces, intricately carved and probably manufactured in Phoenicia."[18] Samaria represents a capital city on a whole new level than anything that archaeologists can point to before it.

The most famous story concerning Ahab may involve his acquisition of Naboth the Jezreelite's vineyard (1 Kgs 21). Elijah condemns Ahab for this land grab. The ability, however, to acquire land and accumulate wealth speaks to a transition from the tribal society to the class-divided society.[19] Ahab and the Omrides display many important signs of the development from a tribal society to a class-divided society.

3. Hezekiah

Hezekiah is one of the great heroes of the biblical text, the greatest king according to the Chronicler, exceeding even Josiah. The Chronicler reports that "Every deed that he began was . . . to seek his God" (2 Chr 31:21). Abundant evidence exists for the interactions of Hezekiah with his contemporaries in the ancient Near East. "His name is variously mentioned in no fewer than seven different biblical books, the annals of the Sargonid king Sennacherib, and a growing corpus of bullae."[20] The threats posed by his adversaries in the ancient Near East lead to perhaps the greatest changes of the monarchic polity of Judah.

---

[17] Mario Liverani, *Israel's History and the History of Israel*, trans. Chiara Peri and Philip R. Davies (London: Equinox, 2005), 108.

[18] James Maxwell Miller and John Haralson Hayes, *A History of Ancient Israel and Judah*, 2nd ed. (Louisville, KY: Westminster John Knox Press, 2006), 303.

[19] Yoffee, *Myths of the Archaic State*, 5: "Class-stratified societies with many different social orientations and occupations and with internally specialized political systems developed from societies in which kin-relations functioned to allocate labor and access to resources; large and densely populated urban systems emerged over time from small habitation sites and villages; ideologies that espoused egalitarian principles gave way to belief systems in which the accumulation of wealth and high status was regarded as normal and natural, as were economic subordination and slavery."

[20] Robb Andrew Young, *Hezekiah in History and Tradition*, Supplements to *Vetus Testamentum* 155 (Leiden/Boston: Brill, 2012), 1.

In the Deuteronomistic History, cult centralization is generally associated with Josiah (2 Kgs 23:4-20). Josiah appears to be the great hero of DH for carrying out this religious policy, but he dies an ignominious death that none of the sources can deny. Hezekiah appears to make a halfhearted attempt at reform and cult centralization according to DH. Yet, even in the Deuteronomistic History, there is evidence that this reform may be much greater than portrayed. In 2 Kings 18:4 and 18:22, we hear of cult centralization: "But if you say to me, we rely on the Lord, our God, is not he the one whose high places and altars Hezekiah has removed, commanding Judah and Jerusalem to worship before this altar in Jerusalem?" (2 Kgs 18:22). We even hear of Manasseh, Hezekiah's son, repairing the "high place" that Hezekiah had destroyed (2 Kgs 21:3).

In an illuminating book by Robb Andrew Young, *Hezekiah in History and Tradition*, he posits that Hezekiah may be responsible for a great political and religious centralization in response to the difficulties of his day. The fall of Samaria caused such a disruption in Jerusalem that the polity was forced to respond at a number of levels. Jerusalem here seems to follow the Mesopotamian model of an urban implosion that leads to stronger city-states and the development of kings.[21] The centralization forced by urban implosion led to larger sites and the need for powerful leaders in war and civil administration. Young argues that the numerous *lmlk* jars of this period "would appear to have been a state-sponsored economic program which spanned several years, a systematic plan of taxation to coincide with the increase in settlement and agricultural buildup throughout the region."[22] The strength of this reform may even go beyond what DH describes, as Young holds that annalistic sources stand behind DH's description.[23] In the famous *Rabshakeh* correspondence, we even hear of Assyrian allusions to the cult centralization (2 Kgs 18:22).[24] Centralization

---

[21] John Baines and Norman Yoffee, "Order, Legitimacy, and Wealth in Ancient Egypt and Mesopotamia," in Feinman and Marcus, *Archaic States*, 208: "The urban implosion of late-fourth- and early-third-millennium Mesopotamia resulted in a massive population shift into large sites."

[22] Young, *Hezekiah in History and Tradition*, 59.

[23] Ibid., 102: "The logic runs that the *waw*-consecutive should be expected at this point, and its absence indicates that a centralization in strict accordance with Deuteronomomic law has been prefixed to an original annalistic note pertaining to the purgation of the Nehushtan."

[24] Ibid., 107.

helped break down the differences between the North and the South after the fall of Samaria. The tribal loyalties to Dan and Bethel must have been strong among the many refugees to Jerusalem; Hezekiah appears to have attempted to break these down for political reasons as much as religious reasons.[25] At the same time, others have seen Hezekiah participating in an Assyrianization of the Levant. Rather than a centralization to strengthen a Judah desiring independence, Hezekiah may have just been a vassal of Assyria for large parts of his reign before he finally revolted.[26] We hear no Deuteronomistic justifications for this centralization, yet there seems to be better archaeological evidence for a general centralization during this period than any other period when we consider the population explosion of Jerusalem and public works projects like the Siloam Tunnel.

4. Manasseh

DH depicts Manasseh "as the worst king in the history of Judah."[27] It may be impossible to come to a complete understanding of him, but he is important for a number of reasons. The Chronicler depicts him in a far different manner from DH. Ernst Knauf argues, "If a good king is a king who brings as much peace, security and prosperity to his people as his times allow, then Manasseh was one of the two best kings Judah ever had."[28] We also see a number of important shifts in the polity at this time. One can argue about the nature of these shifts, but I would agree with Römer's characterization of the polity as increasingly "complex."[29] Centralization becomes very important

---

[25] Ibid., 287: "With rural sanctuaries forcibly and permanently closed, their revenues were redirected to the Judean capital, bolstering the dominance of the king to the detriment of clan leadership elsewhere. Centralization was a logical move to promote reunification of the tribes, as was the invitation extended to those who yet remained in the north to join their brethren in Jerusalem for the Passover."

[26] Miller and Hayes, *History of Ancient Israel and Judah*, 404–5.

[27] Thomas Römer, *The So-Called Deuteronomistic History: A Sociological, Historical and Literary Introduction* (London/New York: T & T Clark, 2005), 70.

[28] Ernst Knauf, "The Glorious Days of Manasseh," in *Good Kings and Bad Kings: The Kingdom of Judah in the Seventh Century BCE*, ed. Lester L. Grabbe, Library of Hebrew Bible/Old Testament Studies 393 (London/New York: T & T Clark, 2005), 173.

[29] Ibid.: "Judah underwent an 'economic revolution,' the traditional system of clan-based and agricultural economics was opposed to a more and more centralized state power. We may therefore assume that Judean administration experienced

under Manasseh. This centralization gets sullied by his religious practices for DH. When centralization ultimately aligns with orthodox religious practices under Josiah, it produces the greatest king of the Deuteronomistic History.

The complexity of the polity under Manasseh can hide behind some putatively countervailing tendencies. A number of commentators note how Manasseh is compared to Ahab.[30] As I have noted, many elements of the Ahab story belied an emergence from a different type of polity. As Ahab followed Omri and expanded Samaria, Manasseh follows Hezekiah and seems responsible for the continuing expansion of Jerusalem. He has been called "Judah's Ahab."[31] For DH, it is hard to know who he is truly facing off against: Ahab, son of Omri, or Manasseh. Much of the criticism of Ahab may simply be a veiled criticism of Manasseh.[32] The Chronicler's redemption of Manasseh may better capture the popular mood of the time. Manasseh's fifty-five-year reign could have captured the popular imagination. The political success of the Omrides is beyond dispute. Perhaps Manasseh was also seen as successful as the Omrides by foreigners and by certain classes and popular elements within Judah.

Another intriguing element in the Manasseh narrative is the mention of tribe within the story. Tribal allegiances rarely come up in the story of the United Monarchy. Even though Judges can be understood as set against the backdrop of a "multi-polity decentralized land," DH seems to go to pains to avoid this backdrop in the book of Kings. The achievement of David and Solomon is to avoid definition by tribes. This reality lurks in the background and may have been much stronger when the events occurred vis-a-vis the actual writing of the stories. Be that as it may, 1 Kings 21:7 reiterates the tribal aspects of Jerusalem

---

an important development during the seventh century and became gradually professionalized. All these observations suggest that for the first time, the royal court in Jerusalem must have attained a certain degree of complexity."

[30] Daniel Fleming, *The Legacy of Israel in Judah's Bible: History, Politics, and the Reinscribing of Tradition* (New York: Cambridge University Press, 2012), 40n4; Römer, *So-Called Deuteronomistic History*, 159.

[31] Francesca Stavrakopoulou, "The Blackballing of Manasseh," in Grabbe, *Good Kings and Bad Kings*, 251.

[32] Fleming, *Legacy of Israel in Judah's Bible*, 112n66: "Walter Dietrich (2000) considers that the biblical Omrides, perhaps for polemical purposes better called 'Ahabides,' were made the Judahite code for the kingdom of Manasseh (696–41). On the historical problems, see Na'aman (1997c)."

as opposed to all of Israel.[33] Even though Manasseh is being criticized here for his religious profanations, we can still understand his other centralizing tendencies through this lens. Jerusalem is the divinely appointed capital of Israel.

Although DH is very critical, we hear of what amounts to a building campaign during his reign (2 Kgs 21:3-4, 7). If we are strictly objective and don't get distracted by all the talk of idolatry, this building campaign denotes a lot of economic activity. We see a strong elite appropriation of order in order to legitimate themselves in Egypt.[34] This may be what we are seeing in Manasseh's building campaign.

5. Josiah

Josiah stands out as the clearest hero of all the kings. Second Kings 23:25 states his superiority to the rest of the kings. Marvin Sweeney affirms that "Josiah is to be regarded as the ideal monarch of the Deuteronomistic History, who alone among the kings of Israel and Judah fully observes YHWH's commands as expressed in 'the Torah of Moses.'"[35] Although the book of Kings leaves no doubt as to his importance, the archaeological record implies another story. "Josiah's reign is almost unique in the seventh century in having no attestation in Assyrian or Egyptian records."[36] Sweeney readily concedes, "[T]he narrative presents many problems, particularly to scholars concerned with assessing the historical reality of Josiah's reign and reform."[37] Surprisingly, scholars are much more limited in what they can say about Josiah as opposed to his predecessor Hezekiah.

---

[33] "The Asherah idol he had made, he set up in the temple, of which the LORD had said to David and to his son Solomon: 'In this temple and in Jerusalem, which I have chosen out of all the tribes of Israel, I shall place my name forever.'" Translation from the *New American Bible*.

[34] Baines and Yoffee, "Order, Legitimacy, and Wealth in Ancient Egypt and Mesopotamia," 213.

[35] Marvin A. Sweeney, *King Josiah of Judah: The Lost Messiah of Israel* (Oxford/New York: Oxford University Press, 2001), 4.

[36] Lester L. Grabbe, "Reflections on the Discussion," in Grabbe, *Good Kings and Bad Kings*, 342.

[37] Sweeney, *King Josiah*, 5.

Many contemporary commentators (Halpern, Miller/Hayes, Ahlström, and Liverani)[38] seem to agree on the importance of Josiah. Among these contemporary commentators, Miller and Hayes take a decidedly different approach to Josiah. They assert that from a strictly historical perspective, he does not merit the treatment he receives.[39] Liverani represents an unusual amalgamation of views, as cautious at times as he is speculative at other times. Liverani describes Josiah as a "reformist king."[40] Nonetheless, he also acknowledges, "[A]rchaeological and epigraphic confirmation of the monotheistic reform of Josiah is not easy to find, due to the difficulty of precise dating (to the decade) of undated ostraca."[41] Surprisingly, Liverani is the only one to offer any evidence of Josiah from a primary source: "[A]n ostracon of unknown provenance (but laboratory analysis confirm its authenticity) records silver furnishing for the temple, ordered by Josiah himself: 'So orders (J)osias ('šyhw) the king: to give, from the hands of Zakaryahu, silver of Tarshish for the temple of Yahweh, 3 shekels.'"[42] Ahlström accentuates the historiographical aspects of the Judean kings. A somewhat cyclical and predictable patina covers the depictions of the good and bad kings in the Deuteronomistic History, with a good king (Hezekiah) followed by a bad king (Manasseh) followed by a good king (Josiah). Ahlström stresses how the ideology of Josiah's reform grows out of a postexilic historiography.

I would like to stress the importance of these three historians. Little extrabiblical evidence exists of Josiah,[43] and even internal evidence

---

[38] Gösta Ahlström, *The History of Ancient Palestine*, ed. Diana V. Edelman (Minneapolis: Fortress Press, 1993); Miller and Hayes, *A History of Ancient Israel and Judah*; Liverani, *Israel's History and the History of Israel*; Baruch Halpern, "Sybil, or the Two Nations? Archaism, Kinship, Alienation, and the Elite Redefinition of Traditional Culture in Judah in the 8th–7th Centuries B.C.E.," in *The Study of the Ancient Near East in the Twenty-First Century: The William Foxwell Albright Centennial Conference*, ed. Jerrold S. Cooper and Glenn M. Schwartz (Winona Lake, IN: Eisenbrauns, 1996), 291–338.

[39] Miller and Hayes, *History of Ancient Israel*, 242.

[40] Liverani, *Israel's History and the History of Israel*, 182.

[41] Ibid., 178.

[42] Ibid., 179.

[43] Lawrence J. Mykytiuk identifies one ostracon sold on the antiquities market that mentions him. See Lawrence J. Mykytiuk, *Identifying Biblical Persons in Northwest Semitic Inscriptions of 1200–539 B.C.E.* (Atlanta: Society of Biblical Literature, 2004), 228.

contradicts the importance of Josiah. As we try to understand the development of the polity, Josiah's kingdom may be showing the signs of stress after much warfare. Hezekiah and Manasseh's accommodations to Assyria are replaced by Josiah's extirpation of all foreign influences in Judah. The archaeological record might not be able to offer a clear assessment of Josiah, but perhaps a more modest assessment of Josiah should be made. Rather than a great centralizer and reformer, perhaps his reforms were much more limited.[44] Na'aman argues very little evidence exists that affirms the picture DH paints of him[45] and "no archaeological evidence associated with the reform has ever been unearthed."[46] The conventional picture of Josiah as a great king must be questioned.

Although the Bible does speak of him often, other great reformers like Jeremiah hardly seem to take notice of him. I consider Jeremiah to be a source as important as 2 Kings. Jeremiah lived during the reign of Josiah and wrote about the historical incidents under examination. Scholars used to believe that Jeremiah was a full-grown man when he first received the prophetic utterance in 627, but more recent scholarship holds this prophetic call was probably more like Samuel's, so he was only a boy of twelve or thirteen when he received the call. Nonetheless, he certainly would have been a fully mature man for the last ten years of Josiah's reign. H. G. M. Williamson states, "[T]he death of Josiah is patterned closely on the account of the death of Ahab in 1 Kgs xxii (22) 30, 34-37."[47] He even dies like Ahab at the bow of an

---

[44] Young, *Hezekiah in History and Tradition*, 108: "The statement in 2 Kgs 23:24 affirms that his actions rightfully fulfilled 'the words of the law which were written in the book that Hilkiah the priest found in the house of Yhwh,' yet the same verse only lauds him for the removal of abominable elements from the land. In short, Josiah's reform was not concerned with centralization, but the extirpation of foreign cults. This is a crucial distinction between the reforms of the two kings, which casts further doubt upon the assertion that the reform of Hezekiah is merely a retrojection of the latter."

[45] Nadav Na'aman, "The Kingdom of Judah under Josiah," *Tel Aviv* 18 (1991): 59; "Our historical conclusions are in line with the lack of descriptive material concerning conquests and expansions in Palestine under Josiah—a lack which has puzzled and perplexed many scholars, and has engendered many and varied explanations."

[46] Nadav Na'aman, "The King Leading Cult Reforms in His Kingdom: Josiah and Other Kings in the Ancient Near East," *Zeitschrift für Altorientalische und Biblische Rechtsgeschichte* 12 (2006): 136.

[47] H. G. M. Williamson, "The Death of Josiah and the Continuing Development of the Deuteronomistic History," *Vetus Testamentum* 32, no. 2 (1982): 246.

archer. Williamson's work suggests the complicated nature of the biblical narrative. It does not lend itself to uncritical use as objective history. Jeremiah's lack of piety in regards to Josiah appears to say more than the piety of the books of Kings and Chronicles.

Josiah seemed to engage in centralizing behavior in the books of Kings and Chronicles, but it could have been limited to only "the extirpation of foreign cults."[48] The archaeological record suggests a reign of limited achievement rather than great successes.[49] Josiah may be the premier example in the Old Testament of the Mesopotamian desire for the historiographic tradition to express a governmental unity that does not correspond to political reality.[50] Perhaps very little information beyond what is already known about the polity may be garnered from the material on Josiah.

C. Kingship in the Psalms

As we explore these kingly figures in chapters to come, we will not be able to consider the influence of the Psalms on these figures because we will be drawing from where the Old Testament deals directly with them. I think it is important in this chapter to think more about kingship through the lens of the Psalms. As I briefly explored in the first chapter, the Psalms give us important background as to how kings were generally perceived in society. Different theological movements varied in their understanding and appreciation of kingship, but Deuteronomy 17's removal of the sacral nature of kingship has left a lasting mark on the scholarly understanding of kingship. I hope to put this shift in the understanding of kingship in perspective by thinking a lot more about kingship in the Psalms. Focusing on Psalms here will give us the opportunity to consider a fuller biblical picture of kingship that can be elusive when we only look at Kings, Chronicles, and the Prophets.

We have even seen a similar movement in downplaying the role of the king in the final form of the Psalter. Jamie Grant will argue for

---

[48] Young, *Hezekiah in History*, 108.

[49] Na'aman, "The Kingdom of Judah under Josiah," 34: "Our conclusions regarding the limited borders of the kingdom of Judah under Josiah are of extreme importance in evaluating his achievements; these conclusions clash with many generally accepted conventions pertinent to the history of his reign."

[50] Yoffee, *Myths of the Archaic State*, 55.

a strong Deuteronomistic influence on the Psalter and the ultimate redaction of the psalms through the editing of the Psalter.[51] He argues, "[W]e see at work here a Deuteronomic redaction in the final shaping of the Psalter—perhaps more specifically, a nomistic [legal] Deuteronomic redaction."[52] Another scholar, Scott Starbuck, will write of the *recontextualization* of the Royal Psalms preceding "even the Hebrew Psalter itself."[53] Ultimately, this is a similar problem to Deuteronomy 17:14-20, which scholars think of as promoting the reconceptualization of kingship. The argument about the redaction and recontextualization of the Psalms is even more speculative than the reconceptualization of kingship, yet like the reconceptualization of kingship, it speaks to the need to get at the original context and text of the Psalms. This will also help us get at the original notion of kingship.

The king has an elevated role within the Psalter. In Psalm 2, a programmatic psalm at the beginning of the Psalter, the psalmist offers a strong contrast between "the kings of the land who rise up and the princes who plot together with them against the Lord and his anointed" (v. 2).[54] So clearly we hear of kingship here as an institution in Israel that is distinguished from the other kings of the ancient Near East. Verse 6 makes this even clearer as it states: "I have installed my king on Zion, my holy mountain." No king is identified here. Some will argue that "Psalm 2 should be heard primarily as an affirmation of God's sovereignty rather than the sovereignty of the Davidic monarchy."[55] I have no problem hearing the affirmation of God's sovereignty here, but the whole of the psalm clearly contrasts Zion's king with the kings and princes of the world. It could be more helpful here to focus on the plain sense of the words. We do not have

---

[51] Jamie A. Grant, *The King as Exemplar: The Function of Deuteronomy's Kingship Law in the Shaping of the Book of Psalms*, Society of Biblical Literature Academia Biblica (Atlanta: Society of Biblical Literature, 2004), 2: "So the central idea of this thesis is that the placement of kingship psalms alongside torah psalms was a deliberate editorial act through which Psalter's redactors intended to reflect the theology of the Deuteronomic Law of the King in the Book of Psalms."

[52] Ibid., 42.

[53] Scott R. A. Starbuck, *Court Oracles in the Psalms: The So-Called Royal Psalms in Their Ancient Near Eastern Context*, Society of Biblical Literature Dissertation Series (Atlanta: Scholars Press, 1999), 3.

[54] Scripture translation by the author.

[55] J. Clinton McCann, *A Theological Introduction to the Book of Psalms: The Psalms as Torah* (Nashville, TN: Abingdon Press, 1993), 43.

a justification for Davidic kingship here, but the plain sense of the words does seem to be justifying kingship in Israel with a strong alliance between Yahweh and his anointed. As we consider earlier points on the body royal, Psalm 2 appears to easily fall within this schema.

1. Development of the Psalms

Recent scholarship on the Psalms has seen important developments in our understanding of them. Gerald Wilson has initiated in his groundbreaking 1985 work a period over the last thirty years that has focused on the editing of the Psalter.[56] While this has helped us come to an understanding of the final form of the Psalter, it may have overly influenced the general study of the Psalms. Most would agree that the Psalter has been edited to carry a certain message and intention that builds up over the 150 psalms, but this can overshadow the original intention of the individual psalm. Although they have come to their decisions independently and in different ways, scholars like Wilson, Claus Westermann, Brevard Childs, and James Mays seem to work from a similar notion that focuses on a secondary interpretation or rereading of the Psalms. "While these scholars admit an original preexilic cultic intentional composition for the Royal Psalms, this original meaning and usage had little to do with the decision to include the psalms in the Psalter."[57] This original meaning and usage is exactly what interests me. It will give us a different sense of kingship than what we find in the book of Kings or the book of Chronicles. Rather than focusing on kingship as a civil institution—as in the book of Deuteronomy—the Psalms will help us get at the sacral elements within kingship.

We also get closer to the actual time of the kings by focusing on the preexilic nature of the Psalms. Deuteronomy 17:14-20's perspective on kingship represents a time that may be at some removal from an actual king. First Samuel 8 and 12 are certainly far removed from King David. If we accept Gerald Wilson's hypothesis of a highly edited Psalter, this too probably was quite removed from actual kings. It is only by examining individual psalms that we can move closer to the time of the kings. I believe this is important to do because concentrating

---

[56] Gerald Henry Wilson, *The Editing of the Hebrew Psalter*, Society of Biblical Literature Dissertation Series (Chico, CA: Scholars Press, 1985).

[57] Starbuck, *Court Oracles in the Psalms*, 61.

on material generated after the time of kings does not represent the world of the kings. There is an almost permanent suspicion toward kingship in the postexilic period that adds a nuance to kingship that may have been quite remote from the actual time of the kings. We will examine the so-called Royal Psalms (2; 18; 20; 21; 45; 72; 89; 101; 110; 132; and 144:1-10) in order to get at the conceptualization of kingship rather than the reconceptualization of kingship in which so much of Kings and Chronicles is steeped.

2. Royal Psalms

Earlier generations of scholars like Hermann Gunkel and Sigmund Mowinckel championed the Royal Psalms as being used over and over again in liturgical or royal ceremonies. This set of beliefs was part of the myth-and-ritual school, which has fallen out of favor. Scholars now are more careful in their judgments and will argue that there is not enough data to prove the existence of royal rituals through these Royal Psalms. We have no proof of the Royal Psalms being used in royal rituals in the northern kingdom of Israel or in Judah.

The Royal Psalms still offer us a challenge in a manner similar to the reconceptualization of kingship. Scott Starbuck will speak about the recontextualization of royal psalms within the Psalter and royal psalms as "psalms whose concern is the institution of the Israelite kingship. Their protagonist is an unspecified king; hence he is a typological representative of the 'office' of the institution."[58] While we may not be able to verify a specific context for these psalms, Starbuck's recontextualization begs us to consider an original context for them. I believe this context merges with the original conceptualization of the king that got replaced by the reconceptualization of the king in Deuteronomy 17:14-10. A careful examination of some of the Royal Psalms will speak to some of the shared attitudes toward kingship throughout the ancient Near East. Before addressing these shared attitudes, we have to come to an understanding of why this view meets such opposition.

As I pointed out in chapter 1, a group of scholars has taken a very strong position against the monarchy representing anything of revelation and inspiration in the Old Testament. This may be best represented by George Mendenhall's view that "the cultic/political system of

---

[58] Ibid., 101.

Jerusalem during the Monarchy had nothing to do with the Yahwist revolution and was actually completely incompatible with that religious movement."[59] Mendenhall's understanding of the monarchy betrays a limited biblical perspective, which is focused on certain books of the Old Testament and completely ignores other books such as the Psalms. This is very much a shared perspective. A few years later, Baruch Halpern wrote about biblical Israel: "[T]he kingship remained a political, rather than a divine office. The humane values affirmed by the subjects and enforced by them on the sovereign remain today models of a commitment to human dignity, to the worth of human ideals."[60] I think this view verges dangerously close to reading contemporary political differences in the Middle East into differences in the ancient Near East. I will argue that the states of the ancient Near East shared more in common than not. Halpern and Mendenhall need to consider the Royal Psalms as they make judgments about kingship in Israel.

When we look at kingship in Israel, it really appears to be a litmus test for a number of scholars. If I may examine another theological turning point, we see similar things happen with views on the historical Jesus. I believe it was Albert Schweitzer who said that a generation of scholars had peered into the well of history in order to discover Jesus and had pale reflections of themselves. A similar thing seems to happen when we look at kingship in Israel. Kingship suddenly becomes a counterrevolutionary force or it becomes something that denies human dignity. The Royal Psalms offer us the chance to construct a more nuanced vision of kingship that takes into regard a fuller picture from biblical sources.

3. Shared Attitudes that Emerge from the Royal Psalms

While we cannot prove the use of the Royal Psalms in an enthronement festival in Israel or Judah, it is important to note the existence of these festivals across the ancient Near East. Many scholars have noted these festivals in Mesopotamia and Egypt.[61] As the superpowers of the ancient Near East resided in these geographical regions, it

---

[59] George E. Mendenhall, "The Monarchy," *Interpretation* 29, no. 2 (1975): 166.

[60] Baruch Halpern, *The Constitution of the Monarchy in Israel*, Harvard Semitic Monographs 25 (Chico, CA: Scholars Press, 1981), 256.

[61] John H. Eaton, *Kingship and the Psalms*, Studies in Biblical Theology (London: SCM Press, 1976), 87–100.

is only logical that we would have many more cultural artifacts from these regions as they had much larger workforces and scribal classes than what we would find in Judah or Israel. Although we have not found the same evidence of an enthronement festival in Judah and Israel as in Egypt and Mesopotamia, many important scholars, such as Sigmund Mowinckel and Hermann Gunkel, have just assumed that they must exist. I would prefer to take a more minimalistic approach and determine what shared attitudes with the rest of the ancient Near East emerge from the Royal Psalms while trying to avoid all elements of patternism.[62]

Many have tried to reconstruct rituals in ancient Israel through the rituals of the nations around them in the ancient Near East. It is imperative to state that "these reconstructions always overlook the fact that the Psalms of the Old Testament do not contain any complete rituals."[63] So rather than trying to reconstruct rituals, I would like to focus on elements of the Royal Psalms that they share with other nations of the ancient Near East. Most scholars agree that the Royal Psalms are 2, 18, 20, 21, 45, 72, 89, 101, 110, 132, and 144:1-11, with some scholars leaving out 132 or another psalm. Another group of scholars would like to include any psalm with David in the title, but these were not considered royal psalms by Gunkel and are not recognized as royal psalms today. Finally, some scholars see another set of psalms carrying forth the royal narrative, but most would consider this too expansive.

1. Autumn New Year's Festival

The autumn New Year's Festival materializes as perhaps the most important commonality throughout the ancient Near East. We see many signs of it in the Old Testament. Richard Clifford points out that in the postbiblical writings of Judaism, New Year's Day was a "solemnity at least as far back as the second century CE (*m. Roš. Haš. 1:2*). Earlier biblical references to an autumn New Year are less explicit

---

[62] Hans-Joachim Kraus, *Theology of the Psalms*, trans. Keith R. Crim (Minneapolis: Augsburg Publishing House, 1986), 107–8: "It is easy to see that the dissolution of the boundaries of clearly distinct categories with the help of the pattern principle was an inappropriate measure which permitted speculation to go beyond all bounds."

[63] Ibid., 111.

but, taken cumulatively, suggest the same."[64] So while we cannot reconstruct a ritual here, we can see similar concerns across the ancient Near East at this time of year.

Although no royal psalms specifically deal with the theme of renewal that accompanies the New Year's Festival, the closely related Enthronement Psalms (24; 29; 47; 93; 95–99) deal with this theme. Psalm 93:1 as well as 47:8, 96:10, 97:1, and 99:1 all declare that Yahweh is king. Psalm 93 will seek to describe how Yahweh became king by overcoming both flood and sea, a somewhat supernatural scenario with echoes of Genesis. Like Genesis, we find God responsible for renewal, a renewal that comes with the autumn rains in Israel and Judah. God as king merits enthronement here and brings order to the—at times—chaotic world.

Many have speculated that Psalms 2, 110, and 132 are especially tied to the autumn New Year's Festival.[65] We will examine the latter two psalms more in terms of enthronement in the next section. While remembering that no complete ritual is present in any psalm, it is easy to recognize that Jerusalem is especially present in Psalm 2 as well as Psalms 46 and 48. Scholars imagine that it is not too hard to imagine the oracle (2:6-9) within Psalm 2 being proclaimed during a New Year's Festival as a warning to any aggressors who may want to attack Jerusalem.[66] While this is speculative at best, we do have many actual rites similar to this in the nations around Jerusalem that promise destruction for their enemies. What is most important here is that the royal nature of this psalm is easily recognized. We see the Lord and his anointed together battling the other kings in verse 2. God has clearly enthroned the king in Jerusalem in verse 6. God's blessings manifest themselves most obviously in the king and are felt throughout the rest of Judah through the king.

2. Enthronement

The actual idea of enthronement differs from the Enthronement Psalms, which focus almost exclusively on Yahweh. "Psalm 110 contains the most clearly recognizable descriptions and texts of an

---

[64] Richard J. Clifford, *Psalms 1–72*, Abingdon Old Testament Commentaries (Nashville, TN: Abingdon Press, 2002), 14.

[65] Eaton, *Kingship and the Psalms*, 127.

[66] Clifford, *Psalms 1–72*, 45.

enthronement festival. The solemn rites of initiation and consecration and the oracles present the picture of an enthronement in a fragmentary, but still impressive, form."[67] This psalm clearly has the sovereign take a throne at the right hand of God (Ps 110:1). This king is ruling from Zion/Jerusalem. His power is derived from God as the Lord crushes his enemies and is the source of his power and authority (110:2, 4). Finally, there seems to be an allusion to an initiation rite in verses 3 and 7, as he is both bedewed and drinks ceremonially from a river. First Kings 1:45 refers to a coronation/anointing ceremony by the river Gihon, to which this may be alluding. Gihon is also seemingly a mythical river in Genesis 2:13, which lends a somewhat spiritual air to this psalm.

Psalm 132 seems to be grounded much more in reality than Psalm 110. Enthronement lies at the heart of the psalm: "The LORD swore an oath to David, a pledge never to be broken: 'Your own offspring I will set upon your throne'" (v. 11). This oath is conditional as the sons have to maintain the covenant. Kraus sees this psalm as genuine and primary as opposed to Psalm 110, which he considers secondary.

3. Basic Legitimation

The Royal Psalms also assert the basic legitimation of the king. Psalm 2 makes this most evident as it states in verse 7: "I will proclaim the decree of the LORD, who said to me, 'You are my son; today I am your father.'" The psalm asserts the proximity of the relationship between the king and God. This assertion is also found in Psalm 110:3b, where we hear, "[L]ike the dew I begot you." Thus, while the language in Psalm 2 is more straightforward, we also hear of the king in Psalm 110 as the product of God's generativity. Both psalms leave no doubt as to God's allegiance to the king.

4. Abasement

While the Royal Psalms give us an important sense of the royal ideal, they also display the kings' utter dependence on God and their human frailty. This human frailty is seen in Psalm 89:48-52, in which the king is subject to scorn and slander. Lest we get too exalted a notion of kingship, we hear how the king is bothered by the insults

---

[67] Kraus, *The Theology of the Psalms*, 111.

of those around him. This is impossible to imagine in Egypt, where no foreigner or commoner was allowed near the king. Hatshepsut, a woman, could become pharaoh and easily portray herself as a king. Whereas the superpowers of Mesopotamia and Egypt would have an enormous distance between the king and commoners, Psalm 89 portrays an environment in which many have easy access to the king. We can imagine the scenarios out of the book of Jeremiah where the king is lashing out at prophets and advisors who don't hesitate to criticize him (Jer 36:31).

Psalm 144 depicts more traditional problems that a king has with foreign enemies. There is a focus on human frailty that one would almost never see in Egyptian writings as we hear in 144:10-11: "You give victory to kings; you delivered David your servant. From the menacing sword deliver me; rescue me from the hands of foreign foes. Their mouths speak untruth; their right hands are raised in lying oaths." Here we see the dependence of the king on God. Foreigners are not to be taken lightly; they can be menacing. The victory is not on account of the king's skill or bravery—God gives victory. The Royal Psalms strike an important balance between the stature of the king at the top of the hierarchy and the frailty of the king who can be easily toppled.

Conclusion

As kingship wanes after the fall of Jerusalem, kingship seems to reemerge as we hear about the "People of the Land" at the end of 2 Kings (2 Kgs 25:22) and in Ezra (4:4) and Nehemiah (9:10). These "People of the Land" may reflect older elements of governance that reemerge in response to chaos. As Ezra and Nehemiah try to impose elements of the monarchic order, they find their competition among the "People of the Land." The competing narratives of centralization and decentralization continue to be played out, as the people of the land can be seen as reaching back to a multipolity decentralized land rather than accept colonial centralization.

Chapter Three

Jeroboam
Heretic or Hero?

A. Introduction

Jeroboam I has become a touchstone in the Hebrew Bible for all that can go wrong with kingship. Few kings are mentioned more frequently than Jeroboam, but few people are more reviled. The ultimate problem with the texts concerning Jeroboam is how far they are removed from their northern kingdom setting.[1] New insights into Jeroboam come to the fore when he is compared to David, especially through a sociological lens. Many consider that an apology has been written into the narrative of David, but David may need an apology that Jeroboam does not need. Later political and theological interests now dominate this story, but the original material may have been neutral or even positive toward Jeroboam, as seen in the Greek Old Testament, the Septuagint.[2] As one draws nearer to the northern kingdom setting, other aspects of Jeroboam come to the fore. Jeroboam does many things expected of an ancient Near Eastern king, such as managing

---

[1] A. Graeme Auld, *Kings without Privilege: David and Moses in the Story of the Bible's Kings* (Edinburgh: T & T Clark, 1994), 172: "Again Jeroboam's new cultic arrangements in Bethel and Dan (1 Kgs 12:25-33) are anticipated—and mocked in advance—in the accounts in Jg 8:24-28 of Gideon's false cult and in Jg 17–18 of the establishment by Danites in the north of a cult stolen from further south."

[2] Alison L. Joseph, *Portrait of the Kings: The Davidic Prototype in Deuteronomistic Poetics* (Minneapolis: Fortress Press, 2015), 133: "[T]he rise and fall of Jeroboam as the potential David and anti-David is a literary strategy only apparent in the MT [the Hebrew Bible]."

troublesome groups of priests and using corvée labor, whereas David fails to do things (for example, building a temple) that may lead to the necessity of an apology.

B. Comparison of Jeroboam and David

There are seven explicit connections that bind David with Jeroboam: (1) flight, (2) forced labor, (3) men of valor, (4) prophetic connections, (5) priestly connections, (6) loss of child, and (7) moving capital. Although not all these categories are of the same strength, they highlight sociological and literary connections between the two men. The sociological characteristics of an emerging leader characterize both David and Jeroboam. Recent work on cultural memory offers an explanation for similarities in the narratives of the two men.[3] Setbacks or incidences of suffering such as the loss of a child may contain actual experiences of a people or group that produced the cultural memory.[4] Such common memories may be what forms groups of people like ancient Israel. We come to encounter many ways in which the stories of the two men coalesce.

(1) Flight: Many commentators have noted the flight motif in the Davidic stories. Some even claim that much of David's story is to be seen as an "exile story."[5] Closer examination of the relevant motifs in David's story demonstrates the importance of flight and his continual struggle with opponents as he tries to maintain his centrality throughout his life and monarchy. This struggle is also a hallmark of Jeroboam. Jeroboam shares character traits with David. The expression, "he returned from," is part of a fixed narrative structure that appears frequently in contexts of flight. This expression of David is used in 1 Samuel 23:14-15 and Jeroboam in 1 Kings 12:2. It also continues the

---

[3] John W. Rogerson, *A Theology of the Old Testament: Cultural Memory, Communication, and Being Human* (Minneapolis: Fortress Press, 2010), 18: "The claim of the narrative view of history is that while we do not invent the past, our narrative accounts of it are affected and shaped by factors such as our very limited knowledge of what happened in the past, and our situatedness in nation, gender, class, political and religious commitment or lack of the same, and aims and interests in wanting to construct narratives about the past."

[4] Ibid.

[5] Barbara Green, *King Saul's Asking*, Interfaces (Collegeville, MN: Liturgical Press, 2003), xiv: "1 Samuel reads best as an exile story."

language of "flight" found first in 1 Kings 11:40 within the Jeroboam story. The idea of flight appears to be the concept that holds together this section of Kings, as it also describes the two other figures found in 1 Kings 11: Rezon and Hadad.

(2) Forced Labor: Both David and Jeroboam are associated with forced labor (2 Sam 20:24; 1 Kgs 11:28). The allusion to it in David is fairly innocuous. As David's administration is described late in his kingship, Adoram is mentioned as being in charge of corvée labor. This institution of corvée labor is portrayed as genuinely hated in Egypt, but it comes to be accepted as a necessity in Joshua and Judges; it was, however, only used on the Canaanites (Josh 17:13; Judg 1:28). The narrator of 2 Samuel 20:24 does not designate who makes up the corvée labor in this case, but similar language in 2 Samuel 12:31 may imply that it was foreigners. This omission may connect David to earlier leaders in Joshua and Judges in a manner that becomes quite clear through a comparison with Solomon. Solomon initiates massive building campaigns in a manner far more characteristic of an ancient Near Eastern king. Although there is no official endorsement of corvée labor in 1 Kings, it is mentioned far more frequently. It seems much more likely to have affected the Israelites themselves (1 Kgs 5:27). Jeroboam emerges as a figure opposed to this system, although he probably gained by it as well. Initially, Solomon puts him in charge of his corvée labor. This may put Jeroboam in a similar role to David. In sociological terms, they both emerge as Weberian charismatic figures (Max Weber, along with Emile Durkheim and Karl Marx, would be considered the founders of sociology). Both David and Jeroboam gain notice through their deeds rather than the administrative offices they hold through inheritance. David is portrayed as killing a skilled warrior, and Jeroboam can organize a work gang. Ultimately, Jeroboam rejects the path associated with corvée labor and rises up with the rest of the Israelites against Rehoboam's implementation of Solomonic corvée labor. We must remember that the frequent condemnation of the "sins of Jeroboam" (1 Kgs 15:30, etc.; twenty times) ignores the fact that he was an opponent of every abuse of corvée labor. Clear grounds emerge for understanding the popularity of Jeroboam based on his support for the people in the North resisting the imposition of corvée labor from the South. Both David and Jeroboam are associated with corvée labor, but neither one of them becomes as associated with it as Solomon.

If we give this issue further consideration, one must look at the building campaigns that Jeroboam undertook after his ascension.

Although both David and Jeroboam are equated with this practice, Jeroboam's skills appear to come to the forefront. Jeroboam becomes associated with building campaigns in three cities (Shechem, Penuel, Tirzah) and two shrines (Dan and Bethel). I shall address the controversy of the exact status of these cities later, but I think Halpern's comment still stands:

> It is to be presumed that these tasks were performed with diplomatic delicacy; at least, Jeroboam selected his capital in such a way as to contribute significantly to the internal unity and external security of the new state. By designating Shechem in Cisjordan and Penuel in Transjordan to share in this prominent position, the northern monarch exerted an effective control upon sectional rivalry within Israel, while emphasizing the patriarchal heritage of his nation (Gen 32:22-32; 35:1-2).[6]

The construction efforts at Shechem also serve to distance Jeroboam from the aniconic tradition at Shiloh.[7] Ahijah serves as a representative of this aniconic tradition, and he initially empowered Jeroboam, but Jeroboam's diplomatic skills become evident as he distances himself from this city that would have southern sympathies. I think the building projects at all these sites imply a continued use of corvée labor.

(3) Men of Valor: Perhaps the association with corvée labor is as a result of their status within their contemporary society. David (1 Sam 16:8) and Jeroboam (1 Kgs 11:28) are described as men of valor. They share this designation with Jephthah and Boaz, among others. This designation is hard to understand, but it seems to go well beyond a military designation. Rather, it seems to imply people wealthy enough to pay a tax. If we combine the idea of "men of valor" with corvée labor, both men appear to be in a similar social class. They seem to be from a type of elite that is both threatening and necessary for a king. Saul

---

[6] Baruch Halpern, "Levitic Participation in the Reform Cult of Jeroboam I." *Journal of Biblical Literature* 95, no. 1 (1976): 31.

[7] Ibid., 39: "Shiloh, scholars agree, was the primary home of the ark of the covenant (1 Sam 4:3), at least during the time of Samuel's religious leadership. The ties between Shiloh and the ark, and the cherub-iconography, appear from the text to be both organic and original (see 2 Sam 6:2). Indeed, A. Alt has suggested that in transferring the ark to Jerusalem, David intended primarily to secure the allegiance of the northern tribes; the Judahite attachment to the ark and the cherubim, by contrast, seems to have been less strong."

and Solomon would need to raise taxes and have compulsory labor, but there probably would not be a large group of men who could fit this type. David and Jeroboam are associated with both of these characteristics. The infrequency of this designation also calls to mind many of the issues around cultural memory. We cannot quite verify all the characteristics of the "men of valor," but this social institution seems to imply some characteristics that bind the holders of this designation together. Since we have a limited knowledge of what happened in the past, the experiences of the people with these men designated as "men of valor" seem to produce a cultural memory that binds figures together such as Jephthah, Boaz, David, and Jeroboam.[8]

(4) Prophetic Connections: The more Jeroboam is understood as reflecting a unique Northern tradition quite removed from the Deuteronomistic editors, the clearer are the similarities with David. Jeremy Hutton's work on the pre-Deuteronomistic material within the Deuteronomistic History accentuates the many independent traditions with which the Deuteronomistic editor ultimately works. He demonstrates that commentators can use a few pericopes to make arguments about all of the Deuteronomistic History.[9] He argues forcefully that independent stories exist within the Deuteronomistic History. These earlier stories contain similar types of stories about Jeroboam and David. As Hutton has suggested, the editor's hand manifests itself much more strongly in 1 Kings than it does in "the loosely conjoined Samuel."[10] Hence, Jeroboam and Josiah become connected in 1 Kings 13:2. The David material never seems to be so blatantly used by DH to make

---

[8] Rogerson, *A Theology of the Old Testament*, 39. Here we see a similar binding together of Joshua, Gideon, Jephthah, Eli, Samuel, David, and Elijah: "All of these set-backs or incidences of suffering can be seen as components of a cultural member or memories that are themselves based upon actual experiences of people or groups within the circle or circles that produced the cultural memory." Ibid.

[9] Jeremy Hutton, *The Transjordanian Palimpsest: The Overwritten Texts of Personal Exile and Transformation in the Deuteronomistic History* (Berlin/New York: Walter de Gruyter, 2009), 133: "Although McKenzie admitted that the refutation of Trabolle's argument here did not constitute adequate evidence to disprove the existence of a pre-Deuteronomistic, prophetic stream of redaction, he systematically challenged the 'prophetic' nature of several key passages in Campbell's PR (1 Kgs 11:29-39; 1 Kgs 14:7-18; 16:1-4, 11-13; 21:21-24; 2 Kgs 9:6-10), insisting that they are to be attributed most readily to the single Nothian Dtr, who crafted the history from an assortment of tradition without relying on an already compiled document."

[10] Ibid.

contemporary or near-contemporary connections. David suffers his condemnation after the Bathsheba incident (2 Sam 11:1-13) at the hands of Nathan and at the hands of Gad after the census (2 Sam 24), but later figures do not appear in this material. Ahijah emerges again in 1 Kings 14 to condemn Jeroboam, but this is radically different from our introduction to him in 1 Kings 11. In chapter 14, Jeroboam is situated in Bethel, a threatening location to a prophet from Shiloh because Bethel has an independent tradition that predates Shiloh and is radically different from its aniconic tradition.

(5) Priestly connections: As becomes obvious from the problems associated with the shrines of Dan and Bethel, Jeroboam becomes associated with much religious controversy. Since David did not build a temple in Jerusalem, he seems to avoid some of this controversy. Jeroboam's various building campaigns embroil him in controversy. When their associations with priests and prophets are carefully examined, the genesis of the problem becomes more apparent. Problems with the priesthood emerge in some of the significant material before David. David's association with the South may help him avoid the problems that bedevil Eli. Eli is associated with a Northern sanctuary (Shiloh) that is not part of David's Southern roots but still holds connections with the aniconic tradition of the South. When things start going badly for Eli because of his sons (1 Sam 2:12), David ultimately appears as a refreshing alternative to this corruption after the misfire with Saul.

David holds much in common with the traditions of Shiloh. In an episode that prefigures Solomon's wisdom in confronting the two women, David must confront two lines of priests. His natural ally would seem to be Zadok.[11] Zadok traces his lineage back to Aaron and the ordered space of the temple,[12] although this is contested. First Chronicles clearly asserts the Aaronid connections, but it is both curious and notable that it never comes up in the Deuteronomistic History. Regardless of whether we believe an indigenous Jebusite background for Zadok or an Aaronid background from Hebron, Zadok has clear affiliations with

---

[11] Baruch Halpern, *David's Secret Demons: Messiah, Murderer, Traitor, King*, The Bible in Its World Series (Grand Rapids, MI: Eerdmans, 2001), 285n6: "Abiathar appears with Zadok, who seems to appear roughly at the time of the Absalom revolt—Zadok is a creature of David's reign."

[12] William R. Millar, *Priesthood in Ancient Israel*, Understanding Biblical Themes Series (St. Louis, MO: Chalice Press, 2001), 33.

the South. Second Samuel 20:26 adds a further level of complexity to this scenario as we hear about another priest of David: Ira the Jairite. Little is known about him, but he would appear to further destabilize the Mushite (Mosaic connections) Levites associated with Moses, as he is a non-Levitical priest descended from Jair of Manasseh (Num 32:41; Deut 3:14). David's other priest, Abiathar, is a Mushite Levite with clear affiliations with the North. The Mushite Levites seem to have been brought into enough disrepute by the stories of Phinehas and Hophni (1 Sam 2:15-17, 22-25) that they could not assert themselves over the Zadokite party. Ultimately Abiathar would try to assert himself by allying with Adonijah rather than perhaps the half-Jebusite Solomon, but this would prove disastrous. One wonders if this move to Adonijah was also a way for Shiloh to challenge the Jerusalem sanctuary. The Mushite Levites are subsequently moved to the periphery.

When we examine Jeroboam's dealings with the Mushite Levites, further polarization becomes apparent. The Mushite Levites may have schemed for years to destabilize Solomon. When they got their chance at the end of his reign, it is no mistake that popular revolt is centered at Shechem, a Levitical city (Josh 21:21) that had fallen back to town status during Solomon's reign (1 Kgs 4:8). Jeroboam seems to do something very similar to David: he either privileged a former line of priests, or he raised a new line of priests. The story that DH tells about David and Jeroboam is similar in this manner. They both elevate a line of priests that ends up competing with the Mushite Levites. The sanctuaries at Bethel and Dan can be seen like Jerusalem: They displace the earlier sanctuary at Shiloh that is so tainted with the corruption of Eli's sons. The Aaronite priesthood associated with Jerusalem was also associated with Shiloh (Josh 22:13, 30-32; 24:33). Dan and Bethel have none of the older taint of Shiloh or the newer taint of Jerusalem, which could have raised resentment in the North as the people there watched their resources flowing in that direction. While "Jeroboam constructs shrines ('high places') and appoints non-Levitical officials to manage their activities,"[13] David can be seen to be participating in similar behavior to a lesser extent. He is not accused of constructing shrines, but he does engage non-Levitical personnel to help him manage the religious activities of his kingdom.

---

[13] Burke O. Long, *1 Kings: With an Introduction to Historical Literature*, Forms of the Old Testament Literature, vol. 9 (Grand Rapids, MI: Eerdmans, 1984), 142.

Here is found a crucial difference between the two kings that highlights their dissimilarities. The Hebrew Bible characterizes Jeroboam's behavior in a particularly negative way by focusing on the construction of shrines, but the reality of independent sanctuaries must also be considered. Can this simply be the propaganda[14] of the Mushite Levite priests against other priests associated with sanctuaries important in the Jacob cycle such as Bethel? In her book on the priesthood, Deborah Rooke claims, "[S]ites such as Shiloh and Bethel had much more ancient and ingrained claims on the people's religious affections, and so it is not really surprising that the idea of centralized worship at Jerusalem took some time to become established."[15] Much recent work on the importance of local sanctuaries speaks to a much more complex picture of priesthood in Israel. Sanctuaries like Shiloh are very important, but the king and other sanctuaries have competing interests. A world emerges in which three competitors, and perhaps four with the emergence of the northern kingdom, compete against any one overarching interpretation of priesthood. Whereas the Deuteronomist seems to be able to live with David's aniconic activity in the South, Jeroboam is represented as worshiping a bull. Gary Knoppers states, "Although the northern king associates the calves with the God of the Exodus, the Deuteronomists associate the creation and deployment of these symbols with idolatry and worshiping other gods (1 Kgs 12:28; 14:10; 2 Kgs 10:29)."[16] Knoppers here guides us between the Northern and Southern perspectives. We must remember that Jeroboam can be seen with a lot of legitimacy from a different perspective. The Hebrew version of Kings paints the most negative picture of him, a picture that is not as negative even in the Greek version of Kings. In a different light, Jeroboam can be seen as having all the components of legitimacy, a perspective not seen in the Bible but hinted at in the archaeological record. Both Patrick Miller and Othmar Keel can see a continuation of tauromorphic imagery from Late Bronze and Iron Age I. Keel says

---

[14] Millar, *Priesthood*, 10: "As a working hypothesis in our point of entry into the world of priests, we will assume that the dominant story in Kings is being told from the perspective of Abiathar of the family of Mushite Levite priests."

[15] Deborah W. Rooke, *Zadok's Heirs: The Role and Development of the High Priesthood in Ancient Israel* (Oxford/New York: Oxford University Press, 2000), 78.

[16] Gary N. Knoppers, *Jews and Samaritans: The Origins and History of Their Early Relations* (New York: Oxford University Press, 2013), 53.

the bull imagery may be a *leftover* from earlier times.[17] Miller allows that this bull imagery may be found in other parts of the northern kingdom, specifically in the tenth-century Taanach Cult Stand.[18] In spite of the harsh condemnation of Jeroboam, he and David may be making similar movements to the popular religiosity of their contexts. Can't Jeroboam be seen here as resorting to the bulls as a conservative and permanent part of the religious infrastructure of the North?

The stories of David and Jeroboam have been examined from the narrative and social perspectives, but it is also important to consider how these stories have been redacted. In general, many would argue that a lighter editorial hand is applied to David, as has been suggested by Jeremy Hutton. Much of the Deuteronomistic criticism of Jeroboam's apostasy seems to be late and formulaic. Two figures that have much in common, as I have postulated, now come to be separated by apostasy. It is important to note that LXX (Septuagint) 1 Kings 12:24:a-z "never presents Jeroboam as king. As a consequence, this text could not conceive of a dynastic perspective, opening onto the future, nor recount a religious schism, since this implies a king, the only one capable of leading a whole nation into another religion."[19] The religious schism seems to be more of a Deuteronomistic bias in order to explain the importance of centralizing religious worship in Jerusalem. The work of Mark Leuchter (and others) focuses on an independent Northern religious tradition that Jeroboam inherited rather than invented.[20] Therefore, we see another similarity between David and Jeroboam, who inherit a number of priestly lines and sanctuaries rather than invent them. They make political moves rather than religious moves in order to consolidate their power.

---

[17] Othmar Keel and Christoph Uehlinger, *Gods, Goddesses, and Images of God in Ancient Israel*, trans. Thomas H. Trapp (Minneapolis: Fortress Press, 1998), 194: "Jeroboam's cultic activities started nothing new—nothing that had to be spread by propaganda and that thus would have called for appropriate small items to be produced—but simply attached new significance to a traditional cultic image that was at Bethel, probably, a *leftover* from the Late Bronze Age or from Iron Age I, which was probably connected originally with El rather than Baal."

[18] Patrick D. Miller, *The Religion of Ancient Israel* (Louisville, KY: Westminster John Knox Press, 2000), 256n258: "The Taanach cult stand may contain a bull relief, though it has been argued that it is an equine figure."

[19] Ibid., 251.

[20] Mark Leuchter, "Jeroboam the Ephratite," *Journal of Biblical Literature* 125, no. 1 (Spring 2006): 51–72.

A general prejudice against Jeroboam persists in the secondary literature where Jeroboam is compared to Sheba, an enemy of David. Jeroboam is never quite so explicitly seen as an enemy of Rehoboam in the early parts of the narrative concerning him. When 1 Kings 12:16 is examined more closely, Jeroboam never appears in the verse. In fact, the writer of this verse has the people proclaim it: "When all Israel saw that the king did not listen to them, and the people answered the king: 'What share have we in David? We have no heritage in the son of Jesse. To your tents, Israel! Now look to your own house, David.' So Israel went off to their tents." This verse clearly has (*h'm*) "the people" (*wyšbw 't hmlk*) "send the word back/answer," and it should be noted that this is a plural verb, so Jeroboam cannot possibly be the subject of it. A careful reading of the MT (Hebrew Bible), especially when one considers the importance of the LXX Alternative Story, militates against making too many negative assumptions about Jeroboam in 1 Kings 11–12. The Alternative Story shares an important feature with Chronicles: "Jeroboam is not introduced to the story till after Solomon's death has been reported. However it goes beyond Chronicles in ascribing blame to Rehoboam as king (end of 12:24a) before mentioning Jeroboam at all (beginning of 12:24b)."[21] The Deuteronomistic redaction of Jeroboam seems hard to overestimate.

(6) Sick Child: In the MT, both Jeroboam and David suffer the loss of a child that the Deuteronomistic editor seems to attribute to their misdeeds. Nathan tells David that since he has spurned the Lord, his child will die (2 Sam 12:14). Ahijah tells Jeroboam's wife that their child will die on account of Jeroboam's sins (1 Kgs 14:12). Interestingly, the LXX offers a dramatically different rendering of the Jeroboam material. Jeroboam's loses a son, but his wife is a daughter of Pharaoh. The Lord condemns the son of Jeroboam through Ahijah, but this condemnation is before Jeroboam commits his famous sins of making calves and establishing them at Dan and Bethel. In this case, the similarities found in the MT between David and Jeroboam are not found in the LXX.

Jan Assmann writes about the struggles in Israel's emerging literacy. These struggles manifest themselves in these different reconstructions of the death of Jeroboam's child in the LXX and MT. Assmann divides Israel's developing literacy into three stages: experience (the

---

[21] Auld, *Kings without Privilege*, 166.

Exodus), repression, and the return of the repressed (finding of the forgotten Book of the Torah). Assmann understands this as part of the "step-by-step transition to a written culture [that] points to a growth in conceptual complexity. . . . Anything that is not used is forgotten, in accordance with the principle of 'structural amnesia.'"[22] Assmann would categorize both David and Jeroboam's experiences as occurring during the second stage of repression. Assmann goes on to make the important point for our understanding of Jeroboam in the LXX: "In writing, what is no longer of its time can endure and speak. It becomes a place of refuge to which the repressed and the inopportune can retreat, and a background from which what is forgotten can reemerge, a place of latency."[23] Egypt was a tremendous enemy at the time of the writing of the Deuteronomistic History, having just killed DH's greatest king, Josiah. The story of Jeremiah and his forced exile to Egypt (Jeremiah 43) can leave no doubt as to how negatively Egypt was perceived by the Deuteronomist and those sympathetic to this school of thought. Certainly, Egypt as an ally of Jeroboam and a place of not only refuge but also hospitality was "no longer of its time." Jeroboam's marriage with Pharaoh's daughter becomes an inopportune memory. Two important prophetic figures in 1 Kings 13 also remain unnamed; perhaps this is a reverse sign of an inopportune memory becoming more opportune. Writing allows these events to reemerge for us and gives us greater insight into the complexities of Israel's past.

Finally, this story points to an important difference between David and Jeroboam, at least in the minds of the final editors. Jerome Walsh reminds us, "Death without burial was a sign of Yhwh's ultimate displeasure. Mentioning Abijah's burial in his familial tomb points up Jeroboam's fate by contrast and demonstrates that the child is blameless and that he dies only because of his father's misdeeds."[24] David's child is equally blameless, but we see that David does not suffer the same fate as Jeroboam. The story of Jeroboam's dead child has more layers and nuances at both the literary and textual levels.

(7) Moving Capital Cities: Both David and Jeroboam appear to establish new capitals. David moves the capital from Hebron to Jeru-

---

[22] Jan Assmann, *Religion and Cultural Memory: Ten Studies*, trans. Rodney Livingstone (Stanford, CA: Stanford University Press, 2006), 98–99.

[23] Ibid., 99.

[24] Jerome T. Walsh, *Old Testament Narrative: A Guide to Interpretation* (Louisville, KY: Westminster John Knox Press, 2009), 137.

salem (1 Sam 5:5). The situation is more confusing with Jeroboam. We are told that he built Shechem and then Penuel (1 Kgs 12:25). He also becomes associated with another city, Tirzah (1 Kgs 14:17), that is understood to be another capital of the northern kingdom. Both men take the bold move of building new cities. Jerusalem was already, pre-David, both a political and religious capital. Jeroboam seems to have built up different religious and political cities rather than having an all-inclusive capital. While Shechem was probably the most important city for him, "The only sure evidence alludes to the fact that Jeroboam had utilized only one city, namely Shechem, as his temporary residence (I Ki. 12:25). Therefore, the generally accepted view of three successive or contemporaneous capitals must indeed be questioned."[25] The MT never states that Jeroboam lived at Penuel. The allusion to Tirzah comes in a strongly Deuteronomistic story. This is a city much more strongly associated with the kings following Jeroboam such as Baasha (1 Kgs 15:21) and the Omrides (1 Kgs 16:23). He builds up Bethel as a religious capital in the South and possibly Dan in the North.

Both sanctuaries are interesting as they share characteristics with the sanctuary in Jerusalem. After Jerusalem, the Hebrew Bible mentions no sanctuary as often as Bethel, and Dan comes up repeatedly in the books of Genesis and Judges. Both Dan and Jerusalem have cultic foundations that are connected with springs. Dan, Bethel, and Jerusalem all had significant histories before the Israelites came to these sites. By moving worship from Jerusalem and perhaps Shiloh to Dan and Bethel, Jeroboam seems to have found places with many similarities to Jerusalem that are also rooted in the ancient past. Leadership emanating from the North is also part of the kingdom of Israel's past. "That some of Israel's key leaders such as Joshua and Samuel come from Ephraim establishes a precedent for the role that Jeroboam is about to play."[26] Initially, Jeroboam will fit into a type of Israelite leader quite comfortably. Jeroboam and David share characteristics that connect them with many powerful leaders of the past and the future who conglomerate power around themselves by moving capital cities.

---

[25] J. P. J. Olivier, "In Search of a Capital for the Northern Kingdom," *Journal of Northwest Semitic Languages* 11 (1983): 121.

[26] Gina Hens-Piazza, *1–2 Kings*, Abingdon Old Testament Commentaries (Nashville, TN: Abingdon Press, 2006), 113.

C. Royal Apologies

As we seek a greater understanding of Jeroboam, it may help to place Jeroboam in the context of other ancient Near Eastern kings. Royal apologies are seen throughout the ancient Near East with some of the best examples found among the Hittites in Asia Minor. Naturally, the assumption behind an apology is some type of controversy or suspicion about the claimant. David raises concerns at a number of levels. He does not reign as the result of proper succession, so his reign must be justified on other grounds. Matthew Suriano holds that there are five elements of an apology.[27] While these elements emerge in both of the stories of David and Jeroboam, crucial differences between David and Jeroboam must also be noted. (1) David replaces a weak Saul, and Jeroboam replaces a Rehoboam weakened by his father's unpopular taxes and his own inability to garner support in the North. (2) Validation through succession is a problem for both of them; they must rely on charismatic qualities of leadership. (3) Both have elements of divine election in their background. David receives the support of Nathan (2 Sam 7:8). Jeroboam receives the support of Ahijah (1 Kgs 11:31-39). (4) David attacks the other claimants through his allies (2 Sam 4:5-7), whereas Jeroboam is part of a popular movement against Rehoboam. (5) David begins his ascent to kingship by killing the Philistine, Goliath. He suppresses both domestic (Absalom) and external forces. Jeroboam is part of a party that kills Rehoboam's attendant Adoram and stands up to Rehoboam. He does not seem to have the same problems with Pharaoh Shishak that Rehoboam (1 Kgs 14:25) has. The first three elements are very strong in both stories, but divergences surface in the final two elements.

Both Jeroboam and David unseat troubled figures who were leading their realms. They both seem to come from nonroyal backgrounds, but they do have leadership qualities as both men are described as a "man of valor." Differences emerge because of the nature of how they unseat their predecessors. David leads a band of guerillas who attack from the margins. David faces a number of usurpers he must overcome.

---

[27] Matthew Suriano, "The Apology of Hazael: A Literary and Historical Analysis of the Tel Dan Inscription," *Journal of Near Eastern Studies* 66, no. 3 (2007): 172: "1. Historical validation to predecessors and their failures (cf. lines 2-4), 2. Validation through succession (cf. line 3), 3. Validation through 'divine election' (cf. lines 4 and 5), 4. Elimination of all claimants to power (line 6), 5. Justification through military prowess (lines 7-13)."

The narrator highlights David's military prowess repeatedly. These elements are largely missing from Jeroboam's story. Jeroboam leads a popular movement against Rehoboam. We do not hear of him facing other domestic usurpers or foreign usurpers apart from Judeans. These different elements seem to point toward different strengths of the two kings.

Ancient Near Eastern expectations toward kings vary. Many kings build temples and other large monumental architecture. Suriano explains to us, "[T]he ideal of kingship in the ancient Levant (and Israel in particular) was founded upon a concept of ancestral identity, the king himself embodied this identity as the living representative of the dynastic line."[28] Subsequently, "[R]oyal capitals of the Israelite kings symbolized their patrimony; whether it was Jerusalem (the city of David), or Samaria (the hill acquired by Omri)."[29] Although David moved the capital to Jerusalem, he is not credited with major building campaigns there. Solomon builds the temple. The narrator emphasizes other strengths that may serve as an apology for the gaps in David's records. These gaps are not in Jeroboam's record. No need exists for an apology after we hear about his numerous building campaigns. The apologetic elements of David's story are largely absent from Jeroboam's story.

David's apology consists of confronting five main charges in the books of Samuel: (1) he advanced himself at court at Saul's expense, (2) he was a deserter, (3) he was an outlaw, (4) he was a Philistine mercenary, and (5) he was implicated in the deaths of Saul, Abner, and Ishbaal. The first three elements call to mind similar events within the biography of Jeroboam. Although Jeroboam is often seen as trying to supplant Solomon, the text clearly explains that he had a reason to rebel against the king as it recounts in 11:40a: "Solomon sought to kill Jeroboam, and Jeroboam arose and fled to Egypt." Similar to David, a prophet was clearly included in his advancement as we can see the vital role the Ahijah plays in this rebellion. Ahijah will become a bitter critic of Jeroboam in 1 Kings 14:2-18, but his alliance with Jeroboam in 1 Kings 11 appears quite positive and argues against Jeroboam seeking to advance himself at Solomon's expense. Jeroboam could be

---

[28] Matthew Suriano, *The Politics of Dead Kings: Dynastic Ancestors in the Book of Kings and Ancient Israel*, Forschungen Zum Alten Testament 2, vol. 48 (Tübingen: Mohr Siebeck, 2010), 12.

[29] Ibid., 45.

accused of deserting Israel for Egypt, but the text explains the reason for this move in Solomon's attempts to kill Jeroboam (1 Kgs 11:40). Jeroboam is also accused of being an outlaw by Rehoboam, who seeks to restore the kingdom to himself (1 Kgs 12:21). Shemiah intervenes here to maintain order and preserve a peace that suits Jeroboam. The accusation of being an outlaw suits Rehoboam, but this does not appear to be a description that the ten Northern tribes would recognize. Later, in 1 Kings 14:8, the text exonerates Jeroboam as it states that God "tore the kingdom away from the House of David and gave it to you." Just as David was connected to foreigners in many ways, Jeroboam has foreign connections. He could not as easily be accused of being a mercenary, but he did spend time in Egypt and, according to some Septuagintal accounts, he desired to start a dynasty of royal blood that was thwarted only by the death of his Egyptian-born son.[30] Finally, Jeroboam is implicated in the death of Adoram (1 Kgs 12:18) much as David was implicated in the death of Saul, Abner, and Ishbaal. Yet, Jeroboam was part of a larger political group rallying against Judean tyranny, and David was involved in more interpersonal plots and machinations.

D. Jeroboam in Kings versus Chronicles

I will examine the different treatment of kings by DH and the Chronicler over the next few chapters. Before scrutinizing Jeroboam, I will open with a short survey of the different approaches to the Chronicler. The Chronicler offers numerous differences with the material in the book of Kings, but the reasons for those differences are disputed. Ultimately, I would like to acknowledge the ideological/theological nature of the book of Chronicles, but I think it is equally important to acknowledge the same nature of the book of Kings.

---

[30] Adrian Schenker, "Jeroboam and the Division of the Kingdom in the Ancient Septuagint: LXX 3 Kingdoms 12.24 A-Z, MT 1 Kings 11-12; 14 and the Deuteronomistic History," in *Israel Constructs Its History: Deuteronomistic Historiography in Recent Research*, ed. Albert de Pury, Thomas Römer, and Jean-Daniel Macchi (Sheffield, UK: Sheffield Academic Press, 2000), 219: "The marriage of Jeroboam with the sister-in-law of the Pharaoh thus represents the social rise of an upstart. This rise is emphasized by accentuating the rank of his wife. She is the (elder) sister of the queen."

1. Theories on Chronicles' Differences with Kings

The Chronicler represents different concerns than those seen in Kings. While both books have a lot of interactions with prophets, we see more concerns with worship in the book of Chronicles. The Chronicler does not hesitate to criticize the king, but we find criticism in more measured tones. "What had happened to the story of a king experienced in lust and adultery. . . . Perhaps the Chronicler was too much a preacher to include a brutally honest picture of David's flaws and familial breakdown. Another explanation also presents itself. . . . [T]he omission of David's weakness fits nicely with the Chronicler's interest in worship."[31] The Chronicler seems to delve less into the personal peccadillos of kings and to focus more on matters of the state: worship and temple. Accordingly, David is criticized for taking a census rather than adultery. We also have to consider the equally tendentious nature of Deuteronomistic History. The sacral perspective of the Royal Psalms is altogether lost in Deuteronomy 17 and much more restrained in the books of Samuel and Kings. We have to ask ourselves if the adultery story is a way to smear Bathsheba, David, and Solomon as we only find it in one source. Its validity is rarely challenged, but a more balanced view on the sources leaves open some doubts.

We see different sources operative within Chronicles and Deuteronomistic History. First Kings 11 gives us the critique of Solomon, and it seems to concern issues closer to adultery than statecraft, similar to the critique of David in Samuel. Different sources are acknowledged in Kings and Chronicles. DH mentions "the book of the Acts of Solomon" (1 Kgs 11:41), whereas Chronicles mentions a source "written in the words of Nathan the Prophet, and in the prophecy of Ahijah the Shilonite, and in the visions of Iddo the Seer" (2 Chr 9:29). This all leads me to concur with the recent trend to view David and Solomon as a unity in Chronicles.[32] Many of the distinguishing features of Solomon and David from Kings are dropped so that some unity is achieved between them. Steven McKenzie has noted the Chronicler's

---

[31] John C. Endres, *Temple, Monarchy and Word of God*, Message of Biblical Spirituality (Wilmington, DE: Michael Glazier, 1988), 95.

[32] Mark A. Throntveit, "The Relationship of Hezekiah to David and Solomon in the Books of Chronicles," in *The Chronicler as Theologian: Essays in Honor of Ralph W. Klein*, ed. M. Patrick Graham, et al., Journal for the Study of the Old Testament Supplement Series 371 (London/New York: T & T Clark International, 2003), 119.

tendency to use prophets more in history writing.³³ Solomon does not receive direct criticism in Chronicles, but the only direct criticism of David or Solomon concerns matters of statecraft rather than their private morality. I find it hard to say too much more than this. We will discover that some believe the Chronicler purposefully alters the stories of DH in order to offer a different view. It does not seem possible to prove whether the Chronicler is simply a redactor or has different sources, but both views deserve consideration.

Isaac Kalimi has proved himself to be the greatest advocate for the view of the Chronicler as redactor. His trenchant insights are firmly rooted in the text. Kalimi maintains:

> [W]e have concluded that these differences between the parallel texts of Samuel-Kings and Chronicles mostly stem from the creative literary involvement of the Chronicler with the earlier texts rather than from his "carelessness" or the "carelessness" of later transmitters and copyists, or even intentional modifications by later scribes or theologians.³⁴

I would like to note here how he emphasizes the "creative literary involvement of the Chronicler." He generally seems to understand the Chronicler as having access to Samuel–Kings. He also stresses the literary technique of the Chronicler rather than any ideology as being responsible for the changes the Chronicler made to earlier sources.³⁵ What I consider to be most important from Kalimi's work is how he equates the Chronicler with DH. He understands both in a manner similar to how Martin Noth understood DH.³⁶ They are not "mere" redactors, but historians who brought together earlier varied sources in order to create a work of history with the limitations of its time. I believe these limitations have not always been recognized, and Kalimi hits an important minatory tone as he "strives to sharpen the historian's awareness of the complexities involved in drawing 'historical

---

³³ Steven L. McKenzie, *1–2 Chronicles*, Abingdon Old Testament Commentaries (Nashville, TN: Abingdon Press, 2004), 53: "The oracles of the prophets in the last two categories are most likely compositions of the Chronicler and fit the warning and judgment functions that he typically assigns to prophetic speeches."

³⁴ Isaac Kalimi, *The Reshaping of Ancient Israelite History in Chronicles* (Winona Lake, IN: Eisenbrauns, 2005), 405.

³⁵ Ibid., 406.

³⁶ Ibid., 409.

conclusions' from these sources."[37] Both Kings and Chronicles are primarily theological works rather than historical works as current scholarship repeatedly echoes.[38]

I will still need to examine each verse on the various kings under inspection in this book. Although Kalimi argues that differences mostly stem from creative literary involvement, we cannot overgeneralize, as he does not overgeneralize. It will be necessary to examine each of the differences, as what may be true for the book of Chronicles as a whole may not be true for an individual king. As we examine the specific texts from Kings and Chronicles on the assorted kings dealt with in this volume, we will examine individual verses to see how the treatment differs. The Chronicler's interest in worship may cause him or her to take the Royal Psalms more seriously. Rather than the negative view of kingship that has prevailed in modern scholarship, Chronicles will display a view of kingship more in keeping with the Royal Psalms and the prevailing notions in the ancient Near East. We will still find searing criticism of the kings in Chronicles, but it is more limited and has surprising differences with Kings.

2. A Sampling of Verses on Jeroboam in Kings and Chronicles

Jeroboam is a more peripheral figure in Chronicles than in Kings and remains at the edge of the story rather than his central position in Kings. Ahijah repeatedly interacts with Jeroboam in Kings at the beginning and ending of his rise to power. We do not just hear reports of it, but we get the whole pericope in 1 Kings 11:29-39. The Chronicler has also been characterized as being reluctant to include prophetical stories in Chronicles.[39] Ahijah is only briefly alluded to in 2 Chronicles 9:29 and 10:15, but any semblance of a prophetical story is missing. The prophets "have become mere spectators to events, their written words providing a retrospective coverage of events rather

---

[37] Ibid., 72.

[38] Mark Leuchter, "Closing Remarks," in *Sounding in Kings: Perspectives and Methods in Contemporary Scholarship*, ed. Mark Leuchter and Klaus-Peter Adam (Minneapolis: Fortress Press, 2010), 144: "When Kings presents a series of events, the text is less a source for reconstructing the historicity of these events and more of an invitation to enter the intellectual culture of authors and audiences alike."

[39] Sara Japhet, *I & II Chronicles: A Commentary*, The Old Testament Library (Louisville, KY: Westminster/John Knox Press, 1993), 33.

than a prospective direction to the narrative action itself."[40] Ahijah's actions seem somewhat arbitrary and neither contribute to a positive and optimistic attitude nor give us a sense of a positive future. Rather, they are somewhat haunting as they allude to future divisions and unhappiness within Israel. The Chronicler's treatment of Jeroboam probably reflects a general aversion or indifference to the North. Jeroboam does not offer us a good way to understand kingship within the book of Chronicles, as the Chronicler seems much more concerned with Jerusalem.

We will also discover fewer reasons for hope in Jeroboam as we read Chronicles. Chronicles only devotes one lengthy pericope to Jeroboam, whereas Kings devotes four lengthy pericopes to Jeroboam. Importantly, he returned ($šwb$) from Egypt to attend the assembly in Shechem in 2 Chronicles 10:2. First Kings 12:2 will have a less interfering Jeroboam who stays in Egypt until he is explicitly called home in the next verse. Chronicles leaves the impression that Jeroboam could have been fomenting rebellion upon his return to the northern kingdom of Israel. These parallel pericopes in Chronicles and Kings end with a slight difference that reinforces the differences at the beginning of the pericope. First Kings 12:20 will emphasize the return of Jeroboam and the people making him king. He had already returned much earlier in the Chronicles story, but he is never explicitly declared king in this Chronicles pericope. In 2 Chronicles 13:1, Jeroboam will be referred to as king, but this is a chronological reference to situate Abijah rather than a legitimating story as we find in 1 Kings 12:20. The final important difference between these two stories is found at the end of the pericope. Both Kings and Chronicles narrate how the prophet Shemaiah warns Rehoboam and the people of Judah not to go to war against "your kinfolk." Chronicles has more specificity at the end of its pericope, as it speaks directly of Jeroboam in 2 Chronicles 12:4 as well, rather than having the people generically turn back from the northern kingdom of Israel without specifying Jeroboam as leader, as in 1 Kings 12:24. This may be partly due to the fact that Kings has Jeroboam return later to Israel, and it is clear that he will be part of this warfare initiated by Rehoboam, whereas he has not been men-

---

[40] Roland T. Boer, "Utopian Politics in 2 Chronicles 10–13," in *The Chronicler as Author: Studies in Text and Texture*, ed. M. Patrick Graham and Steven McKenzie, Journal for the Study of the Old Testament Supplement Series 263 (Sheffield, UK: Sheffield Academic Press, 1999), 391.

tioned since the beginning of 2 Chronicles 10. Both stories reiterate Jeroboam's involvement with the prophet Ahijah and his adversarial relationship with Rehoboam.

Rather than carefully narrate the failed kingship of Jeroboam, Chronicles returns to Jeroboam in an unparalleled pericope involving Rehoboam's successor, Abijah, who is referred to in Kings as Abijam. Kings tells us very little about him other than his being a successor of Rehoboam. First Kings 15:6 seems to mistakenly return to Rehoboam in a passage about Abijam, and it tells us that Jeroboam went to war with Rehoboam. First Chronicles 13:2 seems to clean up this mistake by telling us that Jeroboam went to war with Abijah. It then goes on to narrate an unparalleled pericope about this war.

This pericope contains a number of curious anecdotes—some of which complement the story told in Kings but others of which are quite unique. Jeroboam appears to lead a much stronger army than Abijah, as the archaeology of ancient Israel and Judah would suggest, with greater wealth and population in the North. Abijah has a long, minatory speech in 2 Chronicles 13. As he accuses Jeroboam and all Israel of rebellion and idolatry, he ends up characterizing Jeroboam in a manner similar to some of the accusations leveled against David as he began his rise toward kingship. Second Chronicles 13:7 accuses Jeroboam of attracting worthless men and scoundrels around him. This is not altogether unlike 1 Samuel 22:2, which describes David as gathering everyone in distress, debt, and discontent around him. There are no descriptions of David like this in Chronicles. These negative aspects of David from the Deuteronomistic History all seem to get superimposed only on Jeroboam in the books of Chronicles. We hear none of the pericopes about Jeroboam designating shrines/high places in the northern kingdom of Israel, nor do we hear about the worship of idolatrous bulls. The Chronicler seems to use this story to acquaint us with only this rebellious aspect of Jeroboam. Finally, God is credited with striking down Jeroboam at the end of this war between Jeroboam and Abijah (2 Chr 13:20). His death seems to be peaceful and unremarkable in Kings, but it is quite the opposite in Chronicles.

3. Differences between Jeroboam in Kings and Chronicles

Kings offers a much more complete story about Jeroboam than Chronicles does, as Jeroboam becomes closely associated with sin in Kings, which seems to lead to a number of stories to explicate this relationship.[41] Kings inserts its greatest hero, Josiah, into the midst of this story in 1 Kings 13:2, which does not happen in Chronicles. The Deuteronomist builds up the systematic nature of Jeroboam's apostasy in a manner totally foreign to Chronicles. The sins of Jeroboam almost become a kind of mantra throughout the rest of Kings (1 Kgs 16:31; 2 Kgs 3:3; 2 Kgs 10:29, 31; 2 Kgs 13:2, 11; 2 Kgs 14:24; 2 Kgs 15:5, 8, 24, 28; 2 Kgs 17:22). This is all the more remarkable when one realizes that Chronicles never mentions Jeroboam again after he dies in 2 Chronicles 13. The Jeroboam material in Kings seems to be written in a manner that foreshadows and necessitates the character of Josiah. D. W. Van Winkle claims, "Much of what Jeroboam does, Josiah undoes."[42] Since the Chronicler does not lift Josiah to the same heights as the Deuteronomist, he has no need to demonize him to the same extent. This leaves us with the need to restore Jeroboam to a more appropriate position. The Chronicler may be open to seeing some more royal attributes in Jeroboam. At the same time, Jeroboam clearly has diminished importance in Chronicles. He is not a "man of valor" like in Kings; rather he just seems to have the generic qualities of kingship. If we consider the portrait of a king derived from the Royal Psalms rather than that of Chronicles and Kings, we might be forced to think very differently about Jeroboam. Both Kings and Chronicles leave behind hints that the historical Jeroboam was very different from the Jeroboam of either of these books.

Conclusion

By highlighting forced labor, priestly connections, and moving capital cities, we see three minor motifs in the Davidic Apology that become major motifs in the Jeroboam story. Perhaps David has the good fortune of avoiding the major sites like Dan, Bethel, and Shechem in the North that are so wrought with biblical history. Jerusalem is a kind of tabula rasa that Dan and Bethel can never be. David's use of the aniconic tradition frees him from the priestly criticism emanating from Shiloh. Yet both men work around the Mushite Levites from

---

[41] Joseph, *Portrait of the Kings*, 109: "The entirety of the Jeroboam narrative in these four chapters is purposeful and displays comprehensiveness and completeness."

[42] D. W. Van Winkle, "1 Kings XII 25–XIII 34: Jeroboam's Cultic Innovations and the Man of God from Judah," *Vetus Testamentum* 46, no. 1 (1996): 111.

Shiloh, both men employ corvèe labor, and both men seem to make use of a number of capital cities. These can be seen in David's life, but they come to both define Jeroboam's life and offer a reason for his ultimately idolatrous and polytheistic depiction. Jeroboam represents a tradition that cannot be cleaned up as easily as David's and leads to a number of Northern dynasties that appear to have greater influence and wealth than can be seen in the South. The Deuteronomistic patina comes to define Jeroboam, but a more complicated and textured reality underlays this depiction.

Chapter Four
୨୧

Ahab
Omri's Son or Jezebel's Husband?

Ahab presents us with a conundrum. The reader strikes a rich biblical vein with the abundant material on Ahab in the book of Kings. This material makes him like his predecessors Saul, David, Solomon, and Jeroboam. Multiple chapters are devoted to all these kings, yet the material is mainly of a literary nature rather than a historical nature. In his historical reconstruction of biblical times, John Rogerson demonstrates the counterintuitive nature of the problem: "Frustratingly, whereas it might be expected that the greater availability of evidence both in the Bible and in Assyrian records might ease the task of reconstructing Ahab's reign, the opposite is the case."[1] If we cannot quite reconstruct Ahab's reign, archaeology can tell us considerably more about his time than the times of his predecessors. We may not be able to understand Ahab as well as we would like, but we can understand kingship considerably better.

The book of Kings devotes six chapters to the reign of Ahab (1 Kgs 16:29–22:40). Ahab receives the most attention of the kings of the Omride Dynasty (885–841), which was founded by his father, Omri. Ahab forces us to consider his father and the role of dynasties within Israel. Ahab's kingship will allow us to devote time to understanding the role of the queen, as his wife, Jezebel, is a particularly powerful

---

[1] John W. Rogerson, *Chronicle of the Old Testament Kings: The Reign-by-Reign Record of the Rulers of Ancient Israel* (London: Thames and Hudson, 1999), 103.

queen. Ahab's interactions with Elijah will reinforce the important role of prophets within kingship. We see considerable development of the great cities of the North during his reign, and extensive extrabiblical materials on Ahab will be reviewed. I will conclude the chapter with Jehu's coup that put an end to the Omride Dynasty.

A. Ahab in Kings versus Chronicles

The treatment of Ahab in Chronicles and Kings is radically different. The book of Chronicles mentions him thirteen times, fifty times fewer than the book of Kings. Both books narrate his famous confrontation with the prophet Micaiah and subsequent fiasco with Jehoshaphat, although Kings includes more detail. Both books repeatedly refer to the House of Ahab in 2 Chronicles 22 and 2 Kings 9. From a strictly historical perspective, the book of Chronicles is probably more accurate, as Ahab does not seem to be a prominent king. This accuracy may be accidental, as it is easy to attribute it to the Southern bias of the Chronicler who usually gives short shrift to the Northern kings. We see this same tendency in terms of where the Chronicler only mentions Ahab's father one time, whereas the book of Kings mentions him twelve times. A closer examination of the differences between the books will reveal further insights into the character of Ahab.

The book of Kings narrates numerous stories about Ahab. A consistent theme emerges in many of the stories of Ahab in both books. Ahab has many dealings with the prophets. Whereas his dealings are limited to one prophet in the book of Chronicles, he deals with another prophet in the book of Kings: Elijah. The book of Chronicles has one pericope about Ahab, while there appear to be about eight separate pericopes involving Ahab in Kings. These pericopes have Ahab interacting with numerous individuals involving the full spectrum of characters. We find the holy innocents in Naboth and Obadiah. His wife, Jezebel, is quite common in these stories. We also have him with named and unnamed prophets. He emerges as quite a ridiculous and ultimately ineffectual figure in many of the stories, perhaps even serving as comic relief when he is cuckolded or upbraided by Jezebel.

While it is not easy to piece together a consistent picture of Ahab in Kings and Chronicles, certain pericopes must be ignored. Chronicles confirms many of the most negative stories about Ahab, but it lacks the nuances that we find in Kings. Jerome Walsh has argued for a multiplicity of voices in the stories about Ahab in Kings:

> Unlike chapter 20, chapter 21 does not contain pro-Ahab and anti-Ahab narrative voices in tension with each other; both parts of chapter 21 depict Ahab negatively. This, as we shall see, does not preclude the possibility of multiple narrative voices that are each anti-Ahab, but for different reasons.[2]

Walsh strongly argues for a positive and negative narrator with the negative narrator often redacting the positive pericopes or kernels of pericopes within the book of Kings. We could liken this to the treatment of Jeroboam in the Hebrew Bible and the Septuagint. The Hebrew Bible contains much more hostility to Jeroboam than the Septuagint, but there is a probably a multiplicity of negative voices in the Hebrew Bible. Even though this may be the case, we can see a positive voice in the initial commissioning of Jeroboam in the Hebrew Bible that is accentuated in the Septuagint. Kings will force us to consider a number of different aspects of Ahab. Chronicles usually has a more positive vision of kingship, but Kings will offer us a more positive vision in this instance. We will ultimately try to isolate the positive verses concerning Ahab and consider why they are there. At the same time, the negative narrator of Kings is considerably more negative than Chronicles.

This negativity becomes apparent when Ahab is compared to Jeroboam. Jeroboam is the Deuteronomist's paradigm for the story of an evil king. Yet it appears that Jeroboam had a chance to be a second David. We see him being commissioned by the prophet Ahijah in 1 Kings 11 and being pushed into leadership by the popular will of the people in Shechem as they are disgusted by Rehoboam. He cannot live up to this potential, and his reign ends in disaster as he founds worship sites in the wrong places (Dan and Bethel) with the wrong symbol (bulls). Ahab goes even beyond this level of apostasy. Alison Joseph tell us, "Since Jeroboam is established as the *Unheilsherrscher* in 1 Kings 13–14, to be worse than the prototype of evil (this comparative is articulated twice in the regnal formula, 1 Kgs. 16:30 and 33) sets up Ahab in a position of surpassing Jeroboam in claiming this title."[3] Ahab is unique as he comes up relatively rarely outside the pericopes

---

[2] Jerome T. Walsh, *Ahab: The Construction of a King*, Interfaces (Collegeville, MN: Liturgical Press, 2006), 47.

[3] Alison L. Joseph, *Portrait of the Kings: The Davidic Prototype in Deuteronomistic Poetics* (Minneapolis: Fortress Press, 2015), 145.

devoted to him. Yet we have this mixed material about him, as we do about Jeroboam. This seems to inspire the negative narrator of 1 Kings to highlight the even greater evil of Ahab. He is not part of the narrative arc that we find from Jeroboam to Josiah; rather, he epitomizes the dangers of the wicked king who ultimately ends up worshiping the god of his wife. This was hinted at with Solomon, but it now comes into full relief with Ahab. Ahab's unparalleled evil is depicted as "1 Kings envisages Baal as a foreign deity introduced into Israel from outside by Jezebel and Ahab."[4] The dangers of Jeroboam are fully realized during the Omride Dynasty: "This is especially true after Omri and Ahab (1 Kgs 16), who erected a Baal temple in the new capital city Samaria [brought foreign impurity into Israel]; from this point on, the north is verily contaminated."[5] Jeroboam worshiped at the wrong places in Dan and Bethel and had the wrong religious symbols, but there was no threat of Baalism with him. The Deuteronomist will have that threat realized during the Omride Dynasty. The narrative of 1 Kings might be quite distant from what archaeology tells us between overlapping Canaanite and Israelite cultures, but it is important for us to see the singular concern of the Deuteronomist, a concern not necessarily shared by the Chronicler.

I will focus on the pericope involving Jehoshaphat as both Chronicles and Kings deal with it. The rest of the chapter will develop the other pericopes in Kings. Ahab only receives attention focused on his reign in 2 Chronicles 18. Northern kings like Ahab generally receive little attention, but Ahab is the exception. This attention probably has more to do with the alliance between Jehoshaphat and Ahab than Ahab himself. Ralph Klein believes that Jehoshaphat ultimately receives a final stunning condemnation by the Chronicler because of his previous alliance with Ahab.[6] His final condemnation is based on an event similar to Ahab, except Jehoshaphat is now reaching to Ahaziah in a way too similar to the outreach to Ahab. The Chronicler will have none of it (2 Chr 20:37). Let us carefully examine the details of this relationship.

---

[4] Walsh, *Ahab*, 64.

[5] Walter Dietrich, *The Early Monarchy in Israel: The Tenth Century B.C.E.* (Atlanta: Society of Biblical Literature, 2007), 25.

[6] Ralph Klein, *2 Chronicles: A Commentary*, Hermeneia: A Critical and Historical Commentary on the Bible (Minneapolis: Fortress Press, 2012), 297.

The pericope in 2 Chronicles 18 immediately announces a marriage alliance between Jehoshaphat and Ahab. This information is not present in 1 Kings 22, which narrates the same pericope involving Micaiah. The Chronicler is more interested in telling the story of Jehoshaphat than Ahab. Ahab plays into this story because "the marriage alliance and treaty between the two kingdoms led to joint action and even reciprocal influence."[7] The Chronicler will include both positive and negative material on Jehoshaphat, as he will also discuss the prophet Jehu's rebuke of Jehoshaphat (2 Chr 19:1-3), as well as Jehoshaphat's victory over Moab and Ammon (2 Chr 20:1-30). The former example shows us a surprising difference between the book of Chronicles and the book of Kings. We see tremendous differences in the treatment of early kings like Rehoboam, Abijah, Asa, and Jehoshaphat. These differences involve the introduction of both new prophetic material involving familiar prophets as well as altogether new prophets. The prophet Jehu is known to us in Kings from his involvement with Baasha (1 Kgs 16:1-4). While this is not altogether implausible, it is a bit unusual, as at least a decade separates these two kings. What is more to the point is that Chronicles seems to have a more consistent pattern of good kings who still need to be chastised by prophets.

Jehu offers a mild rebuke of Jehoshaphat. Although he has helped the wicked, he has burned the *asherim* from the land. His alliance with Ahab in 2 Chronicles 18 would seem to militate against him, but he displays good governance in 2 Chronicles 19 when he appoints judges on behalf of the Lord (2 Chr 19:7) as well as priests and Levites to also judge (2 Chr 19:8). We then find him successfully engaging in a number of wars with aggressive Transjordanian powers encroaching on Judah. He quickly proclaims a fast (2 Chr 20:3) and ultimately enjoys success in these battles. Accordingly, we have many examples of Ahab's poor governance, the most notable being the incident with Naboth (1 Kgs 21); the book of Kings, however, seems to be much less interested in governance than the book of Chronicles. Jehu's prophetic rebuke and Jehoshaphat's fast are followed by the "Spirit of the Lord" inspiring a speech (2 Chr 20:14) from a previously unknown figure named "Jahaziel." Jahaziel proceeds to speak for three verses (2 Chr 20:15-17), which is followed by Jehoshaphat's humble bowing down after the words of Jahaziel.

---

[7] Sara Japhet, *The Ideology of the Book of Chronicles and Its Place in Biblical Thought* (Winona Lake, IN: Eisenbrauns, 2009), 244.

Jahaziel seems to be identified as a prophet in 2 Chronicles 20:20 when Jehoshaphat tells the inhabitants of Jerusalem to "believe the prophets" the next day. As the Chronicler has previously demonstrated with David and Rehoboam, we now have an ideal pattern of behavior here. A stronger resemblance may even be found with Solomon, as they both receive the promise of rest in 1 Chronicles 22:9 and 2 Chronicles 20:30.[8] A "message of prayer, repentance and restoration is the central theme of the subsequent presentation in 2 Chronicles 10–36, rather than a supposed theory of divine rewards and punishment."[9] If we consider the promises of the Royal Psalms, they would seem to influence the treatment of the kings in Chronicles much more than they do in Kings. Ahab will have excluded himself from prayer, repentance, and restoration by his idolatrous actions, but Jehoshaphat can still benefit from this. Perhaps the Royal Psalms are more fully realized in the South.

The enhanced role of the prophets in Chronicles is well known, but we see a pattern of intense activity emerge with numerous prophets in the case of Jehoshaphat. The role of prophets in Kings is more selective and parsimonious. Ahab will deal with two named prophets in Kings (Micaiah-ben-Imlah and Elijah), but their roles seem to be much more limited than that of the numerous prophets dealing with Jehoshaphat in Chronicles. Instead of receiving a detailed description of Ahab's rival Jehoshaphat, Kings focuses on Elijah's dealings with Ahab.

The difference between Kings and Chronicles concerns a greater interest with Ahab in Kings than Chronicles. Both books take some interest in Jehoshaphat, but he is a more developed character in Chronicles. Both sources fault Jehoshaphat for his relationship with Ahab, but Chronicles delves deeper into his character. Kings devotes much more interest to Ahab, as we would expect, since Northern interests are largely neglected in Chronicles.

B. The Role of Dynasties

As we consider dynasties, I believe we are invited to consider kingship as an institution rather than an individual. I have already

---

[8] Japhet, *Ideology of the Book of Chronicles*, 306.

[9] Brian E. Kelly, "'Retribution' Revisited: Covenant, Grace and Restoration," in *The Chronicler as Theologian: Essays in Honor of Ralph W. Klein*, ed. M. Patrick Graham, Steven McKenzie, and Gary Knoppers, Journal for the Study of the Old Testament Supplement Series 371 (London/ New York: T & T Clark International, 2003), 217.

outlined this idea in chapter 2. Kingship appears much more stable in the southern kingdom of Judah (where the Bible tells us there was only one dynasty), than in the northern kingdom of Israel (where there were many dynasties). While Ahab is only the second king I have dedicated a chapter to in this book, he represents the third dynasty in the northern kingdom of Israel, which was founded by his father, Omri. Although this chapter focuses on Ahab, Omri's importance cannot be overlooked: "[I]t is clear that even in the late 8th cent BCE—well over a century after the dramatic takeover by Jehu and his descendants—the Assyrians continued to refer to Samaria as the 'House [i.e., dynasty or kingdom] of Omri.'"[10] The previous two dynasties were founded by Jeroboam and Baasha. This type of instability did not exist in the South, as David's dynasty endured during the time of these three dynasties.

I will argue that the transitory nature of the dynasties may represent different attitudes toward governance. While Jeroboam represents a split with the South that may be largely based on resources, something quite different appears to be going on with the dynasty of Omri and Ahab. The narrator represents Jeroboam as using many of the traditional governing structures. His coup comes about as the result of an assembly who nominate him after being rebuffed by Rehoboam. He is portrayed as moving the capital city between Shechem (1 Kgs 12:25), Penuel (1 Kgs 12:25), and Tirzah (1 Kgs 14:17). We see the same thing happen at the beginning of the United States of America as New York, Philadelphia, and Washington, DC, were all the capital city. These moving capitals seem to reflect the instability of a new nation. Even though scholars argue whether this may actually be the case or not, few would doubt the instability of Jeroboam's reign. Something rather different appears to be happening with Omri's dynasty.

A new city is associated with Omri: Samaria. Samaria is first casually mentioned in the story in 1 Kings 13 where the "man of God" comes to Bethel in order to confront Jeroboam. It is rather discordant, as Jeroboam attempted to legitimize the sanctuaries at Bethel and Dan, but Samaria is condemned with Bethel in 1 Kings 13:32. I believe this gives us an idea of the importance of Samaria. Samaria seems to originally have been a lineage-controlled village called Shamir in Judges 10:1-2, which Omri eventually bought from the clan of "Shemir."[11]

---

[10] Ron E. Tappy, "Samaria," in *New Interpreter's Dictionary of the Bible*, ed. Katharine D. Sakenfeld (Nashville, TN: Abingdon Press, 2009), 5:66.

[11] Ibid., 63.

Even though there is no context for the critique of it in 1 Kings 13, it is such an important city in the later history of the northern kingdom that is impossible for it to be overlooked.

A more consistent story about Samaria emerges in 1 Kings 16. Here, the narrator portrays Samaria as a new city, which Ahab's father Omri built after he purchased the land. This portrayal of establishing a new capital bears some resemblance to another story in the Old Testament. The first capital of the southern kingdom appears to be Hebron. David resided here for seven years before he moved to Jerusalem. Hebron is associated with Abraham first in Genesis 13, and he eventually buys some land here in order to bury is wife, Sarah, in Genesis 23:19. Omri's initial acquisition of Samaria would seem to be as modest as Abraham's acquisition. This may be a sign of two origin stories for Samaria: one from the North and one from the South. The Southern tradition is represented in 1 Kings 13, and the Northern tradition is represented in 1 Kings 16.

First Kings diminishes Samaria's importance by identifying Ahab with Samaria rather than Israel. "The first characterization of Ahab [in 1 Kings 21] is easily overlooked. The narrator tells us that he is 'King of Samaria' (21:1), and that he has a palace in Jezreel. The title 'King of Samaria' is very rare in the Hebrew Bible, occurring only here and in 2 Kings 1:3, where it describes Ahab's son Ahaziah."[12] This designation of "king of Samaria" serves to distance both Ahab and the Omride dynasty from the Israelite tradition in which Samaria had only the most tenuous of roots.[13] Samaria can be characterized in Kings as something foreign to both Israel and Judah, hence the powerful dynasty associated with it becomes something equally foreign and less threatening. Samaria represents an important and attractive rival to Jerusalem, so we can see the Deuteronomist's need to attack it in a powerful and sustained manner.

C. The Role of Queen

Jezebel plays a crucial role in the new type of governance that the Omride dynasty represents. Previously, we have heard very little about the role of women in governance. The queen mother certainly plays a role, but it could be argued this role is related more to legitimacy

---

[12] Walsh, *Ahab*, 48.
[13] Ibid.

than to governance. As we explore Jezebel, we will see a queen actively involved in the governance of Israel. We have seen the judge Deborah and her companion Jael play significant roles in the past, as did the sister of Moses, Miriam. Yet these women arose in extraordinary situations where they helped fend off chaos or initiated new patterns of leadership in fluid times.

Jezebel's most provocative role may be in the infamous Naboth story of 1 Kings 21. We can see antecedents for Jezebel in women like Abigail. Yet Abigail plays the role of peacemaker as she calms down David, who could barely endure the slights of Nabal (1 Sam 25). Jezebel exemplifies a different form of governance. Although Ahab can appear cuckolded at times by her, her role is unique in the Old Testament. In 1 Kings 21:7, she will tell her husband, "You now will make kingship over Israel." Jezebel can be seen in a number of different manners. If we allow for just one narrator, the narrator can be seen as portraying her as a foreign woman accustomed to a different type of governance. Unlike the idolatry with which she is normally associated, in 1 Kings 21 Jezebel is the corrupter of Israel's law and morals through her domination of Ahab and the elders of Jezreel.[14] This places an enormous importance on Jezebel—perhaps too much importance.

Ahab does not appear completely out of the blue. The Omride dynasty operated on an international level, seemingly before Jezebel ever arrived on the scene. They warred with the Moabites, and Jezebel represents an alliance with the Phoenicians. Subsequently, she is portrayed as viewing Israelite laws in a different mode than previous kings and queens, using these laws to her own advantage as we would expect from an absolute Canaanite monarch. This authoritarian display ultimately benefits her husband Ahab, but Ahab's strengthened position can only empower her. While there is a mutually agreeable position between the two here, ultimately the Deuteronomist does not seem to want to let Ahab off the hook so easily by placing all the blame on Jezebel. If we identify more than one narrator in 1 Kings 21, we can see the second half of the story even more negatively toward Ahab than the first half. "Yhwh's condemnation not only targets Ahab and passes over Jezebel in silence; it also echoes Jezebel's imperatives in 21:15 to counterpose Ahab and Elijah as principal and opposing

---

[14] Marvin A. Sweeney, *I & II Kings: A Commentary*, The Old Testament Library (Louisville, KY: Westminster John Knox Press, 2007), 250.

figures."¹⁵ While Jezebel represents a new development in the story of kings and their governance, the Deuteronomist will not allow her to be the scapegoat of this story. She plays a nefarious role and receives her brutal punishment, but Ahab still bears the primary responsibility. He is not just a cuckolded man; rather, he is the primary enemy of Elijah and uses Jezebel rather than being used by her.

Jezebel's prominence also models a new type of family. We have had strong women in previous stories, but we repeatedly see Jezebel fearlessly interacting with men in the stories in which she features. If we compare her to Bathsheba, we will find that both women are vital to the interests of their sons, but Jezebel plays a more active role in confronting the enemies of her spouse. While there is still a domestic nature to it, as it involves her spouse, we can understand governance here to be exercised in a broader manner. She is still dependent on her husband, but she takes an active role that bolsters his power. Her role in governance may be implicitly acknowledged by her execution at the time of the coup d'etat. Although the understanding of *gebira* (queen mother) and what it actually means in terms of an official role is hotly contested,¹⁶ Jezebel poses a different kind of threat than any of her predecessors. She is portrayed as being part of a new, more threatening type of leadership that puts prophets on edge and that militantly promotes Baal. Jehu and Elisha must destroy Jezebel in a manner that no previous biblical text has depicted. Her threat as wife and queen mother is unparalleled, as is the violence used to counteract it. The Omride governance leads to a spasm of violence on the international stage as the prophet Elisha reaches out to Damascus as the Phoenician-Israelite alliance is put down.

D. The Role of Prophets

1. Importance of the Murder of Naboth

The Naboth incident appears right in the middle of the Ahab material in 1 Kings 21. We can view the stories around Ahab as operating at a number of different strata—some early and some late. Generally

---

¹⁵ Walsh, *Ahab*, 63.
¹⁶ Datmar Pruin, "What Is in a Text?—Searching for Jezebel," in *Ahab Agonistes: The Rise and Fall of the Omri Dynasty*, ed. Lester L. Grabbe, Library of Hebrew Bible/Old Testament Studies (London: T & T Clark, 2007), 222–23.

the material involving Elijah and Elisha will be later, but the Naboth incident may serve a different function. Ahab represents an important transition from figures like David, Solomon, and Jeroboam, who are primarily literary figures, to Hezekiah, Manasseh, and Josiah, who are firmly embedded in the objective historical record. Ahab is found in the Kurkh Inscriptions, which subsequently makes him the earliest archaeological reference from the Old Testament and makes him a historical contemporary with a foreign leader (Shalmaneser III of Assyria). As a transitionary figure, we are not surprised to see evidence of transition in the texts concerning him. The Naboth incident has been identified as a text that may reflect the transition from a tribal entity to more of a nation-state, as Naboth's understanding of the land is tribal whereas Ahab's understanding is national.[17] Elijah plays a role in the incident—but only after the principals of Ahab and Naboth have squared off.

This familiar text has some surprises when one looks at it more closely. Naboth is not referred to as an Israelite but as a Jezreelite. Jezreel was once a capital of Israel.[18] This is further evidence of the transitory times. Naboth is clearly identified with a more tribal locale. As has been noted, Ahab is identified not as king of Israel but as king of Samaria. As we move through this chapter, Ahab will eventually be identified as the king of Israel in 1 Kings 21:17. It seems to operate as a suture in the text connecting this story with a possibly later master narrative. Finally, Elijah is introduced to us in a different manner as well. When we are first introduced to him in 1 Kings 17:1, we are told he is a Tishbite, who is from Tishbe in Gilead. Rather than a story involving three Israelites, the story can appear to involve three different tribes or geographical locations

Elijah appears on the scene in 1 Kings 21:17. His fight is with Ahab rather than Jezebel. We only have a parenthetical remark concerning Jezebel in 1 Kings 21:23. Rather than idolatry or the larger issues concerning Israel at its inception, we see Elijah acting as a prophet in the mold of Nathan. We have a bitter and very personal conflict here between Elijah and Ahab. We also have a similar result to Nathan's confrontation with David. Ahab winds up weeping and lamenting his ways. Both men murdered their adversaries and both men bitterly regretted their actions. Unlike David, Ahab will go on to be involved

---

[17] Tammi Schneider, "Ahab," in *New Interpreter's Dictionary of the Bible*, ed. Katharine D. Sakenfeld (Nashville, TN: Abingdon Press, 2009), 1:81–82.

[18] Ibid., 81.

in idolatry and other acutely problematic behaviors. If all we had was 1 Kings 21, we might expect a different type of leader in Ahab. In fact, there is considerable archaeological evidence of Ahab's successful leadership, yet the Bible chooses to tell a different story.

First Kings 21 represents an almost unrelentingly negative picture of Ahab. The Deuteronomist is pulling out all the stops in order to leave no doubt as to his character. While Ahab is embedded within the historical record, 1 Kings 21 seems to be, primarily, a late literary creation in which few nuances are left within the portrayal of Ahab; he is almost unremittingly evil here. We have just bad and worse Ahab in this narrative. Glimmers of light are left in his interactions with characters in other stories, but these can be seen as the necessities of history. Certain historical facts cannot be ignored. When we are dealing with more of a literary creation, as in 1 Kings 21, Ahab can appear to be more like Jeroboam. The final literary picture of Jeroboam has his prior positive interaction with Ahijah neatly negated in 1 Kings 14. This literary picture of Ahab also serves to accentuate all his bad qualities.

2. Micaiah

An important pattern emerged with Jeroboam in the role of the prophet. This was a pattern that we saw, to a more limited extent, in David's relationships with his prophets. Prophets can be both supportive and obstructive. Jeroboam's initial interactions with Ahijah were quite positive (1 Kgs 11:31-40), but they quickly moved in a negative direction once Jeroboam assumed leadership of Israel. Ahab represents a variant of that tradition—a much more negative series of relationships.

Although prophets are often presented as mavericks or solitary figures, I reiterate that most of them seem to be embedded in a structure around the king. While this is not as evident with Elijah, it becomes quite apparent in Ahab's relationship with Micaiah ben-Imlah in 1 Kings 22. We start the chapter with a band of prophets advising the two kings, Ahab of Israel and Jehoshaphat of Judah. "Here the biblical text may be useful. First Kings 22:4 suggests that Judah was subordinate to Israel, perhaps being a vassal, as was Moab."[19] Ahab

---

[19] Lester L. Grabbe, "Omri and Son, Incorporated: The Business of History," in *Congress Volume: Helsinki 2010*, ed. Martti Nissinen, Supplements to *Vetus Testamentum* 148 (Leiden: Brill, 2012), 69.

has a keen interest in Judah allying with Israel in its long war against Aram (present-day Syria), Israel's neighbor to the northeast. Judah would not be so interested in waging war against Aram as it has Israel as a buffer. Here we see the prophet emerge as a part of the governance of Israel and Judah.

Prophets function in both an ideal and realistic manner. Prophets are often portrayed very idealistically, but the first part of 1 Kings 22 should disabuse us of any notion that prophets only played an ideal role. In 1 Kings 22:1-6, we see the prophets clearly doing the bidding of King Ahab. Aram and Israel have reached a peace of sorts, but it is a peace that Ahab resents because Aram has control over Ramoth-Gilead. This leaves Israel with depleted resources, and Aram is all that closer to the heartland of Israel in the Cisjordan. The prophets in 1 Kings 22:1-6 serve as less than independent functionaries, as Ahab tries to dupe Jehoshaphat. Jehoshaphat turns the tables after he inquires about Micaiah ben-Imlah. Here we seem to see the more idealized version of the prophet. Rather than someone simply doing the bidding of the king, Micaiah has a measure of independence. Micaiah is a wily advisor of the king. I think we must imagine a political figure who today would have survived many administrations in Washington, DC, serving for both the Democratic and the Republican Parties. Even this ideal prophet is not above lying, as he demonstrably lies in 1 Kings 22:15. After all the buildup to him and the request from Jehoshaphat, we can imagine Micaiah the prophet manipulating both the kings and forcing them to beg the truth from him. When he finally tells them the truth that war against Aram is not advisable, the other prophets react in an equally outraged and violent manner. This only serves to allow him to make his point even more strenuously. As the other prophets protest, he now emerges as a defender of the truth.

We can see the prophet here as the one who has permission to speak the hard truth to the king. In governance, it helps to have a system of checks and balances; the prophet can be a check on the power of the king. This power does not always leave him or her in a comfortable or desirable role, but it does give him or her a necessary role. Many other prophets choose not to play this role and seem to live a comfortable life in the court of the king; the narrators of the Bible imagine something quite different from this role.

This scene also allows a more positive image of Ahab to emerge. This story contains more historical artifacts than what we found in the previous chapter concerning Naboth. There seems to have been a coalition of Syrians (Irueheleni of Hamath and Ben-Hadad of Damascus) aided by Ahab, among others, from the nation-states of the Levant in their battles against Assyria.[20] Although Ahab probably has a grander role in the book of Kings than history would allow, he probably did have some role. Later, this coalition seems to have broken down, and now the Syrians and Israelites are fighting among themselves. Ahab's desire to involve a reluctant Jehoshaphat also makes sense. This portrayal of Ahab starts off in a fairly positive manner before turning negative. In 1 Kings 22:1-4, we see King Ahab with the same expansionistic concerns that will characterize the Deuteronomist's hero, Josiah, at the end of the book of Kings. In much the same way that Josiah is interested in traditional Israelite towns, we see Ahab reminding Jehoshaphat of their traditional inheritance in Ramoth Gilead. The negative narrator returns in 1 Kings 22:5-28, but the positive narrator returns when the battle commences in 1 Kings 22:29.

Walsh insists that Ahab here puts Jehoshaphat in the position of honor, and he is the only one who appears to be king as Ahab goes into battle as a lowly soldier: "Considered in itself, this deed presents Ahab in a positive light. It highlights his courage and willingness to risk himself, and his readiness to offer protection to his vassal."[21] It should also be noted that his death is not altogether unlike Josiah's death at Megiddo, as both of them seem to die by a random arrow. The negative narrator will return in (possibly) verse 37 and definitely verse 38.[22] The overall impression of this chapter on Micaiah and Ahab is quite negative, but it is not the monolithically negative chapter that 1 Kings 21 is. Ahab, like Jeroboam, has admirable qualities of courage and valor that play out on the historical canvas. The literary aspects of this chapter dominate it, however, and complete the portrait of Ahab in a very negative manner.

3. Elijah

The situation with Elijah is radically different from the one with Micaiah. A tradition exists around Elijah and Elisha that is quite different from any other prophetic tradition. "The Elijah and Elisha blocks

---

[20] Gösta Ahlström, *The History of Ancient Palestine*, ed. Diana V. Edelman (Minneapolis: Fortress Press, 1993), 577.
[21] Walsh, *Ahab*, 65.
[22] Ibid., 76.

in 1 Kings 17–2 Kings 9 appear to have roots in Israel, but the material in them that treats king Ahab is less securely Israelite and displays little of its political situation."[23] Although Elisha is particularly involved in governmental affairs at the international level, the traditions around these prophets are very different than what we see with Ahijah or what we will see with Isaiah and Huldah. Many posit that the Elijah and Elisha layers within the book of Kings represent one of the last layers to be part of the book.[24] Both figures maintain a great standing within Kings and the rest of the Bible, even the New Testament. Elijah, in particular, plays a unifying role with many characteristics of Moses. Elijah and Elisha help return the narrative to some of the central religious concerns present at the inception of Israel at Sinai/Horeb. Elijah even returns the narrative to Horeb (1 Kgs 19:8) in case any reader was missing the point.

After the focus on governance with David, Solomon, Rehoboam, and Jeroboam, Elijah brings the narrative to a much more visceral level as he personally struggles with an "evil" king. We do not see him involved in the administration of Israel as a governmental official. Rather, he gets personally involved with some other governmental officials in a most unorthodox fashion. Interestingly, Elijah is from the contested area of Gilead (1 Kgs 17:1). This may add further significance to the area and help explain why Ahab wants to get it back so much. In 1 Kings 18, we see Elijah interacting with one of Ahab's officials, Obadiah. Obadiah has a great loyalty to a group of seemingly Yahwistic prophets who are not faring well under the administration of Ahab and Jezebel. In contrast to the band of prophets with which Micaiah has to contend, we see a band of fiercely Yahwistic prophets whose loyalty does not seem to be so easily compromised.

Elijah's final scene with Ahab in 1 Kings 21 offers a sharp contrast to the rest of his interactions with Elijah and Micaiah. Different sources

---

[23] Daniel Fleming, *The Legacy of Israel in Judah's Bible: History, Politics, and the Reinscribing of Tradition* (New York: Cambridge University Press, 2012), 112.

[24] Ahlström, *The History of Ancient Palestine*, 585: "[T]he stories of the Elijah-Elisha cycle most probably refer to a time later than that of king Ahab. They are not reliable source materials for the social and religious circumstances during Ahab's time. The D-historian has used these traditions for the sole purpose of devaluating Ahab and his entourage as Baal-worshippers, which nobody should be, and to highlight Jezebel's bad influence upon king, court and religious leaders. The purpose is polemical."

color this material, as the attentive reader will note a great disparity in Elijah's opening scene with Ahab as well as Micaiah's scene. First Kings 21 seems to work under the burden of trying to explain the strength and longevity of the Omride Dynasty. The formulaic pattern of the founder (Jeroboam and Baasha) of the dynasty's son being killed in his second year will end with Ahab, who is succeeded by his son.[25] Ahab will be removed from the picture in 1 Kings 22, as we have already discussed, but 1 Kings 21 portrays Ahab in a different light. Perhaps it even foreshadows how the Chronicler will deal with Manasseh. Ahab is not a purely evil character. He will repent. He will also be responsible for the greatest abomination in the North. He remains a deeply ambiguous and ambivalent character. While the authors of Kings and Chronicles have quite different perspectives, Ahab and Manasseh may represent similar struggles. We will deal with Manasseh in a later chapter, but Ahab's treatment in 1 Kings 21 remains a vivid reminder of the dueling tendencies within the book of Kings.

Ahab dies in 1 Kings 22, but this death bears the weight of the material in 1 Kings 21. Unlike the earlier material about Elijah in 1 Kings 17–19, the problem is not Israel's worship of Baal but Ahab himself.[26] Ahab's religiosity, or lack thereof, will dominate 1 Kings 21. The conflict between Ahab and Elijah becomes much more personal and the stakes much higher in the second half of 1 Kings 21. Elijah puts his reputation on the line. As he successfully faced down the prophets of Baal and Asherah in 1 Kings 18, he now confronts Ahab. Given his past performance, there can be little doubt he will succeed here. I believe this focuses the attention on the religious conflict between the two men. Ahab has misremembered Naboth's words to him and understands the conflict as a legal one rather than a religious one: "he leaves out the religious exclamation by which Naboth characterized selling his property as a profanation."[27] Ahab's irreligious attitude will clash with the great prophet of Yahweh, Elijah, who thunders so many of the priorities of Israelite religion.

---

[25] Jerome T. Walsh, *1 Kings*, Berit Olam (Collegeville, MN: Liturgical Press, 1996), 330.

[26] Ibid.: "In chapters 17–19 the horizon of events is all Israel: at issue is Israel's worship of Baal and the drought that has affected the whole people, and Ahab addresses Elijah as the 'troubler of Israel.' Here the horizon is Ahab himself, his sin and his punishment; and he addresses Elijah as 'my enemy.'"

[27] Ibid., 319.

First Kings 21:27 marks the great conversion of Ahab. It utterly reverses all we have previously learned about Ahab. Rather than someone who callously disregarded all those around him, we see how sensitive he can be. Rather than someone who is the epitome of irreligiosity, we see Ahab fasting and in sackcloth. The Lord's oracle to Elijah that we hear in 1 Kings 21:20 is now almost full of marvel at Ahab's humility. This conversion may say as much about Elijah as it says about Ahab. The power of Elijah knows few bounds. His devotion to the Lord is complete, and his success, first against the prophets of Baal and Asherah and now against Ahab, is also complete. The narrator reduces the king to an element within the story of Elijah rather than the opposite, which we found with Jeroboam and David. This pattern will reemerge with Hezekiah and Josiah.

4. Unnamed Prophets

First Kings 20 begins the series of pericopes more concerned with Ahab's governance of Israel than his problematic religiosity. As we have examined in 1 Kings 22, there seems to be a multiplicity of opinion on this governance within the text. Glimmers of light emerge in Micaiah ben-Imlah's dealings with Ahab. They will be quickly extinguished, but they opened us to the idea of more than one narrator within the book, even the pericope. Ahab's dealings with the unnamed prophet of 1 Kings 20:13 open us to a considerably more positive view of Ahab.

First Kings 20 starts positively, as we see Ahab doing everything to avoid war with Ben-hadad, king of Aram. He parries the belligerent requests of Ben-hadad's emissaries in the most diplomatic manner possible (1 Kgs 20:4). When this does not seem to work, he takes the opposite position of Rehoboam and calls a council of elders for advice (1 Kgs 20:7). Ahab is consistently referred to here as the "king of Israel" (1 Kgs 20:2, 4, 7, 11, 13, 21, 28, 31, 32, 40, 41, 43). In the more negative material with Elijah in 1 Kings 21, Ahab is the king of Samaria.

Ahab works well with the unnamed prophet of 1 Kings 20:13. Although Ahab does not seem to have a clear plan at all, he can be seen as submitting to the prophet and following his plan. This plan leads to incontrovertible victory. This prophet reemerges in 1 Kings 20:22 and all seems to be well. I think we see clear parallels with 1 Kings 13 here and Jeroboam's dealings with prophets. Although 1 Kings 13 is almost wholly negative toward Jeroboam, he does recognize and ultimately respects the power of the prophet. We will see a similar thing happen here in 1 Kings 20. Like 1 Kings 13, another prophet/"man of God" will emerge in the story with a much more subtle message. This can be seen as a more negative narrator entering the pericope. Ahab suddenly starts appearing more like King Saul, who does not completely follow the ordinances of God. Like Saul, God delivers an army to him as the "man of God" announces in 1 Kings 20:28. Like Saul, Ahab is merciful to them. A curious incident ends the chapter (1 Kgs 20:35-36), as we see a guild prophet demanding unsuccessfully that his companion strike him. His companion is killed by a lion like the "man of God" in 1 Kings 13:24. This guild prophet then demands another man strike him (v. 37). This time he is struck and now able to disguise himself successfully so that the king cannot recognize him. First Kings 20:42 returns to the implicit comparison of Saul and Ahab. The reference in 1 Kings 20:42 "to *Hērem* is the latest one in the narratives concerning the monarchic period."[28] Ahab's failure to abide by the religious restrictions of Israel once again comes to the fore. Ahab is a multifaceted character like Saul. He never shines as bright as Saul but glimmers of light do come through. Like most of the other pericopes about Ahab, these glimmers of light are quickly extinguished.

Like Jeroboam, these stories are crafted to leave a negative impression of Ahab. His dealing with these three unnamed prophets are ultimately negative. We can see a great reversal with the last two prophets from the initially positive experience of the first unnamed prophet. Walsh argues, "The first step is to recognize two different narrative voices, one strongly favorable to Ahab, the other strongly critical. For one narrator the relationship between Ahab and Yʜᴡʜ is unproblematically positive; for the other, Ahab's mercy toward Ben-hadad makes a lie of his loyalty to Yʜᴡʜ."[29] The final evaluation of Kings is negative toward Ahab, but I would argue it is negative in a manner similar to Saul. Saul still had his admirers in Jabesh-gilead (1 Sam 31:12). While Ahab never receives as much positive attention as Saul, he still must have had his admirers. Their voices are heard in these stories of the unnamed prophets, but they are overwhelmed by the final editor.

---

[28] Mordechai Cogan, *1 Kings: A New Translation with Introduction and Commentary*, Anchor Bible, vol. 10 (New York: Doubleday, 2001), 470.

[29] Walsh, *Ahab*, 45–46.

E. The Role of Archaeology

Archaeology teaches us to be very cautious concerning this material. Even the most cautious scholars will be seen to take much for granted. I agree with Lester Grabbe, who posits, "[R]econstructions of the end of the Omri dynasty and the beginning of the Jehu provide a good illustration of how the Tel Dan stela—with all its problems—and the biblical text —with all its problems—can be utilized in creating a reasonable scenario of what happened."[30] Yet, Grabbe builds this scenario on the conquest of Megiddo by Sheshonq, biblical Shishak (1 Kgs 14:25). While there is a destruction level at Megiddo, our documentary evidence is from the temple of Karnak, a very tendentious location. This still offers us a reasonable scenario, however, but one fraught with difficulties.

Although archaeologists seem to be comfortable with Ahab, archaeology cannot completely verify the life of Jezebel. A seal has been found bearing her name *yzbl*, but it came from the antiquities market rather than an archaeological dig. This adds another note of caution to the historicity of these events.

Archaeology does make it very evident that Ahab is part of a new period of Israelite history in which Israel is more present on the international stage. This presence begins with his father Omri, who became a powerful presence sometime during his reign between 884–873 BCE. Assyrian records from this time start referring "to the northern kingdom as *Bit Humri*, in reference to Omri as the founder of the dominant dynasty or the capital."[31] The archaeological record points to Omri as the founder of this new, more powerful incarnation of the northern kingdom. First Kings 16:24 literally tells us of him buying a hill, fortifying it, and founding the city of Samaria, which would become the great royal acropolis. Franklin believes Samaria encompassed solely an agricultural estate in the time of Omri.[32] The transformative force stands out as Ahab. Finkelstein tells us that the archaeological data from the site of Samaria suggest a "full-scale urban transformation of the capital and the kingdom characterizes the more advanced

---

[30] Lester L. Grabbe, "Reflections on the Discussion," in Grabbe, *Ahab Agonistes*, 340.

[31] Israel Finkelstein, *The Forgotten Kingdom: The Archaeology and History of Northern Israel*, Ancient Near East Monographs (Atlanta: Society of Biblical Literature, 2013), 87.

[32] Norma Franklin, "Samaria: From the Bedrock to the Omride Palace," *Levant* 36 (2004): 189–202.

phase of the Omride dynasty, probably in the days of Ahab (873–852 BCE)."³³ The amount of ink spilled on Ahab would seem to confirm his important role. He may not have been the founder, but he was the transformer.³⁴

F. Religious Reform

We see Ahab and various prophets constantly struggling in the stories of his reign. The Deuteronomist's concerns for religious reform would seem to subject Ahab to a harsh review of his reign. Things appear to be going in the opposite direction of religious reform. Many strong prophets emerge, and eventually they will be able to derail the House of Omri, but it is only destruction. No clear and visible reforms emanate from their interventions.

Ahab represents the greatest existential threat to Yahwistic religion in the books of Kings. As bad as Jeroboam was in the eyes of DH, he did not threaten Israel with idolatrous worship of foreign gods. This may have been a subtext and implicit in the worship at Dan and Bethel, but DH does not present the prophets of Baal and Asherah until Ahab. Archaeology would suggest that these cults were always in the land of Israel, as we can fathom from the book of Judges, but this perspective is distant from the book of Kings, which seems to have a stronger Deuteronomistic influence present within it than does Judges. The final picture of Ahab is of a king who does not take this existential threat seriously. He may have had good qualities, but these quickly evaporate under the pressure of maintaining proper Yahwistic worship in accord with the book of Deuteronomy.

G. Political Reform

Ahab and the House of Omri represent political reform and centralization from the opposite end. Both the Deuteronomist and the Chronicler are more interested in Jerusalem and the South than the

---

[33] Finkelstein, *The Forgotten Kingdom*, 78.

[34] Grabbe, "Omri and Son, Incorporated," 77: "The primary sources indicate that the reigns of both Omri and Ahab were prosperous. Although Omri is not mentioned in Assyrian sources, the kingdom of Israel is most often referred to a 'house of Omri' by them. Ahab is clearly a leading ally in the anti-Assyrian coalition of 12 kings and a powerful ruler as indicated by the size of his military forces."

attempts of alliances between the northern kingdom of Israel and the Phoenicians. We also see attempts at an alliance with Judah, but Judah must stay in the background and allow Israel to set the terms. Ahab is presented as militarily weak, but the reality seems to be that Ahab made strong contributions to the anti-Assyrian coalition[35] and was "a powerful ruler as indicated by the size of his military forces."[36] Samaria reached its heights during his reign, and its demise may have allowed for the huge growth and ultimate centralization in Jerusalem the following century.

Conclusion

Ahab represents the three greatest threats to Yahwistic religion: worship in the wrong place, with the wrong symbol, and of the wrong deity. The book of Kings focuses on these pietistic issues rather than issues of governance. Archaeology will tell us that he is the first figure from Judah or Israel that is recognized in the archaeological record. He was one of the stronger members of the anti-Assyrian coalition. He had the power and stature to marry a foreign princess. Although he represents an existential threat to Yahwistic religion, a focus on the concept of king from the Royal Psalms will force us to see the ambiguity in many of the stories of Ahab. We find an openness to prophets and a positive portrayal of him at the edges of the pericopes. The final editors never allow the positive image to endure, but the Royal Psalms would suggest that the commoner's view of him may have been very different from that of the Chronicler or DH.

---

[35] Ibid., 63: "Ahab had the most chariots (2,000), though fewer foot soldiers than the two leading members of the coalition (Damascus and Hamath). The reading is clear, and the frequent attempts to emend the number to a lower one are unjustified in isolation from the other numbers in the inscription."

[36] Ibid., 77.

Chapter Five

Hezekiah
Religious Reformer and Realist

A. Introduction

Hezekiah is the greatest king according to the book of Chronicles (2 Chr 31:21) and highly esteemed in the book of Kings. Second Chronicles has him, rather than Josiah, reinstitute Passover, as in 2 Kings. He is closely bound to the prophet Isaiah. Although the Bible holds Hezekiah in high esteem, Hezekiah demonstrates the exigencies of kingship. He proves faithful to Isaiah's pleas, but he also seems to have increased tribute to Assyria (2 Kgs 18:14-16). He initiates important reforms within the temple and great engineering feats within the city. His successor, Manasseh, is roundly condemned, but he may be better understood on a continuum with Hezekiah. He did not suffer the same threats as Hezekiah and found a way to coexist with the Assyrians.

B. Hezekiah in Kings versus Chronicles

The treatment of Hezekiah demonstrates the limitations of historiography. Thomas Römer claims, "Kings is not much interested in the political achievements of various rulers."[1] This becomes evident at a number of points in the text, but the case of Hezekiah shows the Deuteronomist's preference for idealistic religious reform over political

---

[1] Thomas Römer, "The Case of the Book of Kings," in *Deuteronomy–Kings as Emerging Authoritative Books: A Conversation*, ed. Diana V. Edelman (Atlanta: Society of Biblical Literature, 2014), 193.

accomplishments and the real religious reform that is so evident in the archaeology of Hezekiah's time. Hezekiah ensured the survival of Jerusalem, but he seemed to be rather pragmatic in how he accomplished this feat. The Deuteronomist will seem to favor idealistic religious reforms and complicated political centralization over political survival.

Great disparity marks the treatment of Hezekiah in Kings and Chronicles. Unlike other kings, where the differences are highly nuanced, much of the coverage of Hezekiah is only found in one book or the other. They even disagree on some basic facts concerning him. Second Kings 18:2 reports that his mother is Abi, but 2 Chronicles 29:1 tells us his mother is Abijah. Perhaps the latter is a lengthening of the former, but one expects agreement on such a distinguished figure as the queen mother. The grandfather seems to be the same for both of them: Zechariah. The divergences continue as we make our way through the two narratives.

Second Kings chooses to focus on the orthodoxy of Hezekiah at the beginning of his narrative. Both narratives have the exact same verse in the opening lines (2 Kgs 18:3; 2 Chr 29:2), which focuses on his righteous or upright nature. Second Kings moves from there to the orthodox nature of Hezekiah. He adheres to all the typical concerns of the narrator of Kings. Hezekiah removes the shrines (the so-called high places) and cuts down the asherah. Second Kings 18:4 tells us that he even "cut up" or destroyed *Nehushtan*, a bronze snake made by Moses, to which the Israelites were offering incense. Second Kings 18:5b conveys the highest praise on him, telling us, "[A]fter him there was no one like him in all the kings of Judah, nor were there any before him." 2 Kings sets him up as unparalleled among all the kings of Judah.

Second Chronicles moves in a different direction with Hezekiah by tying him much more closely to religious piety and worship. The archaeological records certainly seem to be in accord with this characterization, as we see significant reforms at Lachish, Beersheba, and Arad during his reign that serve to increase the importance of Jerusalem.[2] Second Chronicles highlights his role in the restoration of the temple. Rather than highlighting his destruction of heterodox shrines,

---

[2] Benjamin D. Thomas, *Hezekiah and the Compositional History of the Book of Kings*, Forschungen Zum Alten Testament 2 (Tübingen: Mohr Siebeck, 2014), 398–401, 410: "The breadth and strength of the evidence produced in favor of Hezekiah's cultic reform is unparalleled for any other king of Judah, particularly, Josiah."

we find Hezekiah deeply involved in repairing the temple and interacting with Levites and priests (2 Chr 29:3-4). This role of builder is common with many of his predecessors, and he will share it with his son Manasseh only in Chronicles. This role represents an important virtue in Chronicles that differentiates it from Kings.

The rest of 2 Chronicles 29 consists of material unique to Chronicles. The Chronicler does not share Kings' interest in the fate of the northern kingdom of Israel (2 Kgs 18:9-12). Instead, the Chronicler focuses on religious worship and the king's role in encouraging and safeguarding it. What becomes apparent is an important theme in Chronicles: the alliance between the people and the king. The Chronicler pays special attention to the role of the Levites, mentioning fourteen by name and telling us, "[T]hey were more righteous of heart in consecrating than then the priests" (2 Chr 29:34b). The chapter paints a picture of a great number of people participating in many different aspects of worship. The chapter also concludes with an important and characteristic quality of the Chronicler: "Hezekiah and all the people rejoiced" (2 Chr 29:36b). We will come to see the depiction of a much stronger relationship between the king and the people in Chronicles. Rather than constant prominence being given to the relationship between the prophet and the king, the Chronicler will not only give attention to prophets but also noticeably focus on the general people.

Passover may be the most difficult incident to reconcile between Chronicles and Kings. Many scholars have looked at the Chronicler's attribution of Passover to Hezekiah as a creation out of whole cloth, or less subtly put, a fabrication. Sara Japhet argues against this line of thinking: "[S]ome of the data easily pass the test of historical probability for the very period in which they are ascribed."[3] Ralph Klein seems to be more skeptical of its historicity,[4] but he still claims: "None of the material in this chapter came from the *Vorlage* in 2 Kings."[5] Although Hezekiah may not have been responsible for the restoration of Passover, the Chronicler has clearly made this festival uniquely his or her own. A spirit of joy[6] comes through in this chapter like nothing

---

[3] Sara Japhet, *I & II Chronicles: A Commentary*, The Old Testament Library (Louisville, KY: Westminster/John Knox Press, 1993), 935.

[4] Ralph W. Klein, *2 Chronicles: A Commentary*, Hermeneia (Minneapolis: Fortress Press, 2012), 429.

[5] Ibid., 429.

[6] Ibid., 430.

in Kings, where the word only appears once (1 Kgs 1:40). It appears three times in this chapter alone.

Second Kings spends very little time on worship. Rather, it focuses on significant historical events. Second Kings 18:13-37 highlights the invasion of Sennacherib. Second Chronicles 32:1-19 is also concerned with this event, but it only describes it after almost three chapters devoted almost entirely to religious matters. The two books choose to highlight different aspects of Sennacherib's invasion. Second Chronicles 32 devotes considerable attention to Hezekiah's preparation for this invasion. Unlike 2 Kings, the Chronicler chooses to depict Hezekiah strategizing and taking counsel with his officials and warriors (2 Chr 32:3). Similar to 2 Chronicles 29, Hezekiah is once again depicted as a builder here, as he strengthens and rebuilds the walls around the Millo of the City of David (2 Chr 32:5). He also appoints officers (2 Chr 32:6). Once again we see many more people involved with the king than in Kings' portrayals of him.

Second Kings 18 dwells on the Rabshakeh incident in the buildup to the invasion of Sennacherib. There are a number of interpretations of this incident, but it is another incident unique to Kings and Isaiah. No reference to Rabshakeh exists in 2 Chronicles. Both historians choose to highlight different aspects of Sennacherib's invasion into Judah, just agreeing on the broad outlines of the invasion. Both accounts describe Hezekiah's great trust in Yahweh (2 Kgs 18:22; 2 Chr 32:11-12), and in this case, they both stress that Hezekiah had removed the shrines and altars.

The Rabshakeh incident portrays an important distance between the king and the people. Important advisors to the king, Eliakim and Joah, urge Rabshakeh to speak in Aramaic rather than "Judahite" so that the people will not understand the threats of the king of Assyria (2 Kgs 18:26). Although this story appears to be ultimately told to demonstrate Hezekiah's great trust in the Lord, it also displays a very different relationship between Hezekiah and the people than we have seen in Chronicles. Hezekiah's advisors try to keep the people in ignorance of what is really happening. While they fail in this endeavor, it is hard to imagine the Chronicler describing a similar scenario for one of his heroes. The Chronicler accentuates a unity between the king and his people that seems to be outside of the experience of the Kings' author.

The author of Kings chooses to accentuate the relationship between Hezekiah and the prophet Isaiah. What makes this so unique is that the Chronicler only once recounts an incident between Hezekiah and Isaiah. Chronicles mentions Isaiah two other times (1 Chr 25:15; 2 Chr 32:32), but both references are to the book of Isaiah rather than the person. The Chronicler will actually mention many more prophets than the author of Kings, but they do not receive the same prominence as in Kings. Steven McKenzie has noted the Chronicler's use of prophets more in history writing.[7] The ten references to Isaiah in 2 Kings 19–20 are about the person of Isaiah and his interactions with Hezekiah or Hezekiah's advisors. Let us examine the role Isaiah plays in 2 Kings' story of Isaiah.

We are introduced to Isaiah in 2 Kings 19:2 as a figure that Hezekiah consults in times of crisis. After his counselors return to him with Rabshakeh's dreaded message, he tears his clothes in distress and mourning before sending for Isaiah. Isaiah plays a role of someone with even more faith and trust in God than his uniquely faithful king. As has occurred repeatedly throughout Kings, the greatest leadership and faith is often found in the prophets, whether it is Elijah, Elisha, Micaiah ben-Imlah, or in this case, Isaiah. Hezekiah is obviously discouraged after Rabshakeh's message, but Isaiah's trust in God never wavers. We hear a strident message in 2 Kings 19:6-7 of dismissal of any threat that could possibly exist from the king of Assyria. It is also connected to the author of Kings' characteristic concern of improper religious conduct, in this case, blasphemy. Isaiah assures everyone that the king of Assyria will suffer divine punishment on account of his blasphemy.

Chronicles and Kings both recount an incident involving Hezekiah, Isaiah, and prayer (2 Kgs 19:20; 2 Chr 32:20). Once again, they move in different directions with this incident and their relationship that ultimately presents a much different picture of Hezekiah as king and Isaiah as prophet. Kings offers a picture of their relationship and the proceedings that is pretty consistent with what we have seen so far. Hezekiah is informed of the insults of Sennacherib, the king of Assyria. He utters a confident prayer to Yahweh (2 Kgs 19:15-20). Isaiah responds to this prayer in one of the most traditional roles of a prophet or *nabi* as a spokesperson for God. Isaiah seems to send a message to Hezekiah,

---

[7] Steven L. McKenzie, *1–2 Chronicles*, Abingdon Old Testament Commentaries (Nashville, TN: Abingdon Press, 2004), 53: "The oracles of the prophets in the last two categories are most likely compositions of the Chronicler and fit the warning and judgment functions that he typically assigns to prophetic speeches."

letting him know that God has heard the message (2 Kgs 19:20). He then utters a long oracle reminding Hezekiah and the audience of God's mighty acts within salvation history (2 Kgs 19:21-34). The characters of Isaiah and Hezekiah remain pretty consistent to the story Kings has told us. Isaiah clearly has the upper hand, and he serves to reassure Hezekiah that his faith in Yahweh is warranted. Hezekiah echoes Isaiah's earlier concern with blasphemy (2 Kgs 19:6) when he calls attention to the insulting words of Sennacherib concerning Yahweh (2 Kgs 19:16). Neither man appears terribly concerned with the situation—we only see a little more concern from Hezekiah, which allows Isaiah to better play his seemingly designated role of stalwart servant of God. This picture diverges significantly from that of Chronicles.

Second Chronicles 32:20 depicts Hezekiah and Isaiah praying together and crying out to heaven. They seem to be together, unlike in Kings. Sennacherib, through his servants, has just been addressing the people of Jerusalem (2 Chr 32:10-19) with many warnings and threats, even using the "Judahite" language to terrify and frighten the people (2 Chr 32:18). Perhaps Hezekiah and Isaiah have also been terrified as they pray and cry out to God. Whether this is the case or not, they certainly are not brimming over with the unbridled confidence that we see in Kings. This picture of Isaiah and Hezekiah seems pretty realistic when we consider the well-earned terrible reputation of the Assyrians.[8] Their terror is rooted historically in the constant presence of the Assyrian war machine:

> [T]he Assyrian kings invaded the Levant 67 times. The first campaign took place in the reign of Assurnasirpal II (between 876 and 869 BCE). The last campaign was carried out in 645 BCE by Assurbanipal. In these approximately 230 years and during the 67 campaigns the majority of the Western states lost their independence.[9]

---

[8] Mordechai Cogan, "Into Exile: From the Assyrian Conquest of Israel to the Fall of Babylon," in *The Oxford History of the Biblical World*, ed. Michael D. Coogan (Oxford/New York: Oxford University Press, 1998), 249: "[W]hen the Assyrian empire was shaken by Sargon II's death on the battlefield while campaigning in distant Anatolia. . . . That mighty Assyrian king, infamous for his merciless use of force."

[9] Angelika Berlejung, "The Assyrians in the West," in *Congress Volume: Helsinki 2010*, ed. Martti Nissinen, Supplements to *Vetus Testamentum* 148 (Leiden/Boston: Brill, 2012), 22.

What is even more important is the apparently equal status of Isaiah and Hezekiah. We do not find the glorification of the prophet here, as is so often the case in Kings, nor do we find Hezekiah as totally dependent on the prophet. Rather, we find two men supporting each other and turning to God in their hour of need. Chronicles offers a picture of kingship that employs the support of the people or prophet as appropriate. Chronicles also depicts the prophet as part of the king's court but not superior to the king in this incident.

Both Kings and Chronicles relate an incident concerning a grave illness of Hezekiah (2 Kgs 20:1-11; 2 Chr 32:24-26), but they focus on radically different details that will not be a surprise to us at this stage. Kings narrates Hezekiah's illness and the important role the prophet Isaiah plays in overcoming it. Chronicles tells us of Hezekiah's illness (2 Chr 32:24), but it does not describe any intermediaries. Hezekiah prays directly to God. He does not receive relief immediately because of his pride (2 Chr 32:25), but both he and, importantly, the inhabitants of Jerusalem humble themselves. This seems to avert the wrath of God. We see a characteristic move of the Chronicler to align the fate of the king and the people. The Chronicler's Hezekiah both relies on and needs the support of the people.

Kings moves in both an opposite direction and characteristic theme. Rather than aligning the fate of Hezekiah with the people, the fate of Hezekiah is very much dependent on the prophet Isaiah. No sooner do we hear of Hezekiah's illness than we hear Isaiah giving him an oracle to get his house in order (2 Kgs 20:1). Hezekiah will then pray like in Chronicles, but his prayer is very much at the prompting of Isaiah. Once again, we find a prophet, in this case Isaiah, to be the dominant persona in this pericope. Whereas Hezekiah initiates his prayer in Chronicles and ultimately teams with the people to conclude the supplication to God, Hezekiah seems beholden to Isaiah in Kings. Yahweh speaks to Hezekiah and gives him a sign in Chronicles (2 Chr 32:24), but Yahweh only speaks to Isaiah in this pericope in Kings. Isaiah stops being a vocal intermediary in Hezekiah's recovery and becomes directly involved in his healing as he seemingly directs the servants of Hezekiah to take a lump of pressed figs and place them on a boil (2 Kgs 20:7). Instead of directly receiving a sign from Yahweh, Isaiah tells him the sign will be a shadow turning back ten steps (2 Kgs 20:9). Isaiah ultimately cries out to Yahweh for this sign, and it happens at the end of 2 Kings 20:11. Yet again we see similar circumstances in Kings and Chronicles but a radically different understanding of the role of the king and people as well as the necessity of a prophet.

Kings' final pericope about Hezekiah also features Isaiah in a dominant role. It presents Hezekiah receiving envoys from Babylon after he has recovered from his illness of the previous pericope. Hezekiah seems to naively give them a tour of the palace and especially the treasury (*'wcr*) (2 Kgs 20:13). Isaiah then asks him three questions focusing on what they said, where they came from, and what they have seen (2 Kgs 20:14-15) that seems to add up to an accusation of incompetence, as Hezekiah has shown them everything. Isaiah then utters an oracle that indicates this is a sign of things to come, as everything in the palace will ultimately be taken to Babylon in the time of his sons or descendants (2 Kgs 20:17-18). Curiously, Hezekiah seems to be relieved by this as it seems to promise him a secure future. Once again, Isaiah appears to be the more responsible figure, while Hezekiah is in need of guidance.

Chronicles briefly alludes to this same incident in 2 Chronicles 32:31. The Chronicler does not go into nearly the same detail and is much more ambiguous in his verdict of this event. We simply hear that "God abandoned him in order to test him for knowledge of all his heart" (2 Chr 32:31b). When we compare this event to Kings, we find some crucial differences. The envoys in Kings presented a gift, so perhaps there is more a sense of him being fooled or avarice coming into play in Kings. Isaiah plays a vital role in the Kings episode, but he is not mentioned in Chronicles at all. I believe we can understand this episode as another and final episode in Chronicles where Hezekiah makes crucial decisions on his own recognizance rather than with the help of a prophet. Here, he does not have the help of the people either.

Second Chronicles 32:31 is sandwiched between verses celebrating the acumen and riches of Hezekiah, so this also colors it. We hear of riches, and more importantly, of his prowess in supplying water for Jerusalem in 2 Chronicles 32:27-30. His ability to attain the water continues the narrative of Hezekiah as a builder, and evidence of this exists in the archaeological record as well. We only hear of Hezekiah's famous tunnel in the death notice of Hezekiah in 2 Kings 20:20. Characteristically, the death notice in Chronicles elaborates more details and explicitly connects him in death with the people as it did in life. We hear that "all Judah and the inhabitants of Jerusalem did him glory in his death" (2 Chr 32:33ba). The connection with the people remains explicit even in his death, and his status seems to be much greater in Chronicles than in Kings.

C. The Role of Historiography

Our considerations of Hezekiah in Chronicles and Kings have raised some issues that we have not had to deal with heretofore. Ahab and Jeroboam receive much less treatment in Chronicles than they do in Kings. This forces us to think about why they receive less treatment and how we should use this relatively new abundance of material about Hezekiah. We also discover divergences between the archaeological and biblical material. Accordingly, we must think about what the book of Kings and the book of Chronicles are trying to do. This may diverge with what we expect from a modern historian, but it is common among ancient Greek and Roman historians.

Hayden White argues, "[H]istorical narratives are verbal fictions, the contents of which are as much *invented* as *found* and the forms of which have more in common with their counterparts in literature than they have with those in the sciences."[10] Language theory argues that the text has no reference to an external reality but is contained within itself.[11] I am interested in looking at the impact of the linguistic turn on our understanding of events in the book of Kings. Many current histories of Israel and Judah reflect the increasing awareness of the limits of objectivity. On the other hand, the Bible does refer to people and events found in the archaeological record. King lists were displayed on the walls of temples, and the temple itself is an important artifact referred to in historical narratives. As we consider the book of Kings, we should remember that the "style of list-repetition observed in the framework is paralleled by king-lists from Mesopotamia and the Levant (Tryian King List)."[12] This forces the historian to look more cautiously at biblical literature without completely discounting it.

Many current histories of Israel and Judah reflect the increasing awareness of the limits of objectivity. Megan Moore and Brad Kelle declare: "[R]eassessments of the nature of the HB/OT texts within biblical scholarship in the last three decades have emphasized that these texts are first and foremost literary constructions, produced many

---

[10] Hayden V. White, "The Historical Text as Literary Artifact," in *Tropics of Discourse: Essays in Cultural Criticism* (Baltimore: Johns Hopkins University Press, 1978), 82.

[11] Georg G. Iggers, *Historiography in the Twentieth Century: From Scientific Objectivity to the Postmodern Challenge* (Hanover, NH: Wesleyan University Press, 1997), 121.

[12] Thomas, *Hezekiah and the Compositional History*, 411.

years later than the events they describe in order to serve particular ideological agendas."[13] Historians have noted that genealogy restored to medieval historiography the linear consciousness of history.[14] Genealogy is prominent within both 1–2 Kings and 1–2 Chronicles. It allows for a linear arc to the material while still respecting the linguistic turn and fictive nature of history. I would like to use the genealogies present in the Jeroboam and Hezekiah stories, as well as the role of Egypt (explicit and implicit) in these stories, as potential test cases for Jeroboam's historical narrative as invented and Hezekiah's historical narrative as found. Since an invented narrative has no external references, we can see it as constructed by a later editor. Nicholas Dirks offers us another way to think of this invented narrative: "To historicize is to accept that the past is constructed, that things are not given but made and made sense of."[15] The found narrative builds off of external references. Just as genealogy restored to medieval historiography a sense of the linear consciousness of history, the Hebrew Bible offers many genealogies from which to choose and test this hypothesis. The linguistic turn has challenged some of the realities that traditionally underlie comprehensive histories of ancient Israel, but not all historical narratives within the Hebrew Bible are equal.

The formulaic character of genealogies found in Kings stands out as an important aspect of them. Diana Edelman notes: "Scholars have also long noted an alternating pattern of good King–bad King within the larger narrative dealing with the Judahite kings Ahaz–Hezekiah–Manasseh–Josiah."[16] This type of pattern indicates a motivation to the book of Kings that we do not often consider. Perhaps the writer is trying to control the material in a way that we would not expect. Yet,

---

[13] Megan Bishop Moore and Brad E. Kelle, *Biblical History and Israel's Past: The Changing Study of the Bible and History* (Grand Rapids, MI: Eerdmans, 2011), 150.

[14] Gabrielle M. Spiegel, "History, Historicism, and the Social Logic of the Text in the Middle Ages," *Speculum* 65 (January 1990): 80: "Genealogy restored to medieval historiography the linear consciousness of history which, as Erich Auerbach brilliantly demonstrated, was destroyed by the adoption of figuration as the basic strategy of historical interpretation in the early Middle Ages. Genealogy necessarily fashions history as linear narrative, for what after all is a *lignage* if not a line?"

[15] Nicholas B. Dirks, "Is Vice Versa? Historical Anthropologies and Anthropological Histories," in *The Historic Turn in the Human Sciences*, ed. Terrence McDonald (Ann Arbor, MI: University of Michigan Press, 1996), 32.

[16] Diana Edelman, "Hezekiah's Alleged Cultic Centralization," *Journal for the Study of the Old Testament* 32, no. 4 (2008): 397.

this is obviously not a motivation for the writer of Chronicles, who ultimately presents Manasseh as a good king. Both king lists in Kings and Chronicles share a desire to lift the South over the North. One of the most recent commentators on Hezekiah, Benjamin Thomas, contends: "These formulae provide evidence that the Hezekian historian combined a northern kinglist and a southern kinglist to contrast the enduring existence of Jerusalem and the unbroken chain of succession of Judahite kings down to Hezekiah with the demise of Tirzah and Samaria and its royal houses."[17] Genealogies serve to give us a linear consciousness of history, but the other motivations behind them may distort some of the value of the linear consciousness that we obtain.

As I have stated earlier, language theory argues that the text has no reference to an external reality but is contained within itself. The Hezekiah material may show the limits of language theory. The external reality of both temples and genealogies in the ancient Near East may have an effect on how this material is received. We must remember that king lists were publicly displayed in Egypt at sites like the Abydos Temple. As we consider the role of temples in Egypt, one observer notes:

> It is little wonder that the Greeks named each Egyptian city after the main god of its temple, as the temples at their center would have seemed like the pulsating heart of the settlement, and the officiants of cult as the knowledgeable, somewhat mysterious, guardians of traditions and wisdom. This was to be the view transmitted through the ancient Mediterranean.[18]

This view comes into full relief in the Hezekiah material. Perhaps Jeroboam was appealing to this belief when he acknowledged and elevated the status of Dan and Bethel. Yet these sites were still removed from the palace. In Jerusalem, the powerful triad of kingship, creation, and temple are present in a manner not seen in Dan or Bethel of Israel. When we look to the historical past of Jerusalem, even the Jebusites seemed to believe in the inviolability of their Jerusalem.[19] The role of the temple in Jerusalem transforms the city and gives it a status that

---

[17] Thomas, *Hezekiah and the Compositional History*, 411.

[18] Neal Spencer, "Priests and Temples: Pharaonic," in *A Companion to Ancient Egypt*, ed. Alan Lloyd, Blackwell Companions to the Ancient World (Malden, MA: Wiley-Blackwell, 2010), 272.

[19] Jon Levenson, *Sinai and Zion: An Entry into the Jewish Bible* (San Francisco: Harper & Row, 1987), 94.

appeals to the ordered world created by gods in a way that the kings of the North are not portrayed in the text as being able to appeal to. Accordingly, this material also shows the power of language theory as a reality about the North as constructed in the text that may bear little validity to the reality of the day. Samaria may have had just as powerful of a combination of king, creation, and temple; we just do not see much evidence of it in the text.

D. Temple Restoration and Archaeology

Although we have seen different circumstances highlighted about Hezekiah in the various sources, we see an important narrative of Hezekiah as a builder emerge from both the biblical sources and the archaeological sources. Hezekiah's internal motivations are very hard to fully understand, but there seems to be some consensus on his physical accomplishments. Different sources will credit that to his relationship with Isaiah or the efficacy of his personal prayer, but I would like to use this section to consider how the sources seem to overlap on emphasizing certain parts of his life. While I will focus on trying to create a positive picture of what we can say, it will also be important to determine some of the reasons for conflict in the sources. We will ultimately see a conflict that I have already noted between the emphasis on the king and the prophet and the emphasis on the king and the people. Many elements of great concern to the prophets are not necessarily of great concern to the people. I will try to reexamine some of these theological concerns with an effort to understand recent developments in the study of Hezekiah.

Cultic centralization often accompanies temple restoration. Many scholars in the past have focused on the narrative of 2 Kings 18:4, where he removes the so-called high places, or shrines, and destroys idolatrous objects like Nehushtan. We do not find anything quite like this specificity in 2 Chronicles, although we do find Israel going out to the cities of Judah and Benjamin in 2 Chronicles 31:1 in order to destroy the shrines. The differences in these sources seem to be the attention to Jerusalem itself. Marvin Sweeney understands the Nehushtan as "a fixture of the Jerusalem temple prior to the time of Hezekiah."[20] Second Chronicles focuses on activities outside of Jerusa-

---

[20] Marvin A. Sweeney, *I & II Kings: A Commentary*, The Old Testament Library (Louisville, KY: Westminster John Knox Press, 2007), 403.

lem rather than inside Jerusalem. This disparity in Hezekiah's actual actions leads us to consider the importance of cult centralization.

Diana Edelman has written an article titled "Hezekiah's Alleged Cultic Centralization" that looks at Assyrian as well as biblical sources. The article's title betrays her position, which reflects a position much more critical of the sources. Edelman is very concerned with historiography, the writing of history. She argues that a central concern of both Kings and Chronicles is to explain the fates of the northern kingdom of Israel and the southern kingdom of Judah. Rather than try to accurately reflect every detail of history, "The author of Kings has ostensibly composed his account of the reign of Hezekiah in such a way as to compare and contrast the fates of Israel and Judah at the hands of the Assyrians."[21] Edelman notes that Hezekiah is depicted as working closely with Isaiah,[22] and as I have already highlighted, I believe it depicts a subordinate relationship with Isaiah as the dominant figure rather than a relationship between equals as we find in Chronicles. Given all these ideological concerns, Edelman argues that this text does not offer an accurate picture of cult centralization because "cult centralization would not have made sense under the monarchy. To deprive the national God of his outlying sanctuaries would have been tantamount to eliminating his claims to those lands, which his physical presence in sacred spaces would have symbolized."[23] The people clearly seem to have had a popular religiosity founded on shrines and images in the countryside that does not accord with the Ten Commandments and many other elements in the book of Deuteronomy and the Pentateuch. The writer of Kings displays much more concern with this than does the writer of Chronicles.

I believe Edelman makes many good points, but centralization has its appeals. We know there was much bitterness during the time of Hezekiah on the part of the rural regions of Judah. Micah seems to imply that too much was sacrificed for Jerusalem. He decries the arrogance of the leaders in Micah 3:11, who appear to think Jerusalem is invulnerable and argue that no evil can come upon it. Centralization allowed for a transferal of resources that may have helped Jerusalem survive the Assyrian siege that devastated many other parts of Judah and led to the fall of the northern kingdom of Israel. If Arad, Beersheba,

---

[21] Edelman, "Hezekiah's Alleged Cultic Centralization," 397.
[22] Ibid.
[23] Ibid., 429.

and Lachish were decommissioned, this was all income that would naturally go to Jerusalem.

> It is useful to see an overlap of motivations between Hezekiah's religious goals and his political objectives, since pulling together all cultic revenue into Jerusalem would have provided him with the means to strengthen the capital and surrounding Judah against outside attack. . . . The flow of cultic revenue would have aided Hezekiah in sending tribute as a vassal to Assyria.[24]

Since we know Hezekiah both sent tribute and strengthened the infrastructure of the city, cult centralization seems to explain a lot. The archaeological record bears it out. We can move beyond the text and see the tunnel that he was so famous for. The Chronicler also greatly emphasized the pietistic motivations behind it.

The reality beyond the text may indicate that Hezekiah's motivations were more practical than pietistic. This may be what accounts for the more measured account of Hezekiah in the Deuteronomistic History. "The Law of the King in Deuteronomy 17:14-20 is not even remotely in the background of Hezekiah's reform."[25] Hezekiah centralizes, but he generally ignores the inside of the temple.[26] We will have to wait until we study Josiah to find a king who is motivated by the ideals of the book of Deuteronomy. These ideals do not seem to be embraced by Hezekiah, and the prophet Isaiah in the book of Kings serves to keep a watchful eye on him. The archaeological record would seem to confirm that Hezekiah paid tribute to Assyria in order to survive rather than embrace the pure ideals of the book of Deuteronomy.

E. The Role of Egypt and Assyria

Hezekiah is one of the great heroes of the biblical text, the greatest king according to the Chronicler, exceeding even Josiah. The Chronicler reports, "Every deed that he began was . . . to seek his God" (2 Chr 31:21). Abundant evidence exists for the interactions of Hezekiah with his contemporaries in the ancient Near East. "His name is variously mentioned in no fewer than seven different biblical books, the annals

---

[24] Thomas, *Hezekiah and the Compositional History*, 411.
[25] Ibid., 415.
[26] Ibid.

of the Sargonid king Sennacherib, and a growing corpus of bullae."[27] The threats posed by his adversaries in the ancient Near East lead to perhaps the greatest changes of the monarchic polity of Judah. All these external references offer a sharp contrast with Jeroboam. Certainly the influence of later editing is found, but it builds on objective external references.

We must remember that there were two superpowers in the ancient Near East at this time: Egypt and Assyria. Different superpowers arose in both regions between 3,000 BCE and 333 BCE. Egypt was generally controlled by native Egyptians, but Asians, Libyans, and Nubians controlled Egypt for short periods. This was one of those periods in which Egypt was controlled by Nubians. Mesopotamia saw a succession of Assyrian and Babylonian kingdoms between 2300 BCE and 539 BCE, with interludes of other local powers controlling this region. The Persians under Cyrus the Great invaded Mesopotamia in 539, which spelled an end to the succession of Babylonian and Assyrian kingdoms. Israel was always on the border of the Egyptian and Mesopotamian spheres of influence, and conflict emerged at a number of times over whose client state Israel would be. This seems to be a particularly important issue during the reign of Hezekiah, as 2 Kings 19:9 states: "The king of Assyria heard a report that Tirhakah [Taharqo], king of Ethiopia, had come out to fight against him. Again he sent envoys to Hezekiah with this message." Accordingly, we see a contest for the loyalty of Hezekiah between Taharqo and Sennacherib, the king of Assyria. Sennacherib sends messengers to Hezekiah in order to remind him of how powerful Assyria is and the destruction it has caused. Although many seem to have understood Egypt to be trying to assert itself at this moment, it was very weakened and would ultimately be overrun by Assyria in 663 BCE, as is alluded to in the book of Nahum (3:8-10).

This particular time called for a lot of discernment from King Hezekiah. While his ancestors generally had to worry a lot more about Egyptians (as we saw with Jeroboam), the Assyrians had been menacing the northern kingdom of Israel for some time and had probably been receiving tribute from both Israel and Judah for a long time. "Eight times over a period of 37 years [starting in 738 BCE], Assyria,

---

[27] Robb Andrew Young, *Hezekiah in History and Tradition*, Supplements to *Vetus Testamentum* 155 (Leiden/Boston: Brill, 2012), 1.

history's first military state, had dispatched armies to the region to conquer its people and, when they dared rebel, punish them by ravaging the land."[28] Ultimately, Assyria toppled the northern kingdom of Israel and its capital city Samaria in 722BCE. The Assyrians created havoc in Judah and the surrounding states at this time. They were the more powerful kingdom, but Israel's history with Egypt cannot be easily negated. We find a long history of oracles against Egypt starting with Isaiah 19 and continuing in Jeremiah 46 and Ezekiel 29–32. This betrays an anxiety about Egypt rooted in Israel's long history with it and the presence of a number of important Egyptian colonial centers in the near past such as Beth-Shan at the all-important junction of the Jezreel and Jordan valleys.

1. Taharqo

Scholars have recently reconsidered the role of Taharqo and Egypt in the time of Hezekiah. Rather than seeing Egypt as simply trying to blunt Assyrian interests in Judah, evidence emerges of many smaller states around Judah reaching out to Egypt for aid. These pleas come to the knowledge of Assyria, and we read of the negative propaganda concerning Egypt. This propaganda is most famously realized in 2 Kings 18:21, with Egypt being described as "[T]his crushed reed which pierces the palm of any man who leans on it." Our challenge is to discern the propaganda from the reality. What were Taharqo's and Egypt's true aspirations?

The kingdom of Kush (Nubia) had moved up the Nile and taken over Egypt during this period. They controlled Egypt from about 760 to 656 BCE. Kush had a different perspective and foreign policy than Egypt. While their knowledge of Egyptian history, religion, and literature was superior, they had their own set of relations with the powers of the ancient Near East and a distinct set of influences on them. Kush should not be thought of in simply Egyptological terms, as it had a much different topography, a much smaller population, and important influences from the Sahara that were quite different from Egypt. "Kush was rather located at the junction of two perpendicular axes—one Nilotic and the other Sahelian—both of which played significant roles in its development and both of which differentiated the environment

---

[28] Henry Aubin, *The Rescue of Jerusalem: The Alliance between Hebrews and Africans in 701 BC* (New York: Soho Press, 2002), 274.

of Kush from that of Egypt."²⁹ The imperialism often associated with New Kingdom Egypt is a distant memory and should not be used to characterize Egypt at this time.

I believe we must first consider Israel's problems within the larger context of the Levant. Two Philistine princes, Jamani of Ashdod and Chanunu of Gaza, fled to Egypt for refuge when Assyrian forces overran their kingdoms. Chanunu of Gaza involved himself in an alliance with the northern kingdom of Israel and emerges in 734 as the head of a coalition that was trying to avoid Assyrian domination.³⁰ After suffering defeat at the hands of the Assyrian leader Tiglath-pileser III, he fled to Egypt where he made a remarkable recovery. He returned from Egypt and came back to Gaza as an Assyrian vassal. He then organized another rebellion against Tiglath-pileser III's successor, Sargon II. He was deported to Assyria this time and never heard from again. Jamani of Ashdod similarly revolted against Assyria in 712 and fled to Egypt. He receives much different treatment than Chanunu, as he is deported by the king of Kush to the Assyrians at the climax of a series of overt and covert actions against Assyria by Kush.³¹ Egypt during the Kushite Dynasty 25 played an important role as a place of refuge to blunt the power of Assyria, but it seems to exercise much more soft power than military power.

Kush seems to exercise more economic than military power at this time. While many military campaigns have been hypothesized,³² we only have strong evidence for trading relations between Kush and the Levant as well as the use of Egypt as a place of refuge or as host for meetings of conspirators, including one of the last kings of the

---

²⁹ Jeremy Pope, "Beyond the Broken Reed: Kushite Intervention and the Limits of L'histoire Événementielle," in *Sennacherib at the Gates of Jerusalem: Story, History and Historiography*, ed. Isaac Kalimi and Seth Richardson, Culture and History of the Ancient Near East (Leiden: Brill, 2014), 142.

³⁰ Bernd Ulrich Schipper, *Israel Und Ägypten in Der Königszeit: Die Kulturellen Kontakte Von Salomo Bis Zum Fall Jerusalems*, Orbis Biblicus Et Orientalis 170 (Freiburg, Schweiz: Universitätsverlag; Göttingen: Vandenhoeck & Ruprecht, 1999), 153.

³¹ Anthony Spalinger, "The Year 712 B.C. and Its Implications for Egyptian History," *Journal of the American Research Center in Egypt* 10 (1973): 204.

³² Pope, "Beyond the Broken Reed," 158: "[T]he Kushite documentary and iconographic record of the eighth and seventh centuries B.C.E. undermines the assumption made by Kitchen, Morkot, Redford, and Moyter that the 25th Dynasty would have entertained imperial ambitions of territorial acquisition and administrative overrule in Western Asia."

northern kingdom of Israel, Hoshea. Second Kings 17:4 notes: "But the kings of Assyria found Hoshea guilty of conspiracy for sending envoys to the king of Egypt at Sais, and for failure to pay the annual tribute to his Assyrian overlord." Hosea 12:2 witnesses friendly relations between Ephraim and Egypt. We find Kushite connections in Zephaniah 1:1, and Moses marries a Kushite woman in Numbers 12:1. From the Kushite perspective, the Levant was a source of important prestige goods that were redistributed to local elites and then reciprocated through soldiers, agricultural workers, and general workers in this less populated part of the Nile. While Taharqo never recounts Asiatic wars or rebellions, he does mention loss of tribute from the Levant.[33] He is mentioned with good reason in the Bible, but not for the reasons that the historical record would lead us to believe. Now we will have to consider why he is mentioned in Kings but not in Chronicles.

Commentators are generally in agreement that the Kushite king here could not be Taharqo. Marvin Sweeney explains, "[T]he notice that Sennacherib had gone to fight Tirhaqah is anachronistic, since Tirhaqah did not rule Egypt until 690–689 B.C.E."[34] Aubin will grant that Taharqo could not have been pharaoh at this stage, based on the reference to him by Strabo, the Greek historian, over six hundred years later. Nevertheless, the Kushite pharaoh Shebitku, his uncle, gave him control over the second army that journeyed to the Levant and surrounded him with strong military men.[35] While it is possible that this is the case, what the Kushite annals and inscriptions "reveal most clearly is historians' eagerness for an explicit Kushite account of their campaigns(s) in 701 B.C.E.—despite the Kushite record's apparent refusal to provide one."[36] I think it would be much safer to see pesky Kushite interference here rather than full-scale war. The Kushites provided refuge at this time and fomented indigenous insurgencies and insurgents, but since they did not memorialize any victories over the Assyrians at this stage, I think we have to question how involved they were in Jerusalem and just what kind of "victory" happened here.

Perhaps Chronicles gives us a better picture of the proceedings here than Kings. Although both Kings and Chronicles credit an angel with annihilating Sennacherib's army (2 Kgs 19:35; 2 Chr 32:21), they build

---

[33] Ibid., 148.
[34] Sweeney, *I & II Kings*, 417.
[35] Aubin, *The Rescue of Jerusalem*, 115.
[36] Pope, "Beyond the Broken Reed," 118.

up to this scene quite differently. There is great intrigue in Kings, as an envoy of Sennacherib, Rabshakeh, argues, threatens, and seems to provide a lot of the international background to these events, including the mention of Taharqo. Little of this appears in Chronicles. Rather, we find Hezekiah and his officials dutifully preparing for siege in 2 Chronicles 32:1-19. I think this could also be part of the negotiations with Sennacherib. If Jerusalem was prepared to withstand a siege for a number of years, how hungry would Sennacherib be for this fight? Perhaps the envoys sent to Jerusalem who were as insulting and threatening as Rabshakeh also did more negotiation than we hear about in the text. Regardless, we hear about no pesky Kushite interference in Chronicles, a fact that mirrors the Kushite record far better than Kings. While the scholarly consensus is that Chronicles is a later history than Kings, there are obviously parts of Kings that reflect late sources and perhaps pericopes that have been far more edited than we find in Chronicles.

We find similar testimony about Hezekiah in the book of Sirach. Hezekiah seems to be primarily memorialized in the book of Sirach as a builder (48:17), one of the traditional roles of a king that we have previously considered. Sirach also recounts God's miraculous deliverance of Zion, but in a manner that bridges Chronicles and Kings. All three of the major players are remembered here: Hezekiah, Isaiah, and the people. Like Chronicles, we hear of the people praying to God (48:20), not just Isaiah and Hezekiah. Although Sirach also memorializes certain prophets, he would seem to be closer to the Chronicler in his perspective by giving a little more attention to priests (45:20-25) and the people rather than a much more heightened attention to prophets.

2. Rabshakeh

Sirach also seems to serve as a middle ground on the issue of Rabshakeh. Although the Chronicler does not mention him, he plays a major role in the Kings narrative and is mentioned in Sirach 48:18. Ehud Ben Zvi argues that the Rabshakeh speech (2 Kgs 18:19-25, esp. 18:22-24 with its focus on the Deuteronomist's concerns with Hezekiah's cult reforms) emanates from a later Deuteronomistic stage in the editing of Kings, perhaps even a post-Josianic stage.[37] This offers

---

[37] Ehud Ben Zvi, "Who Wrote the Speech of Rabshakeh and When?" *Journal of Biblical Literature* 109 (1990): 91.

further evidence for an understanding of Chronicles that may be missing some of the later, Deuteronomistic sources from Kings.

Jerome Walsh argues for the importance of seeing the literary character of Rabshakeh. He will identify different voices with 2 Kings 18:19-25 with a later redaction present in 2 Kings 18:22b-24. He finds urgency and concrete realism in this later redaction.[38] He ultimately sees Rabshakeh as an admirable "literary achievement"[39] that has obviously caught the attention of many over the ages. As great of a literary achievement as it is, it can distract from the question of Hezekiah's own achievements. Hezekiah seems to have been more than ready for Sennacherib's envoys, and rather than for resting on the "broken reed" of Egypt or relying on the other Levantine potentates around him, he is remembered in Chronicles, Sirach, and Kings for building his tunnel.

Conclusion

We see three different understandings of Hezekiah in Kings, Chronicles, and Sirach. Although Kings offers us some of the most colorful detail, it seems to be highly redacted and at the service of a strong Deuteronomistic agenda. DH accentuates the role of Isaiah, but we see Isaiah as a milder character in both Chronicles and Sirach. Chronicles' silence on a number of important issues concerning Egypt and Assyria may not be of service to historians who generally seem to be reliant on Kings, but it may better reflect what we actually know about this time.

---

[38] Jerome T. Walsh, "The Rab Šāqēh between Rhetoric and Redaction," *Journal of Biblical Literature* 130, no. 2 (Summer 2011): 278.
[39] Ibid., 279.

Chapter Six
ॐ

Manasseh
Evil Incarnate?

A. Introduction

Manasseh represents for us one of the greatest enigmas within the Old Testament. The book of Kings vilifies him in terms similar to Ahab except there is no repentance for Manasseh; he is an unmitigated disaster from the beginning to the end of his reign. The book of Chronicles also starts its description of him in a very negative fashion, but it redeems him in an equally positive fashion. The depiction of Manasseh may display the theological imperatives behind the portrayal of kings more clearly than the narratives of any other king. Hezekiah's son Manasseh reigned longer than any other king in the Bible. The Bible understands this long reign in starkly different terms in the books of Kings and Chronicles. Many have condemned Manasseh's reign as one of subservience and religious syncretism, but the material culture of this reign argues for an understanding of a Manasseh who managed to preserve some semblance of peace after the difficulties of his father's reign. The realpolitik of Hezekiah's reign may have been continued and consolidated under Manasseh.

Manasseh can be understood as preserving the temple and the prophets rather than being completely subservient. The prosperity of his reign and the important archaeological findings necessitate a more nuanced understanding of Manasseh. Much recent research has demonstrated the ideological depiction of the kings. Deuteronomy 17:14-20 delimits and describes the role of the king in much the same fashion as Deuteronomy 34:10 offers Moses as the premiere prophet. I believe the Deuteronomist has been much more successful in controlling the narrative when we speak about biblical kings today than when we speak about biblical prophets. Current scholarship more readily acknowledges the ideological biases of the different narrators. Manasseh can be seen as an almost necessary persona in the movement to King Josiah. Gary Knoppers will tell us that Manasseh's "unprecedented apostasy calls for strong counter-measures. The buildup to Josiah's reign is carefully contrived."[1] This analysis will try to appreciate Manasseh on his own terms as much as possible. It may not be possible to get beyond the ideology, but we must recognize the extent of the ideology that has colored the depiction of Manasseh both in the Bible and its reception.

Many scholars now recognize that "the portrait of Manasseh within the Hebrew Bible and later traditions differs greatly depending upon the portrait painter."[2] This chapter will attempt to balance the different perspectives within the Old Testament. I will pay special attention to King Ahab from the North and consider how much the depiction of King Ahab may influence the depiction of Manasseh. Although the book of Kings associates few prophets with Manasseh, the critique of Manasseh resembles the prophet Jeremiah's critique of popular religiosity. These diverse sources may help us to arrive at a fuller picture of Manasseh.

B. Manasseh in Kings and Chronicles

A comparison of Manasseh in Kings and Chronicles reveals two very different stories. Commentators have long noted the differences between the two, and the Kings story has generally been considered to be the more accurate. Kings and Chronicles reveal a troubled character from the second verse of their description of him. A great divergence occurs halfway through the story. Manasseh continues his evil ways unabated in Kings, but he experiences enormous difficulties in Chronicles that ultimately lead to a conversion experience. These

---

[1] Gary N. Knoppers, *Two Nations under God: The Deuteronomistic History of Solomon and the Dual Monarchies*, vol. 2, *The Reign of Jeroboam, the Fall of Israel, and the Reign of Josiah*, Harvard Semitic Monographs 53 (Atlanta: Scholars Press, 1994), 146.

[2] Francesca Stavrakopoulou, *King Manasseh and Child Sacrifice: Biblical Distortions of Historical Realities*, Beihefte zur Zeitschrift für die alttestamentliche Wissenschaft 338 (Berlin/New York: Walter de Gruyter, 2004), 9.

different narratives are well known, but a closer inspection of these stories shows a number of subtle differences worth exploring.

Kings begins its description of him in the standard manner by naming his mother, Hephzibah. Both Chronicles and Kings do this with Hezekiah. Yet Chronicles diverges from this standard description and does not tell us the name of Manasseh's mother. The story in Chronicles will contain a number of surprising divergences from the story of past kings; this is just the first of them.

Second Chronicles 33:3 uses the more normative word for pulling down (*nṣ*) the shrines made to Baal and Asherah. Kings generally uses this same language for Josiah, Hezekiah, and Jehu, but 2 Kings uses much less specific language in this instance (*ʾbd*), which is normally translated as "destroy." This word is occasionally equated with Hezekiah and Jehu, but it is far from normative. I think we can perhaps see the Chronicler stylizing this story a little bit.

Second Chronicles 33:3 also has the foreign gods as plurals: Baalim and Asheroth. They are in the singular in Kings' rendition of this story. The surprising element of Kings is that the writer makes a comparison between Ahab and Manasseh. The Chronicler's failure to make this comparison may foreshadow how this rendition of the story will change so drastically. Bernard Levinson argues that "Deuteronomy submits a utopian manifesto for a constitutional monarchy that sharply delimits the power of the king."[3] I believe part of this utopian manifesto also works in reverse as a dystopian manifesto. Kings is going to work many of the kings into this framework, with the two leading kings obviously being Ahab and Manasseh. Chronicles works from a different framework and perhaps has a more realistic notion of kingship. The book of Kings seems to be more ideological here. Most scholars will accept at least two different editorial hands at work in the Kings story of Manasseh: Dtr[1] and Dtr[2]. Dtr[1] is a preexilic editor who is concerned with the Jeroboam–Josiah arc. This editor focuses on a few kings like David, Solomon, Jeroboam, and Josiah, who "fill unique roles in the history, embodying the Davidic prototype and its antitype."[4] Manasseh is equated with the final figure of Jeroboam in

---

[3] Bernard M. Levinson, "The Reconceptualization of Kingship in Deuteronomy and the Deuteronomistic History's Transformation of Torah." *Vetus Testamentum* 51 (2001): 511.

[4] Alison L. Joseph, *Portrait of the Kings: The Davidic Prototype in Deuteronomistic Poetics* (Minneapolis: Fortress Press, 2015), 191.

this redaction of the story according to some. Without necessarily accepting the framework of the two redactions, one can see the generic nature of Manasseh as opposed to Ahab and Jeroboam. The reader is given little access to anything beyond the generic nature of Manasseh in Kings, which is quite different from all the vivid details concerning Ahab, Jeroboam, and their contretemps.[5] Manasseh is an archvillain in Dtr² according to the putative postexilic editor who "establishes Manasseh as an evil king, on par with those of northern Israel. Then, in order to express his theological concerns (the problem of idolatry and foreign worship), he constructs Manasseh in the model of Ahab rather than Jeroboam, the anti-David and prototype of the evil king in the preexilic tradition."[6] The destruction of Jerusalem seems to lead to a dystopian reappraisal of Manasseh in Kings by Dtr². This raises the question of whether Kings (especially in its final edition) has room for a king who does not match up to this utopian manifesto. We saw the ambivalence toward Hezekiah in the previous last chapter. Isaiah guides him carefully and takes on many of the heroic qualities of Hezekiah that we find in Chronicles. Hezekiah's reforms do not match the Deuteronomistic reforms perfectly, and he does not seem to be fully trusted by DH. Would the final editor of Kings be able to exhibit all the positive qualities that Chronicles will go on to attribute to Manasseh, or is the author just too ideological?

If we return to the Jeroboam–Josiah arc, the most important person for understanding Manasseh according to Kings may be Josiah. Rather than paralleling Jeroboam or Ahab, Kings' understanding of Manasseh may be dictated by Josiah. In an insightful essay on Manasseh, Stuart Lasine maintains: "I would suggest that the Manasseh of 2 Kings 21 is DH's 'antisovereign,' the inverted image of a glorified Josiah. The fact that he is so extraordinarily and unequivocally evil indicates that his function is to represent the limiting case of an anti-king."[7]

---

[5] Stuart Lasine, "Manasseh as Villain and Scapegoat," in *The New Literary Criticism and the Hebrew Bible*, ed. J. Cheryl Exum and David J. A. Clines, Journal for the Study of the Old Testament Supplement Series 143 (Sheffield, UK: JSOT Press, 1993), 164: "The chapter includes no quoted speeches of the king, let alone descriptions of his emotions similar to those reported of his fellow-apostate Ahab. Nor does the narrator describe any interaction between Manasseh and the 'people,' opposition parties, specific prophets, or rival leaders, as he did for Jeroboam and Ahab."

[6] Joseph, *Portrait of the Kings*, 196.

[7] Lasine, "Manasseh as Villain," 177.

Lasine's idea of an antisovereign seems to operate well within the later scholarly ideas of the reconceptualization and recontextualization of kingship. The antisovereign may not be something that could really exist during the actual time of the kings. After the destruction of Jerusalem, a scapegoat was needed and found by the book of Kings in Manasseh. The Chronicler refused to accede to that vision.

The sixth verse in both narratives specifies the sins of Manasseh, but Chronicles goes into more detail. This is generally the opposite phenomenon of 2 Chronicles 33:3 and 2 Kings 21:3, where Kings goes into more detail. This greater detail is unusual in Kings and may be another sign of how tendentious the material is. We even have a direct reference to Ahab in 2 Kings 21:3. Here we see the Chronicler customarily being more specific about place and the sins in which Manasseh engaged. There is one sin unique to the Chronicler (*kšp*), a word used twice in Exodus and six times in the Writing Prophets to connote one who practices some type of sinful magic, which is associated with Pharaoh's magicians in Exodus 7:22.[8] It does not add much as it generally matches the other sins mentioned in Kings. The specificity about Valley of Ben Hinnom is unique to the Chronicler. This toponym only comes up once in Kings as a place that Josiah defiles (2 Kgs 23:10). We find it twice in Chronicles associated with Manasseh and Ahaz (2 Chr 28:3). The prophet Jeremiah refers to it five times, so it certainly seems to be gaining currency just after the time of Josiah, and it would make sense as a later addition to the story.

The specificity reverses in the seventh verse of the story. Second Chronicles 33:7 simply speaks about the image of a generic idol, whereas 2 Kings 21:7 speaks about the image of "asherah." While we can never be quite sure of what an "asherah" is, it often appears as a female deity and consort of a male deity. It has been connected with Baal earlier in the Kings narrative, and its plural has been connected with Baalim earlier in the Chronicles narrative. Alison Joseph relates in her book a conversation on this subject with Mark Smith: "Because this expression is unique, Mark Smith suggests that we do not necessarily know that this is a statue of the goddess Asherah, as many have argued. It is possible that it 'may have been a more elaborate form of

---

[8] G. André, "Kashap," in *Theological Dictionary of the Old Testament*, ed. G. Botterweck, Helmer Ringgren, and Heinz-Josef Fabry, trans. David E. Green (Grand Rapids, MI: Eerdmans, 1995), 7:365.

the asherah in the royal cult of Jerusalem.'"[9] This uniqueness forces us to acknowledge that, once again, both stories may be adding to an original story. Alison Joseph associates this unique sentiment to Dtr².[10] Perhaps Chronicles was not familiar with Dtr² but only Dtr¹.

Chronicles may not always reflect a later reading than Kings, and Kings may be just as ideological as Chronicles. The ideology in Chronicles has been recognized for a long time, but it is rarer to discuss the ideology present in Kings. Many of the standard histories of the time period are based on Kings, so a more measured approach to its historical veracity is needed.

Verse eight in both narratives has a couple of surprises. The verse serves the same purpose in both narratives of reinforcing the promises of the covenant and the mechanisms for keeping the covenant. Chronicles goes into more specificity, as we have generally come to expect, by mentioning not only the Torah but also statutes and customs. Ironically, Chronicles uses more Deuteronomistic language with the verbs "to turn aside" (*swr*) and "to assign or set up" (*ʿmd*). The reason this is such Deuteronomistic language is that it is the same verb (*swr*) used in the Deuteronomistic reconceptualization of kingship found in Deuteronomy 17:20. This is an example of the Chronicler's profound indebtedness to the Deuteronomistic History.[11] The former verb (*swr*) can even be translated as "disappear," and the "Deuteronomic History asserts formulaically that although the kings acted properly and were believers during their reigns, nonetheless the high places did not 'disappear.'"[12] Deuteronomistic History also uses *swr* in the usually negative evaluation of Northern kings in the stereotypical formula connoting refusal to deviate from the ways of their sinful fathers.[13] It is rather intriguing that the Chronicler is using the language of the Deuteronomist often associated with Kings, but the Chronicler may be quite ironic here, as we could be set up to see another evil king through this language in order to be surprised by the ultimate result.

---

[9] Joseph, *Portrait of the Kings*, 204.
[10] Ibid., 205.
[11] Knoppers, "The Relationship of the Deuteronomistic History to Chronicles," 310.
[12] L. A. Snijders, "Sûr," in *Theological Dictionary of the Old Testament*, ed. G. Botterweck, Helmer Ringgren, and Heinz-Josef Fabry, trans. David E. Green and Douglas W. Stott (Grand Rapids, MI: Eerdmans, 1999), 10:202.
[13] Ibid., 204–5.

I believe the Chronicler may be building drama in order to set us up for a great reversal, and he uses the language of the Deuteronomist to create the expectations normally associated with that language before moving to a very different denouement.

The Deuteronomist will blame Manasseh for Israel's exile in Babylon. Second Kings 21:8 demonstrates this phenomenon by the language it uses. Rather than using *swr*, the author of Kings will use *nûd*, which has a considerably different connotation of wandering or causing to seek refuge. "The hiphil in 2 K. 21.8 [this is a reference to *nûd*] . . . cites Yahweh's promise to David (2 S. 7:10?) that he will never 'cause Israel to seek refuge' from his land if the people keep his commandments—obviously a Deuteronomistic commentary on Manasseh's idolatry."[14] Verse 8 in both the narratives of Kings and Chronicles is the turning point. Chronicles is setting us up for a great surprise. Kings evokes some of the most important promises of the Old Testament to explain how everything went wrong and how this particular example is supremely important. We have a verb, *nûd*, rarely used in Deuteronomistic History, being exploited to put all the blame at Manasseh's feet.

Verse 9 in both stories exhibits a characteristic difference between Chronicles and Kings. Manasseh causes a generic group to err in Kings, but he causes Judah and the inhabitants of Jerusalem to err in Chronicles. Although I would imagine both writers to be talking about a similar group, Chronicles characteristically focuses on Jerusalem and Judah in explicit detail. After this verse, the two narratives start to diverge with dramatically different results and important differences in method.

Although Yahweh has been quoted before in the two narratives, Yahweh now emerges as an overt character in the narratives. Verse 10 of both narratives has Yahweh speaking with characters, but they are different characters. Prophets play a significant role in both books, but Yahweh only speaks to prophets in the Kings version of this story. Yahweh will speak directly to Manasseh in Chronicles. This direct discussion launches the Kings narrative in a radically different direction.

Yahweh speaks through his servants the prophets in Kings. The narrative returns to Ahab again in 2 Kings 21:13. We hear about Ahab a second time in reference to the "House of Ahab," and it is clear that

---

[14] H. Ringgren, "Nûd," in *Theological Dictionary of the Old Testament*, ed. G. Botterweck, Helmer Ringgren, and Heinz-Josef Fabry, trans. David E. Green (Grand Rapids, MI: Eerdmans, 1999), 9:271.

the two are being grouped together. It begs the question of which king is really the prototype for the wicked king. Much more space is devoted to Ahab, but Manasseh would be a better figure, much closer to the time of DH. Regardless, the die is cast, and the inhabitants of Judah and Jerusalem will lose their inheritance as a result of Manasseh.

The story develops in a much different manner in Chronicles. While Yahweh speaks directly to Manasseh and the people in Chronicles, they initially pay no attention. Although it is obvious that Yahweh speaks to Manasseh rather than the prophets, what is not so obvious is that the people (*'m*) are included in this message. The "people" are never mentioned in the Kings narrative of Manasseh. The "people" are in both 2 Chronicles 33:10 and in 2 Chronicles 33:17, where they continue sacrificing at the popular shrines, the so-called high places. The reconstruction of these high places has been a source of controversy from the start of the Manasseh narrative. Chronicles seems to allow room for these shrines at the end of the Manasseh narrative after his redemption. We read in 2 Chronicles 33:17: "The people were still sacrificing in the high places, but only to the LORD God." Chronicles also appears to acknowledge a legitimacy to these shrines that we rarely see in the Old Testament. God speaks directly to Manasseh and the people. They both respond as the people no longer sacrifice to foreign gods, and Manasseh ultimately turns his life around. Popular religiosity is both altered and maintained with a new emphasis.

I want to emphasize the importance of the "people" here; this is especially the case with Chronicles. Chronicles gives us access to a different perspective on kingship. The book of Kings' view of kingship is influenced by Deuteronomy 17. Although scholars will debate just how extensive the influence of Deuteronomy is on Kings, almost all scholars will acknowledge some influence, especially where national decline is emphasized in texts like 1 Kings 9:6-9 and 2 Kings 17:7-20.[15] It is important to note that "the text of Deuteronomy 17 carefully avoids any *positive* reference to the king's political, military, and economic roles. The conception is further developed in vv. 18-19, where the sole positive duty that is specified for the king is the daily reading of his copy of the Mosaic Torah."[16] We see how Deuteronomy clearly circumscribes

---

[15] Christophe Nihan, "Rewriting Kingship in Samuel: 1 Samuel 8 and 12 and the Law of the King (Deuteronomy 17)," *Hebrew Bible and Ancient Israel* 2, no. 3 (2013): 321.

[16] Ibid., 328.

the role of the king. This circumscription is found in Kings, but there is considerably more cynicism toward the king in Deuteronomy and even the book of Samuel. Chronicles reflects a different tradition that is not so influenced by Deuteronomy. The cynicism toward the king can be clearly seen in 1 Samuel 8:1-18, where the people are warned that a king will take their sons for soldiers and their daughters for ointment makers, cooks, and bakers, as well as taking the best of their land. While there are many similar passages in the book of Samuel and in Chronicles, there is no parallel passage for this section of Chronicles. This section of Chronicles starts from a different vantage point.

This vantage point would appear to reflect the more common view toward kingship across the ancient Near East. Kingship is the normal means of government from Egypt to the kingdoms of Assyria and Babylonia that inhabited Mesopotamia, as well as the smaller states like Moab and Ammon that bordered Israel and Judah. Stuart Lasine will quote the eminent Egyptologist Henri Frankfort as he argues: "In the ancient Near East, kingship is not the most common form of government, it is 'the very basis of civilization.'"[17] The critical stance toward kingship probably reflects some of the literati and clerics of ancient Israel and Judah, a very small percentage of the population. This perspective was not necessarily shared by the common people. Since the common people were illiterate, it is very hard to access their perspective, but the common people around Israel and Judah certainly learned to live with kingship if not enthusiastically participate in it. Chronicles reflects a bond between the king and the people that may be much more normative than what we find in Kings. Let us now turn to how Manasseh changes.

Manasseh changed only in Chronicles, but it was neither immediate nor painless. After Yahweh spoke with him in 2 Chronicles 33:10, Manasseh paid no attention to him, and Yahweh used the Assyrians against him; he was taken in captivity to Babylon (2 Chr 33:11). In a fashion similar to Jeroboam in 1 Kings 13:6 and using the same verb ($ḥlh$), he appeals for mercy. Whereas Jeroboam appealed to a "man of God," Manasseh appeals directly to Yahweh. He not only appeals to Yahweh but also humbles ($knʿ$) himself before God. Second Kings 22:19 uses the same verb to describe Josiah's attitude after the finding of the Book of the Law, so Manasseh finds himself in illustrious company.

---

[17] Stuart Lasine, *Knowing Kings: Knowledge, Power, and Narcissism in the Hebrew Bible*, Semeia Studies (Atlanta: Society of Biblical Literature, 2001), 8.

Manasseh then seems to reverse a lot of his behavior from the beginning of the Chronicles' narratives about him. In 2 Chronicles 33:3, he rebuilds the shrines that Hezekiah destroyed, but now all his building is legitimate. In 2 Chronicles 33:14-16, he builds up the city in a legitimate manner without any of the shrines to foreign gods. In 2 Chronicles 33:14, we see Manasseh building an outer wall for Jerusalem in a manner similar to Solomon in 1 Kings 3:1 and his father, Hezekiah, in 2 Chronicles 32:5. The Chronicler seems to be going out of his way to draw parallels between Manasseh and the great kings of ancient Israel.

Kings takes its narrative of Manasseh in the opposite direction of Chronicles. In language reminiscent of Lamentations 2:8, we see 2 Kings 21:13 threatening to stretch out a plumbline (qw) to destroy the city as a result of Manasseh's evil actions. We could easily understand Lamentations 2:8 as the fulfillment of this oracle. Second Kings 21:11-17 piles on the accusations against Manasseh. The House of Ahab is invoked again in verse 13. We also hear of much innocent blood being spilled in verse 17.

Both narratives end on a similar and familiar note. As is customary at the end of the life of a king, a formula is used to denote his death and the end of his reign. Second Chronicles 33:18 focuses on Manasseh's prayer, and 2 Kings 21:17 focuses on Manasseh's sin. They also reference different sources for their accounts of Manasseh, with Chronicles using the Annals of the Kings of Israel and Kings using the book of the Chronicles of the Kings of Judah. Second Chronicles 33:19 gives a more holistic account of the good and bad of Manasseh and references the words of Hozai, which some translate as "seers." Finally, the last verse of each narrative is very formulaic, without any reference to the good or bad of Manasseh. There is a reference to Uzzah in the Kings narrative; this could be a reference to the figure from 2 Samuel 6:6 who was tragically killed after he reflexively tried to stabilize the ark when it was about to fall down. This final verse reflects almost none of the ideology found in both stories apart from a generic deference to the king.

C. The Role of the Institution

Another interesting aspect of Chronicles is the increased attention it gives to fortified cities. We hear of fortified cities only once in 2 Kings (18:3), but we hear of them four times in 2 Chronicles (17:2; 19:5; 32:1;

33:14). Most importantly for our considerations, we hear of Manasseh using fortified cities. Ziony Zevit tells us: "Adjudicators whose authority derived from royal appointment may have been deployed in fortified cities (Deut 17:9, 12), including Jerusalem (2 Chr 19:5-6, 8)."[18] These adjudicators, or more commonly known as "judges," could generally be seen as part of Deuteronomy 17's program to prescribe the limits of the king, yet we find Chronicles making more use of fortified cities. I believe Manasseh's use of fortified cities in 2 Chronicles 33:14 helps give us a further sense of the seeming alliance between the king and the people that we heard about in 2 Chronicles 33:10. Manasseh's long reign may have been prefaced on the successful implementation of institutions like the judges and fortified cities. While we do not hear about judges here, we do hear about the fortified cities where they were thought to hold court. We will evaluate the success of Manasseh's kingship later in the section on archaeology, but the use of fortified cities strikes me as a vital part of a successful kingship. It also paints a picture of kingship that is much more than a great man but rather an intricate institution with many moving parts.

The institution of the kingship calls the reader to consider more than the texts that simply mention a king like Manasseh. While these texts tell us important things, we also have to consider the larger role of the king in society to which texts like Kings and Chronicles are often reacting. There are many elements of the institution that lie under the surface of Kings and Chronicles but are nonetheless undeniable. An important element would be coronation.

Reflecting on Psalms 2, 45, and 110, Mark Hamilton tells us: "The coronation created a king for whom 'dominance is a sort of norm,' a ruler set on Zion able to face down all foreign enemies because Yahweh has trained him for war, giving him not only the right anatomy, but the right martial disciplines and weapons for dominating all attackers."[19] Accordingly, coronation cuts both ways. Certainly the Deuteronomist could be justified in his disgust with and dismissal of Manasseh as he sees failure to face down foreign enemies. While the Deuteronomist

---

[18] Ziony Zevit, "The Textual and Social Embeddedness of Israelite Family Religion: Who Were the Players? Where Were the Stages?," in *Family and Household Religion: Toward a Synthesis of Old Testament Studies, Archaeology, Epigraphy, and Cultural Studies*, ed. Rainer Albertz et al. (Winona Lakes, IN: Eisenbrauns, 2014), 296.

[19] Mark W. Hamilton, *The Body Royal: The Social Poetics of Kingship in Ancient Israel*, Biblical Interpretation Series (Leiden/Boston: Brill, 2005), 268.

does not mention this instability, it is a well-known feature of the time. The Chronicler could be so caught up in the dominance ascribed to the king with coronation that he overlooks the failures of the king in order to transmit this narrative of dominance. The narrative of dominance accurately reflects the finale of the story in Chronicles.

Another important role of the kings is as builder. We have already seen the importance of this role in the life of Hezekiah. This role is also important for Manasseh, and it appears to be much more contested during his lifetime, as he is only portrayed as a builder of idolatrous shrines, objects, and altars in 2 Kings 21:3-5. Second Chronicles 33:14 reports his many building campaigns, which go unreported in 2 Kings. Like the idea of coronation, this idea has roots in the Psalms. Psalm 132 seems to be prefaced on a tradition of temple building associated with David rather than Solomon, as it explains his concern for finding "a home for the Lord, a dwelling for the Mighty One of Jacob" (132:5). Psalm 132 celebrates Jerusalem with a theology of invincibility (132:13-14), and the "king, precisely as ruler of his loyal subjects, builds in imitation of Yahweh the builder of the cosmos; the king fights alongside the warrior deity."[20] While we do not have a sense of Manasseh fighting, we do have a sense of him both building around Jerusalem (2 Chr 33:14) and establishing altars to the Lord around all of Judah (2 Chr 33:16). Accordingly, Manasseh is represented as strengthening Jerusalem, a city whose invincibility is treated in a much different way than in Kings. While Kings will blame the destruction of Jerusalem on Manasseh (2 Kgs 21:13), 2 Chronicles 36:21 uses the idea of a sabbatical for the temporary difficulties of Jerusalem. It could almost be seen as an incubation period, an experience many kings of the ancient Near East had to go through. After seventy years of lying in waste in order to retrieve the lost sabbaths, Jerusalem will reemerge. The king as builder of an invincible city is an important part of the Chronicler's understanding of kingship, an understanding foreign to the Deuteronomist but quite conventional in the rest of the ancient Near East.

D. The Role of Geopolitics

Manasseh lived during a very complicated time. The Chronicles narrative offers more evidence of these complications than does the Kings narrative. The Kings narrative seems more preoccupied with

---

[20] Ibid., 83.

explaining the demise of Jerusalem than situating Manasseh in his ancient Near Eastern context. Second Kings 21:13 alludes to Samaria and Ahab as the prototype for what will happen to Jerusalem, perhaps a Deuteronomistic *vaticinium ex eventu*. Chronicles reflects the realpolitik of the time. Assyria had conquered most of Judah during the reign of Manasseh's father, Hezekiah. While it is not "historically credible"[21] that Manasseh was deported to Babylon, I believe the story may interact with another biblical text. The Chronicler may be depicting that Manasseh was taken to Babylon by the Assyrians (2 Chr 33:11) in much the same fashion as his descendant Zedekiah would be (2 Kgs 25:6) in a far more historically credible text. Although Manasseh is not the villain that he appears to be in Kings, a need for repentance exists in much the same fashion as we find in the case of Zedekiah. Just as Zedekiah had done "evil in the eyes of the LORD" (2 Kgs 24:19), we have already heard in the exact same language that Manasseh has done "evil in the eyes of the Lord" (2 Chr 33:2; 2 Kgs 24:2). Accordingly, there may be some interaction between these texts.

Francesca Stavrakopoulou will distinguish between the Manasseh of Kings, the Manasseh of Chronicles, and the historical Manasseh.[22] The historical Manasseh finds himself in the midst of the demands of the ancient Near East that are not accurately reflected in either text, but they are alluded to in Chronicles and the prophecy of Isaiah in 2 Kings 19:9b-37. Assyria is a mighty power that cannot be overlooked. Second Kings 22 and Jeremiah 15:4 will present Manasseh as an egregious sinner, but the historical Manasseh seems to be something else. By trying to understand the ancient Near Eastern context a little better, we may come to a clearer understanding of the differences between the historical Manasseh and the Manasseh of Kings and Jeremiah.

There seem to be conflicting historiographies at work within the various books of the Bible. Although there is a concern with sin across all of these books, the book of Jeremiah and 2 Kings may share a similar concern with trying to explain the demise of Jerusalem through the sins of Manasseh. Parts of Jeremiah display a complex theodicy that shares much in common with the book of Job. At other times, we see Jeremiah with a theodicy more emblematic of 2 Kings and the Deuteronomistic History. Jeremiah 15:4 really does not explain to us

---

[21] Stavrakopoulou, *King Manasseh and Child Sacrifice*, 115.
[22] Ibid., 98.

what Manasseh did, but I think we can safely assume that they are the same sins explicated in both 2 Chronicles and 2 Kings. Jeremiah and 2 Kings share a great concern with idolatry, perhaps such a great concern that the picture of Manasseh gets obscured, as an explanation for the demise of Jerusalem becomes much more important.

Jeremiah 7:18 and 44:17-25 demonstrate the intensity of this concern. Jeremiah sees idolatry as both a problem in the land of Israel and with the so-called bad figs who go into exile in Egypt. While Manasseh precedes Jeremiah, Jeremiah has obviously inherited a worldview much more similar to 2 Kings than 2 Chronicles, as he holds Manasseh accountable for the Lord's wrath in Jeremiah 15:4. We may be able to trace this perspective to 2 Kings 21:11, where the Lord speaks through his prophets in order to condemn Manasseh. I have already pointed to the importance of this verse before as we see a sharp differentiation between the audience of 2 Kings (the prophets) and the audience of the similar verse in 2 Chronicles (the kings and the people). These different audiences may suggest a different understanding of idolatry and popular religiosity. Second Chronicles 33:17 will insist that the people continued to sacrifice at the so-called high places, or shrines. What this seems to represent is that 2 Chronicles and 2 Kings placed different importance on the centralization of worship. Does 2 Kings represent a view of opposition to any foreign involvement? Does 2 Chronicles represent an accommodationist view similar to Ezra and Nehemiah? Different geopolitical realities may be behind these books.

Both Kings and Chronicles ultimately represent a trajectory of diminishing Judahite sovereignty. Both books will initially project Israel and Judah as deeply involved on the world stage. In 1 Kings 11:40 and 2 Chronicles 12:3, Shishak, the king of Egypt, attacks Israel. This gives the impression of Israel as being a player on the world stage. We will see them struggling later with the Moabites, a much more modest power, perhaps akin to Israel and Judah at the time. As we progress through the books of Kings and Chronicles, Judah will transform from a tribal state into a city-state.[23] Ernst Knauf will speculate as to whether Athaliah, Hezekiah, or Uzziah start this process, but he ar-

---

[23] Ernst Knauf, "The Glorious Days of Manasseh," in *Good Kings and Bad Kings: The Kingdom of Judah in the Seventh Century BCE*, ed. Lester L. Grabbe, Library of Hebrew Bible/Old Testament Studies 393 (London/New York: T & T Clark International, 2005), 168.

gues vigorously that "it was Manasseh who completed this process."[24] Whereas 2 Kings may see the completion of this process as a negative thing, with Judah completely subjugated to a foreign kingdom, Chronicles may view this process as eventually leading to peace, security, and prosperity. If we think about Ezra and Nehemiah, they seem to have shared a similar vision of Jerusalem under the Persian Empire. It seems to have been impossible to imagine an independent Jerusalem for Ezra and Nehemiah; perhaps it was equally impossible for the Chronicler. The author of 2 Kings still held out for this possibility, but it was soon to become an impossibility.

E. Archaeology

The archaeology of Manasseh's time period tells a much different story to us than the biblical text tells. While this is not atypical (or all that surprising), it is important to note the differences. Although Kings focuses on the sins of Manasseh, the writer does not give us any sense of instability during his time. The writer of Kings highlights that Manasseh was guilty of sacrificing his own son (2 Kgs 21:6). The archaeological record does not show any widespread practice of child sacrifice in Israel, Judah, or the entire ancient Near East during this period. Punic Carthage is the only place where this seems to be a credible charge, and that was around five hundred years after this period. While this is a common accusation against enemies, rarely is there substantive proof of episodes like this.

Second Chronicles does not make any accusations of child sacrifice, but it does depict a time of great instability. We see Manasseh deported to Babylon (2 Chr 33:11), and he returns to initiate an impressive building campaign around Jerusalem (2 Chr 33:14). The archaeological record does not seem to depict any evidence of this type of instability, but it does seem to suggest the possibility of a major building campaign during the lifetime of Manasseh.

Both Kings and Chronicles tell us that Manasseh reigned for a long fifty-five years, the longest reign claimed for any king of Israel or Judah. A long reign implies a certain amount of peace and prosperity. We see long reigns in Egypt associated with peace and prosperity, but they are often followed by tumultuous periods of instability, as two generations

---

[24] Ibid.

vie for power in the vacuum after the death of the king. We know that both of the successors of Manasseh, Amon and Josiah, suffered violent deaths after him and did not live very long as king—especially Amon.

The archaeological record shows signs of security, prosperity, and peace during this long reign. Marvin Sweeney tells us: "[T]he large number of olive presses in the city [of Jerusalem] during the seventh century BCE indicates sufficient capacity to supply the needs of the entire Assyrian empire."[25] We have a sense of Judah and Jerusalem playing a role as a dependable Assyrian colony during this time, which paid dividends that Manasseh may have been responsible for.[26] Although Kings will fight hard for an understanding of Judah as independent, its history can easily be understood as almost always being dependent. During the time of Omri and Ahab, we see Judah rebelling against its inferior role to Israel by refusing to ally with Israel. Many scholars see this as a tacit acknowledgment of Judah resisting its normal role as second fiddle to Israel. This inferior status changes at the fall of Samaria from dependence on Israel to dependence on Israel's clear conqueror, Assyria. If this understanding is correct, then Francesca Stavrakopoulou can correctly claim that "recent historical reconstructions of Manasseh's reign have emphasized that Manasseh was probably one of Judah's most successful monarchs."[27] Realpolitik would determine that a successful monarch of this period ensures the people's safety and well-being rather than their independence. Independence may have been a longing of the intellectual class and the exiles in foreign lands, but the real world of Manasseh determined something much different as success.

F. Theology and Ideology

The contrasting stories of Manasseh offer a unique challenge to the biblical reader. Unlike the chapters on Jeroboam, Ahab, and Hezekiah,

---

[25] Marvin Sweeney, "King Manasseh of Judah and the Problem of Theodicy in the Deuteronomistic History," in Grabbe, *Good Kings and Bad Kings*, 270.

[26] Israel Finkelstein and Neil Asher Silberman, *The Bible Unearthed: Archaeology's New Vision of Ancient Israel and the Origin of Its Sacred Texts* (New York/London: Free Press, 2001), 265: "[A] seventh century text reporting tribute given by south Levantine states to the Assyrian king indicates that Judah's tribute was considerably smaller than that paid by neighboring, poorer Assyrian vassal Ammon and Moab."

[27] Francesca Stavrakopoulou, "The Blackballing of Manasseh," in Grabbe, *Good Kings and Bad Kings*, 248.

Chronicles and Kings propose radically different outcomes to the story of Manasseh. This forces the biblical reader to consider the genres from which we receive information about Manasseh and about the king in general. I have looked to a number of psalms in this chapter that would be identified as poetry and subsequently allow a different understanding of the king to emerge because of the nature of this genre. The poetry helps us understand the ideals of the society and the expectations that the king was anticipated to fulfill or, at least, had the opportunity to fulfill. Although poetry is important, most of this chapter and book focus on narrative.

Narrative theory distinguishes between the primary world and the secondary world. The world in which the real author writes is the primary world and "the world of the story the 'secondary world.'"[28] While there is usually some disparity between the primary world and the secondary world, the disparity is acute in the case of King Manasseh, as we really seem to have two primary worlds and two secondary worlds. Thus, we have accepted the distinction of Francesca Stavrakopoulou between the Manasseh of Kings, the Manasseh of Chronicles, and the Manasseh of history. While narrative theory does not seek to get at the primary world, it does help us to think about the theology and ideology present in the secondary worlds that we have considered. The secondary world of Kings has often been taken to possess a verisimilitude with the historical world of Manasseh. Narrative theory helps us to recognize that both the primary worlds of Chronicles and Kings must be taken with equal seriousness. The choice to privilege one primary world over the other is an ideological choice that must be greeted with considerably more caution than has often been the case.

Narrative is generally understood to have a quality of truth to it that differentiates it from others genres of literatures. Cristiano Grottanelli claims: "This quality of truth that is consistently attributed by authors and readers to the biblical narrative is central both on the level of their literal faithfulness to historical events, and the level of their symbolic value."[29] This makes the biblical narrative considerably different from the other historical narratives of the ancient Near East

---

[28] Jerome T. Walsh, *Old Testament Narrative: A Guide to Interpretation* (Louisville, KY: Westminster John Knox Press, 2009), 7.

[29] Cristiano Grottanelli, *Kings and Prophets: Monarchic Power, Inspired Leadership, and Sacred Text in Biblical Narrative* (New York/Oxford: Oxford University Press, 1999), 161.

or the Mediterranean. While Greek literature produced desacralized historical narratives, the biblical narratives told "demythicized stories about their ancestors and founding heroes, but the stories they had demythicized and rationalized never became desacralized history or desacralized and dehistoricized fiction."[30] Thus, the Manasseh narratives produce some difficulties as they highlight contrasting sacralized histories. For too long, the sacralized history of Chronicles has not been taken seriously enough. In researching for this book, it was amazing to see the number of scholars that left Chronicles completely out of their methodology; but Chronicles may offer us a sacralized history more consistent with the Psalms and other parts of the Old Testament such as Wisdom literature.

Kings represents the more normative sacralized history that corresponds with many of the prophets. Scholars have embraced this view, and the figure of the prophet has often been romanticized in academic culture vis-à-vis the king. If one examines Chronicles, the careful reader will note the presence of many prophets not even mentioned in Kings; yet, the role of the prophets is not as important and vital as it is in Kings. The sacralized history of Chronicles preserves a more hopeful outlook on the potential of humanity. John Endres argues, "The Chronicler grounds a generous view of repentance and restoration in a vision of the merciful God whom Israel is called to worship."[31] Rather than trying to explain the destruction of Israel, the Chronicler "offers a hopeful narrative in place of the prophetic condemnation in 2 Kings 21:10-16, thus portraying Manasseh's life as a paradigm for the possibility of repentance, forgiveness, and grace available for the text's postexilic Judean audience."[32] Ultimately, we see the power of narrative here. Narrative allows humans to explain or make meaning of the situation in which they find themselves. The Chronicler opts for a narrative of healing, grace, and compassion. We find a theodicy present here much closer to that of Job or Qoheleth than the mechanistic punishments so prominent in Kings.

---

[30] Ibid.

[31] John C. Endres, "The Spiritual Vision of Chronicles: Wholehearted, Joy-filled Worship of God," *Catholic Biblical Quarterly* 69, no. 1 (2007): 1–2.

[32] Ibid., 9.

Conclusion

Manasseh demonstrates the limits of the book of Kings. Although the archaeological record would suggest that he appeased the Assyrians in a manner similar to his father Hezekiah, he receives an entirely different treatment than Hezekiah. We could see glimmers of hope in Kings' portrayal of every other king under study in the book, but DH is unremitting in his negativity toward Manasseh. The portrayal of Manasseh in the Deuteronomistic History moves the reader toward darkness and despair, which will almost immediately be relieved by the figure predicted during the reign of Jeroboam, Josiah. The formulaic nature of Kings is shattered by the presentation of Manasseh in Chronicles. The Chronicler offers us a far different story. It starts in a similar fashion, but it ends with redemption, restoration, and grace. The royal psalms would seem to echo in the background to the presentation of Manasseh. Finally, the historical Manasseh may be a much tamer figure. The archaeological record points to Judah as an efficient colony of Assyria at this time. Manasseh seems to have avoided the wars that plagued his father and enjoyed a long life, unlike his successors to come.

Chapter Seven

Josiah
A Perfect King?

A. Introduction

Manasseh's grandson Josiah (640–609) continues to find himself as a heroic reforming king in much recent scholarship and the greatest king Israel ever knew according to 2 Kings 23:25, a verdict not found in Chronicles. The picture of Josiah becomes considerably clouded when one combines a theological lens with a critical historical methodology. The limitations of what can be said about the multiple, diverging sources need to be acknowledged. A clear understanding of what Josiah actually accomplished in terms of reforms and how this accomplishment is viewed in the Old Testament is crucial for understanding the confines of what we can say of this period. The reforms attributed to Josiah are far from anomalous. Josiah follows a long line of ancient Near Eastern monarchs who made major religious reforms. Josiah's kingship is unique in Israel but bears some striking resemblances outside Israel.

Although the Old Testament attributes great reforms to Josiah, the archaeological record does not reflect the importance of Josiah in the same way as it reflects the importance of Hezekiah. We clearly find Hezekiah mentioned in the Assyrian Chronicles. We clearly see the tunnel credited to him in Jerusalem and can see the Siloam Inscription (the epigraphic evidence for it) in the Istanbul Archaeological Museum today. Kings, Chronicles, and Sirach will all speak positively about him, but the lacuna of evidence for him outside the Bible calls for caution and perhaps a revision of some of the claims that have been made for him.

B. Josiah in Kings versus Chronicles

Second Kings 22:1 and 2 Chronicles 34:1 both start by emphasizing Josiah's early accession to the monarchy at the age of eight and how he "did right in the eyes of Yahweh" (2 Kgs 22:2; 2 Chr 34:2). Kings will quickly move on to the discovery of the "book" in the temple, whereas Chronicles will immediately focus on Josiah's reforms. This chronological difference betrays different ideologies behind the two books. Josiah is remembered as a reformer in both of these books (and in Sirach 49:2 as well), but Kings will give him a much more unique role in these reforms than will the other books.

Kings describes a Josiah fundamentally different before and after the discovery of the Book of the Torah. We only have two verses describing Josiah before the discovery of the book in Kings. Chronicles offers a sharp contrast to this narrative as we have seven verses of description of Josiah before the discovery of the book. Rather than describing an epiphany like Kings, Chronicles describes him in terms more reminiscent of Hezekiah. Both Chronicles and Kings tell us that Hezekiah also "did right in the eyes of Yahweh" (2 Kgs 18:3; 2 Chr 29:2) in the opening lines of their description of him. They both go on to catalog these righteous deeds in much the same way as Chronicles does with Josiah.

Both books are clear that the Book of the Law was discovered in the eighteenth year of his reign. This discovery almost seems to be a part of an iterative process for Josiah in Chronicles, as we hear of a deeper relationship with God beginning in the eighth year of his reign (2 Chr 34:3a), when he would have been sixteen. This progresses to cleansing the so-called high places of their *asherim*, carved-metal images, and cast-metal idols in the twelfth year of his reign, when he was twenty. Hezekiah is described in similar terms in 2 Kings 18:4 and 2 Chronicles 31:1. Second Chronicles 34:4 narrates Josiah breaking down pagan shrines, something that Hezekiah is never described as doing in Kings, but 2 Chronicles 31:1 does describe Hezekiah as doing this. Josiah then burns the bones of the pagan priests on their altars in 2 Chronicles 34:5. This would seem to be a clear reference to 1 Kings 13:2, which could easily be seen as a *vaticinium ex eventu*. Nothing like 1 Kings 13 appears in Chronicles. Kings will have a similar reference after the discovery of the Book of the Law in 2 Kings 23:16. When looking at the similar verses in 2 Kings 23:16-20, Alison Joseph will state: "It is clear that these verses were composed in conjunction with the events and composition of 1 Kings 13."[1] Finally, Josiah's ambitions are pitched at an equally high level in Chronicles as Kings, which both depict him traveling through the former northern kingdom of Israel in order to purify the shrines there in a like manner as to what he was doing in Judah and Jerusalem. We are left with some similarities in the depiction of Josiah in Chronicles and Kings, but the differences are equally important.

Both present him as a fundamentally good man. Chronicles depicts him as a lifelong reformer. Kings only briefly describes him before the finding of the Book of the Law. Kings leaves us to surmise that this was a much more profound experience for him than Chronicles would suggest. We have less of a sense of his almost missionary nature in Chronicles, as there is no mention of specific cities of the former northern kingdom of Israel, rather cities of Manasseh, Ephraim, and Simeon (2 Chr 34:5). Second Kings has him go pointedly and explicitly to Bethel, where one of the altars constructed by Jeroboam (2 Kgs 23:15) was located. As I mentioned in the previous paragraph, there is a continuity to the pericope around Bethel that does not exist in Chronicles. Second Kings is obviously putting much more importance on the finding of the Book of the Law. Second Kings would also appear to be much more stylized than Chronicles as questions emanating from unique pericopes in 1 Kings are resolved in 2 Kings.

Both Chronicles and Kings recount the discovery of the Book of the Law. They start with different premises, and Chronicles will include many more people in the story as we have become accustomed to by now. Many more people are involved in the administration of the monarchy in Chronicles. Second Chronicles 34:8 highlights that this discovery happened either in the midst or after the cleansing of the land, which was described in the verses preceding this verse. Second Kings 22:3-8 narrates the discovery in a different fashion. It simply describes seemingly normal events taking place in the administration of the temple. Josiah was a righteous king, but he did not seem to have any plans for purifying the land. Fundamentally, Chronicles and Kings understand Josiah differently.

As Chronicles continues, it persists in viewing the king in a much less individualistic fashion than we find in Kings. I have noted in earlier chapters that we often find the grouping of the "king and the

---

[1] Alison L. Joseph, *Portrait of the Kings: The Davidic Prototype in Deuteronomistic Poetics* (Minneapolis: Fortress Press, 2015), 174.

people" in Chronicles, but we seldom find these two groups together in Kings, where the king generally seems much more dependent on prophets. Whereas Josiah is simply interacting with Shaphan in the first line of this pericope in 2 Kings 22:3, we find him interacting not only with Shaphan in the parallel line of 2 Chronicles 34:8 but also with Maaseiah and Joah. He is also sending the three of them explicitly "to repair" or "to restore" the temple. The same project is taking place in Kings (22:5), but we get to it slightly later in a section that is further explicated in Chronicles (34:10) as well. Accordingly, Chronicles seems to highlight Josiah's roles as a reformer before, during, and after the discovery of the Book of the Law.

Both books focus on the discovery of the law during the repair of the temple. Interestingly, they both initially agree on Hilkiah the high priest stating: "I have found the book of the Torah" (2 Kgs 22:8; 2 Chr 34:15). Shortly after these verses, Kings will consistently refer to "the words of the book of the Torah" (2 Kgs 22:11), but Chronicles will refer now to only "the words of the Torah" (2 Chr 34:19). The law of brevity that textual criticism demands would suggest that the Chronicles formulation may be the original formulation, with words added to the Kings story. I believe this is further evidence of Chronicles, at times, reflecting a source behind both it and the book of Kings.

Chronicles and Kings will both narrate the approval of the Book of the Torah by the prophetess, Huldah. Surprisingly, 2 Kings 22:14 names five individuals being sent to visit Huldah in 2 Kings 22:14, whereas 2 Chronicles 34:22 just tells us Hilkiah went with some anonymous individuals belonging to the king, but the Chronicler does not name them. Huldah proclaims an important oracle approving the discovered book, which is now named in both sources as the "Book of the Covenant" (2 Kgs 23:3; 2 Chr 24:30). King Josiah then reads this book to the inhabitants, but as we would suspect, Kings articulates that he read it to "priests and prophets," whereas Chronicles tells us he read it to "priests and Levites" (2 Kgs 23:3; 2 Chr 24:30). We see DH's continual emphasis on prophets, which is not shared by the Chronicler. Chronicles concludes this pericope by expanding the audience feeling the impact of this discovery to those from Benjamin (2 Chr 34:32), and by Josiah continuing to remove abominations from all the lands that belong to the Israelites, a formulation which suggests a continuing interest in the North that we heard of in 2 Chronicles 34:6.

Josiah only becomes a reformer after the approval of the Book of the Torah in Kings. We hear of Josiah's reforming nature in the introduction to Chronicles' narration of him. Both Kings and Chronicles follow their introductions with the discovery of the Book of the Torah, but we have five verses describing Josiah's reforms and interest in the North in Chronicles. Second Kings 23:4-20 elaborates and expands on these reforms mentioned in the introductory material in Chronicles. Kings is much more explicit than Chronicles that the problem is in the temple of Yahweh itself (2 Kgs 23:4) rather than simply cleansing Judah and Jerusalem (2 Chr 34:4). Chronicles' interest in cleansing Judah and Jerusalem would seem to be consistent with the actions of Hezekiah in 2 Chronicles 31:1. There is a general concern here that does not quite match the Deuteronomistic concern with the inside of the temple. Josiah will distinguish himself with this concern in Kings, a concern that is not as important in Chronicles. We also see Josiah's actions as part of a more hierarchical movement, including Hilkiah the high priest and the so-called priests of the second order and other attendants in 2 Kings 23:4. We have seen more of an alliance between the king and the people in Chronicles, whereas Kings describes the king as closer to prophets or priests at times. This especially manifests itself at the end of Kings' pericope of reform. Josiah continues his reforms in the North as in Chronicles, but 2 Kings 23:17 pays special attention to the "man of God" from the Jeroboam narrative in 1 Kings 13. There are four terms that can be translated as prophet—"man of God" is one of them. This reference to the "man of God" episode highlights the unique importance of prophetic figures in the Kings account.

This reform pericope (2 Kgs 23:4-20) also goes into much more detail about the problems of idolatry. Second Kings 23:5 describes an attack on the presence of idol-priests, a group we only hear of in Hosea (10:5; 11:8) and Zephaniah (1:4). Chronicles mentions *asherim* three times (1 Chr 34: 3, 4, 7), but 2 Kings mentions *Asherah* four times and *asherim* another time. We find much more detail about the idolatrous cult in Kings. We focus on the evil kings before the two reforming kings in 2 Kings 23:12 (Hezekiah follows Ahaz, and Josiah follows Manasseh), where the upper chamber of Ahaz and the altars of Manasseh are torn down and removed. The polemic against Manasseh started a couple verses earlier, in 2 Kings 23:10, where Josiah neutralizes the idolatrous site of Topheth, a place it may be assumed that the writer of Kings believes Manasseh sacrificed his son (2 Kgs 21:6). This stands in stark contrast to the Chronicler's understanding of Manasseh. The memory of another evil king, Jeroboam, is condemned in 2 Kings 23:15. All in all, Kings presents a very disturbing picture of popular religiosity in the time of Josiah.

The final element of the reform is Passover. We have not heard of Passover in the Deuteronomistic History since the time of Joshua (Josh 5:10-12). The Chronicler focuses on Passover here as well. He never mentions it at all until the time of Hezekiah (2 Chr 30:1). We see a crucial difference in their perspectives here. Kings reserves Passover to Josiah, but Chronicles initiates its reinstitution with Hezekiah. Kings wants to tie it to the "discovered book," which is now referred to as "this book of this covenant" (2 Kgs 23:21). We first heard a similar title for it in 2 Kings 23:2-3, when it seemed to stop being referred to as the Book of the Law. The Chronicler also shifts language in 2 Chronicles 34:30-32. This genesis for the reinstitution of Passover makes no sense in the Chronicler's schema. Accordingly, we see Passover as a very significant marker associated with the most important king for each of these writers: Hezekiah for the Chronicler and Josiah for Kings.

Both the Chronicler and Kings agree on the importance of this Passover. The Chronicler reaches back to Samuel the prophet (2 Chr 35:18), and Kings states that nothing like this happened since the days of the judges (2 Kgs 23:22). Second Chronicles 30:1-18 describes Hezekiah's reinstitution of Passover and some of the difficulties in trying to celebrate it. The Chronicler has a lot more to say about Passover in the time of Josiah than Kings has to say about it. A chief difference is the role of the Levites in it. Kings mentions Levites only two times, and both instances are long before Josiah or Hezekiah. Levites come up throughout the books of Chronicles with perhaps no one more associated with them than Hezekiah. They are mentioned twenty-four times in material associated with him, about a fifth of the references in the book. They also play a large role in the story of Josiah, especially Passover. Their inclusion in the stories of Passover suggests an alliance between kings and lower elements of the hierarchy that we do not see in the books of Kings. Finally, both Kings and Chronicles agree on Passover happening in the eighteenth year of Josiah.

Chronicles and Kings both agree that Josiah died in battle with Pharaoh Neco (2 Chr 35:24; 2 Kgs 23:29). Chronicles seems to inherit Kings' story, as it appears to add to the details present in Kings with one exception. Second Kings 23:29 implies that Pharaoh Neco personally kills Josiah. Second Chronicles 35:23 will place the blame on the archers of Pharaoh Neco. Chronicles will also go into more detail about the specifics of the battle. Rather than simply hearing that Neco went up to support "the king of Assyria at the river Euphrates" (2 Kgs 23:29), we hear that Neco went up to do battle at Carchemish on the

Euphrates (2 Chr 35:20). The expansion in Chronicles also appears to minimize the responsibility of Pharaoh Neco as he tries to dissuade Josiah from entering into battle with him (2 Chr 35:21).

Chronicles seems to display a consistently more accepting view of Egypt. This would be uniform with the treatment of Egypt in the material associated with Hezekiah. Egypt is famously a "bruised reed" in 2 Kings 18:21. Kings rarely fails to take advantage of an opportunity to put scorn on Egypt. Chronicles offers a more nuanced view that may display a different set of interests at work. We never hear of Solomon's enemy Hadad the Edomite taking refuge in Egypt. When Pharaoh Shishak invades Israel in the fifth year of King Rehoboam (ca. 925 BCE), only Chronicles will tell us that he did this because Jerusalem had been unfaithful to Yahweh (2 Chr 12:6). First Kings 14:25-28 simply describes this as an act of war. Chronicles ultimately may help prepare us to understand reasons for the flight to Egypt that Jeremiah the prophet so vehemently opposed. Jeremiah constantly contrasts those who trust in God with those who seek refuge in Egypt. Though we find a similar scenario at the end of the book of Kings and the Baruch Scroll (Jer 36–45), Jeremiah presents consistently negative portrayals of Egypt as a place of refuge throughout his book, whereas Kings can be quite ambivalent in its portrayal of Egypt as a place of refuge. The prophets are very negative toward Egypt as we see in the oracles against Egypt in Isaiah, Jeremiah, and Ezekiel, but the monarchy's interests were different from DH's and from prophets only loosely affiliated with the king like Jeremiah. Chronicles ends up being even more ambiguous than any of these sources.

Finally, Chronicles paints Jeremiah as lamenting for Josiah in 2 Chronicles 35:25. This verse implies that this is a lament which can be found in the book of Lamentations. Today we generally understand the book of Lamentations to be written by a different author than Jeremiah. When we carefully read through the book of Jeremiah, we find only a few references to Josiah, and these references are rather ambiguous. I believe it is just as easy to see Jeremiah's references to Josiah as damning him with faint praise. The Chronicler wants to present the prophets and kings as far more allied than we will find in the book of Jeremiah. Egypt may have been a place where this alliance broke down, as we see its more critical treatment in the books of Kings and Jeremiah, as well as a number of minor prophets like Nahum and Amos.

C. The Role of Archaeology

Scholars have started looking much more carefully at the historicity of 2 Kings' claims about Josiah. The field of biblical studies has seen a sea change in approaches toward the background of Josiah. Previous generations have looked at 1–2 Kings as much more objective than the supposedly more subjective and theological 2 Chronicles. Over the last three chapters of this book, we have seen considerable theological and subjective content in both Kings and Chronicles. Many commentators of an earlier generation (Halpern, Miller/Hayes, Ahlström, and Liverani) have agreed on the importance of Josiah. They consistently describe his actions, which included the removal of all idolatrous items from the Jerusalem temple, the disestablishment of all high places, and the execution of all priests of the high places as reforms. Halpern will go so far in his descriptions of Josiah as labeling him as a reformer and describing him as similar to Calvin, Cromwell, and Akhenaten.[2]

Each of the writers approaches Josiah's reforms in a different manner. Halpern describes the reforms as personal attributes of Josiah and speaks of Josiah with elaborate detail. Although the other writers speak of Josiah's reforms, they speak more cautiously than Halpern. Some even doubt what truly can be said of the reforms. The other writers also discuss the difficulty of understanding how Kings was edited as well as the general problems of Kings as historiography. Halpern never acknowledges these difficulties in his description of Josiah.

These difficulties have come to the foreground of contemporary scholarship on Josiah. Nadav Na'aman has written a series of trenchant articles on the Josiah material over the last decade. He highlights the literary aspects of the Josiah material that others have seen, but he initiates this discussion at a deeper level as he displays similar phenomena across the ancient Near East. Na'aman focuses on the importance of cult reform and zeroes in on the "discovery" of the lost book. Na'aman is unwilling to go as far as Katherine Stott, who sees

---

[2] Baruch Halpern, "Sybil, or the Two Nations? Archaism, Kinship, Alienation, and the Elite Redefinition of Traditional Culture in Judah in the 8th–7th Centuries B.C.E.," in *The Study of the Ancient Near East in the Twenty-First Century: The William Foxwell Albright Centennial Conference*, ed. Jerrold S. Cooper and Glenn M. Schwartz (Winona Lake, IN: Eisenbrauns, 1996), 329: "Josiah's iconoclasm parallels not just the program of Akhenaten, of Thutmosis III against Hatshepsut, but that of Ahmose against the Hyksos; but it was a systematic effort to erase from the nation's history the memory not just of a rural predecessor but of a whole culture."

the lost book as "fictional" literature.³ Stott states: "Just as classical stories about lost and found books serve the purpose of bolstering the credibility of the narratives in which they are embedded, so too the story of the book of the law may serve such a purpose in the biblical literature."⁴ Na'aman, rather, points to the pious fraud of the discovery of the Memphite Theology in Egypt less than a century before the finding of the "Book of the Law" in Jerusalem.⁵ Stott's focus on classical literature is helpful, but I think Na'aman's focus on ancient Near Eastern literature is more important. Na'aman will point out,

> [T]ext manipulations of many forms and functions, all of them real artifacts, are attested from (at least) the early second millennium onward. In this light, the search for an original location for the topos of scroll/book/tablet "discoveries" is useless. The episode of the "finding" of the scroll in the time of Josiah should be studied in its own right.⁶

Accordingly, Na'aman appears to see both the Memphite Theology and the Book of the Law as important mechanisms to legitimate a reform rather than as objects leading to a reform. The book of Chronicles helps sustain this argument, as Josiah is introduced as a reformer long before the discovery of the Book of the Law. The book of Kings would have Josiah's inspiration coming from this discovery.

This discovery is just a part of the larger cult reform. We have seen a number of reformers, but the book of Kings wants to isolate Josiah as the most important reformer. We must come to terms with one of Na'aman's most important and telling claims: "No archaeological evidence associated with the reform has ever been unearthed."⁷ So we have seen the difficulties with the "discovery" of the Book of the Law, but now these can be seen within the larger difficulties of the

---

³ Katherine Stott, "Finding the Lost Book of the Law: Re-Reading the Story of 'The Book of the Law' (Deuteronomy–2 Kings) in Light of Classical Literature," *Journal for the Study of the Old Testament* 30, no. 2 (December 2005): 161.

⁴ Ibid., 166.

⁵ Nadav Na'aman, "The 'Discovered Book' and the Legitimation of Josiah's Reform," *Journal of Biblical Literature* 130, no. 1 (Spring 2011): 51.

⁶ Ibid., 53.

⁷ Nadav Na'aman, "The King Leading Cult Reforms in His Kingdom: Josiah and Other Kings in the Ancient Near East," *Zeitschrift für altorientalische und biblische Rechtsgeschichte* 12 (2006): 136.

reform itself and the different descriptions of the reform in Kings and Chronicles.

Josiah must be understood within the narrative arc of Jeroboam to Josiah. Rather than a fully fleshed out character, we discover a reformer who perfectly embodies the hopes of the book of Deuteronomy. He does this more perfectly than any other king, including David. He resonates more with Joshua[8] and Moses than any king. Josiah "is the only king to comply with the law of the king (Deut. 17:15-20)."[9] He fulfills the prescriptions of Deuteronomy 12:3 in terms of tearing down *masseboth* and *asherim* and Deuteronomy 16 in terms of celebrating Passover. Rather than the concept of a king familiar from the Royal Psalms, Josiah embodies the reconceptualization of the king. Alison Joseph explicitly points to the rhetorical nature of the Josiah material and its place on the Jeroboam–Josiah narrative arc:

> Josiah is the only one to walk in all the ways of David, parallel to and contrasting those bad kings of Israel who walk in the way of the anti-David, Jeroboam. This is a highly rhetorical collocation, functioning as one of the first indicators that Josiah and his reform are set up to oppose Jeroboam and undo his sin.[10]

Where we could point to many clear signs of Hezekiah in the archaeological record, such as Hezekiah's Tunnel and the *lmlk* storage jars,[11] the material culture associated with Josiah appears to be much more elusive. Benjamin Thomas will point to Beersheba and Arad as demonstrating the credentials of Hezekiah's reforms, but we really cannot point to any archaeological sites that demonstrate what Josiah did. The Deuteronomist ultimately credits Josiah with enormous and

---

[8] Joseph, *Portrait of the Kings*, 168: "Josiah's covenant is based on the written word. Joshua in Josh. 8:30-35 also celebrates a covenant renewal, connecting the portraits of Josiah and Joshua. Just as Josiah's covenant is presented as better than Jehoida's, throughout the history of the monarchy, when a figure mounts a reform, Dtr makes sure that Josiah's measures supersede those of the others."

[9] Joseph, *Portrait of the Kings*, 153.

[10] Ibid., 155.

[11] Robb Andrew Young, *Hezekiah in History and Tradition*, Supplements to *Vetus Testamentum* 155 (Leiden/Boston: Brill, 2012), 58: "The Type 484 storage jars designated as *lmlk* 'royal property' may now be securely placed under the auspices of king Hezekiah, thanks to the redating of the end of Level III at Lachish to 701 B.C.E."

much-needed reforms. He must finish the job that Hezekiah inadequately started. But does ideology trump material culture here? This leaves us with unanswered questions as to the where and how of Josiah's reforms. "These unanswered questions highlight the literary, rather than historical, value of the report of the Passover celebration,"[12] among many other reforms. Josiah remains almost impossible to reconstruct beyond the biblical text.

Na'aman remains a firm believer in Josiah's reform. He tells us, "[T]he reform as related in 23:4-15 should be regarded as an historical event which must have taken place roughly the way it is described in the history of Josiah, the last of the great kings who ruled the kingdom of Judah during the First Temple period."[13] I believe the problem here is the disparity between Chronicles and Kings, as well as similar disparities in the description of Hezekiah. Josiah begins his reforms before the discovery of any book in Chronicles, and these reforms quickly move to the northern "cities of Manasseh, Ephraim and Simeon and as far as Naphtali" (2 Chr 34:6). Na'aman considers the nationalistic qualities of this reform, but he only deals with the source from Kings. He will admit, "[A]longside the motive of faith, strong national feelings swelled in the kingdom of Judah."[14] Yet when we examine Chronicles, these strong national feelings emerge very early in his reign. I think it is very hard to move beyond the structural aspects of the book of Kings that demand Josiah to be a good king and demand that he be understood as a reformer despite the lack of evidence and even the contrasting evidence of Chronicles.

D. The Role of Theology

Josiah continues to find himself as a heroic reforming king in much recent scholarship,[15] but a lacuna in the scholarship with respect to the

---

[12] Joseph, *Portrait of the Kings*, 183.

[13] Na'aman, "The King Leading Cult Reforms in His Kingdom," 168.

[14] Ibid., 141.

[15] Marvin A. Sweeney, *King Josiah of Judah: The Lost Messiah of Israel* (Oxford: Oxford University Press, 2001), 20: "Josiah lays the foundation for the exilic thinkers and movements that ultimately rescued Judaism from the obscurity and anonymity of Babylonian defeat and exile and saw to the restoration of the post-exilic Jewish community in the land of Judah. Although there may well have been "conspiracy of silence" concerning the death of Josiah, there has been

treatment of Josiah's death must be filled. As a new understanding of Judah in the late seventh century has emerged, the understanding of Josiah and the critical examination of his death have not changed to reflect this understanding. Both Egyptologists and Biblicists have examined parts of Josiah's death and cite each other in their writings on Josiah. One generally fails to see an appraisal of the theological content of the material from the Hebrew Bible by Egyptologists; nonetheless, the Egyptological contribution remains important. The picture of Josiah becomes considerably clouded when one combines a theological lens with a historical-critical method. The limitations of what can be said about the multiple, diverging sources need to be acknowledged. A clear understanding of what Josiah actually accomplished in terms of reforms and how this accomplishment is viewed in the Hebrew Bible is crucial for understanding the confines of what we, as well as Egyptologists, can say about this period.

Although two kings dominate the second half of the seventh century in Judah (Manasseh and Josiah), a general lack of stability reigns in this period. Manasseh concluded his lengthy reign about the year 642. Amon commenced his short reign at this time, and 2 Kings 21:23 reports that he was killed by his own servants in the second year of his reign. Josiah succeeded him as a child of eight and reigned until 609. Three of his sons reigned for short periods after him, but dynastic succession came to an end with the final one of these sons.

Egypt demonstrates much greater stability during this period. The Saite Dynasty, or Dynasty 26, came to power with Psammetichus I in 664.[16] This northern kingdom overthrew the Kushites who ruled Egypt in the Twenty-Fifth Dynasty. They ushered in the epoch known as the Late Period, during which pharaonic vitality displayed itself over the course of five dynasties of both native and foreign rulers. Like Manasseh, Psammetichus reigned for nearly half a century. Necho II

---

considerable conversation about the significance of this great monarch, both in antiquity and in the present."

[16] Douglas J. Brewer and Emily Teeter, *Egypt and the Egyptians* (Cambridge/New York: Cambridge University Press, 2007), 58: "Dynasty 26, also called the Saite Period after Sais, the home of the kings of the era, was a time of tremendous artistic achievement."; Alan Lloyd, "The Late Period (664–332 BC)," in *The Oxford History of Ancient Egypt*, ed. Ian Shaw (Oxford/New York: Oxford University Press, 2000), 371: "[T]he 26th Dynasty achieved spectacular success, which was to be crowned with nothing less than the resurgence of Egypt as a major international power."

succeeded him and reigned for about fifteen years until 595. Second Kings 23:29 claims that he personally killed Josiah, whereas 2 Chronicles 35:23 more sympathetically asserts that an archer of Necho killed Josiah. Jeremiah 46:3 merely mentions that Necho imprisoned Josiah's son, Jehoiakim. After Necho, Psammetichus II ruled for about five years. Then Apries ruled for nearly twenty years until 570. Ahmose II succeeded him and reigned for nearly fifty years. The Persians defeated Psammetichus III the year after he came to power and initiated Dynasty 27.

Historians rely exclusively on the Hebrew Bible for the reconstruction of Josiah. The Hebrew Bible refers to Josiah fifty-five times, chiefly in Jeremiah, 2 Chronicles, and 2 Kings. The house of Josiah rather than the individual is responsible for the last three of these fifty-five citations in Zephaniah and Zechariah, as well as many of the citations in Jeremiah. Second Kings and 2 Chronicles serve as the basis for the common understanding of Josiah as a religious reformer enforcing long forgotten Deuteronomistic laws within Jerusalem and Judah. These reforms included a purge of syncretistic worship sites, the covenant renewal ceremony, and the celebration of Passover. The king lists of Egypt confirm one aspect of this reconstruction—that Necho II was active in this period. Others use the archaeological findings at the small coastal fort of Mesad Hashavyahu to confirm the general background of Josiah's historical epoch and to conjecture that he employed these Greek mercenaries.[17] A scholarly consensus has not formed around the findings of Meṣad Ḥashavyahu.[18] The simple proposition concerning Josiah's untimely death becomes far more complicated when we try to understand exactly how he died.

---

[17] Ephraim Stern, *Archaeology of the Land of the Bible*, vol. 2, *The Assyrian, Babylonian, and Persian Periods, 732–332 BCE*, Anchor Bible Reference Library (New York: Doubleday, 2001), 107: "[W]hen the Assyrian administration in Palestine collapsed totally around 640 BCE, the Egyptians penetrated Philistia and replaced the Assyrians, except perhaps in the northern part of the kingdom of Ashdod, which fell for a short time into the hands of Josiah king of Judah (according to the finds at Meẓad Ḥashavyahu and perhaps also those of Tell Qasile)."

[18] J. Maxwell Miller and John H. Hayes, *A History of Ancient Israel and Judah*, 2nd ed. (Louisville, KY: Westminster John Knox Press, 2006), 460: "The argument that Josiah had Kittim (Greeks/Cypriots) as mercenary troops under his control and gained a foothold on the Mediterranean, based on the Mesad Hashavyahu finds, can no longer be accepted."

The treatment of Josiah by Egyptologists offers an excellent example of the assumptions underlying various histories of the Saite period. Egyptologists play an important role in the understanding of this epoch of the history of ancient Israel. Histories of ancient Israel frequently cite Egyptologists because evidence of Egypt's engagement in the Levant is considered crucial for a reconstruction of events. Ironically, most Egyptological literature views Josiah solely through the lens of the Bible. We arrive at the problem of a circular argument as Egyptologists accept the biblical premise, and Biblicists support their views through these Egyptologists. Both Egyptologists and Biblicists must take a more critical view of the Bible's theological portrait of Josiah, rather than accepting this portrait uncritically as they mostly do.

1. Egyptological Treatments of Josiah

One of the pivotal books concerning this period is Donald Redford's *Egypt, Canaan, and Israel in Ancient Times*. Redford states that "Josiah's intervention at the Megiddo pass, though a courageous move, failed at the cost of the thirty-nine-year-old king's life."[19] Although he cites nothing, he must be basing his views on 2 Kings 23. Redford's views develop the conventional understanding of this event as we see in earlier articles and books by Anthony Spalinger, Abraham Malamat, and Anson Rainey. While Malamat and Rainey are not primarily Egyptologists, Egyptological literature frequently cites them. All these writers rely solely on the biblical evidence, but the contradictory nature of the biblical evidence goes unmentioned. Redford warns the reader earlier in his book, "[T]he author of 1–2 Kings has produced his work from the vantage point of a much later age,"[20] yet he does not heed his own warning. The biblical portrayal of Josiah demands careful examination. Many of these authors also speak of the importance of Josiah's reforms, but they are basing this solely on the biblical record. No discussion about discrepancies in the biblical record is found.

Anthony Spalinger has written important articles on this time period that provide the backbone for many who cover the period. His view on Josiah pushes beyond the limits of what his sources can support. He argues "that some type of alliance existed between Josiah of

---

[19] Donald B. Redford, *Egypt, Canaan, and Israel in Ancient Times* (Princeton, NJ: Princeton University Press, 1992), 448.

[20] Ibid., 320.

Judah and Psammetichus, even though the Bible is silent concerning any collusion between these two kings."[21] Egyptian records would also appear to be silent concerning this collusion. He states further that Egypt needed to have a pledge of neutrality from Josiah in order to secure the *via maris*.[22] Again, this seems to be an inference. Many think of Judah as an inland empire at this stage.[23] Spalinger goes on to state: "The Jewish king was more concerned with his religious reformation than to foolhardily risk another defeat by the Egyptians, especially since in the 620's and early 610's Egypt was the only power in Palestine."[24] While all three of these assertions may be true, and some of them reflect certain aspects of the biblical record, they do not reflect the entire biblical record. We must ask ourselves, was a later biblical writer more concerned about religious reformation than Josiah was? There is a fictive element to many of the stories concerning Josiah that cannot easily be discounted. Chronicles and Kings understand the nature of his reforms in a different manner. It does not seem to me that Spalinger takes any of these considerations into account.

Egyptian sources offer no evidence of Necho's encounter with Josiah. In fact, as Hooker and Hayes note, "[N]o known Egyptian text refers to any northern campaign through Syria-Palestine by Neco II."[25] Egyptian sources do not refer to Josiah. The Babylonian Chronicles do not seem to mention Josiah, either. The Babylonian Chronicles "in-

---

[21] Anthony Spalinger, "Egypt and Babylonia: A Survey (c. 620 B.C.–550 B.C.)," *Studien zur Altägyptischen Kultur* 5 (1977): 223.

[22] Ibid.

[23] Mario Liverani, *Israel's History and the History of Israel* (London: Equinox, 2005), 173–74: "The most common indicators of material culture show that the kingdom of Judah consolidated between Bethel and Beer-sheba, but without any spread visible to the north nor to the Mediterranean coast."; Diana Edelman, "Hezekiah's Alleged Cultic Centralization," *Journal for the Study of the Old Testament* 32 (2008): 425: "It is likely after 701 BCE, the territory of the kingdom of Judah was probably limited to the immediate environs of Jerusalem. This situation, which resulted in the temporary 'centralization' of the cult of Yahweh in Jerusalem, is most likely what prompted the author or a subsequent editor of Kings to credit Hezekiah with a voluntary cultic centralization that followed the call in Torah for a single place where Yahweh would choose to place his name to dwell."

[24] Spalinger, "Egypt and Babylonia," 223.

[25] P. Hooker and J. Hayes, "The Year of Josiah's Death: 609 or 610 BCE?," in *The Land that I Will Show You: Essays on the History and Archaeology of the Ancient Near East in Honor of J. Maxwell Miller* (Sheffield, UK: Sheffield University Press, 2001), 99.

clude coverage of the years 626–623 and 616–594 B.C.E."[26] Miller and Hayes put it best: "[W]e really possess little material about Josiah's reign except for the extensive accounts in II Kings and II Chronicles of his religious reform."[27] This circumstantial perspective is never shared with us in the work of Egyptologists like Redford and Spalinger, yet it is fundamental for evaluating the activities of Necho.

2. Biblical Treatments of Josiah

A recent atlas on biblical Israel demonstrates the problem of the Egyptological influence on biblical studies. This atlas has an excellent bibliography and was written by a preeminent Biblicist. We are told the "king of Judah had hoped to stop the Egyptian advance by opposing Necho's army in the valley of Jezreel at Megiddo. . . . [B]ut an archer struck the fatal blow."[28] Rainey bases this claim primarily on the biblical record from 2 Chronicles, but he also cites Anthony Spalinger, Abraham Malamat, and Redford. We see the depth of the problem here, as Rainey buttresses his argument with a number of secondary sources. We have already considered the influence of Spalinger on biblical studies. I will now examine the Malamat article in order to demonstrate how influential it has been on Redford and the field.

Another important Biblicist, Abraham Malamat, uses parts of the biblical record to compose a similar picture. He begins his portrayal of Josiah by stating that the "assassination of Josiah's father, Amon, was undoubtedly of Egyptian instigation, and already then Egypt seems to have been intriguing to install a sympathetic regime in Judah."[29] Apart from the fact that Amon was assassinated, he offers no evidence for these statements, biblical or otherwise. While Amon was assassinated by court attendants, no evidence exists that they were under Egyptian influence. At this time (641), Egypt was having a lot of its own internal difficulties, as Psammetichus I struggled to consolidate power in the early years of the Saite Dynasty. Scholars seem to feel that there was

---

[26] Miller and Hayes, *A History of Ancient Israel and Judah*, 441.
[27] Ibid.
[28] Anson Rainey and R. S. Notley, *The Sacred Bridge: Carta's Atlas of the Biblical World* (Jerusalem: Carta, 2006), 259.
[29] Abraham Malamat, "The Twilight of Judah: In the Egyptian-Babylonian Maelstrom," in *Congress Volume: Edinburgh 1974*, Supplements to *Vetus Testamentum* 28 (Leiden: Brill, 1975), 126.

not enough stability for Egypt to engage in foreign intervention until the close of the seventh century.[30] Malamat then states:

> Josiah was able to launch his annexation policy only after initiating his reform (around 628 B.C.; cf. II Chron. xxxiv(34) 6), and he seems to have gained control solely over the former Assyrian province of *Samerina* and to have established a corridor reaching the coast in the northern Shephelah, as possibly witnessed by the Hebrew epigraphic finds at Mecad Hashavyahu.[31]

Although Malamat cites Chronicles here, he certainly seems to be under the influence of Kings. Josiah is constantly reforming throughout Chronicles, whereas he initiates reforms after the discovery of the Book of the Law in Kings. Malamat and Spalinger combine to give us a picture of Josiah as a reforming king who judiciously averted conflict with an Egypt that was interfering in domestic Judean concerns. Yet, Miller and Hayes have come to cast doubt on this picture: "The argument that Josiah had Kittim (Greeks/Cypriots) as mercenary troops under his control and gained a foothold on the Mediterranean, based on the Meṣad Ḥashavyahu finds, can no longer be accepted."[32] Let us now examine the biblical material.

Although Malamat and Spalinger do not consider him, I consider Jeremiah to be a source as important as 2 Kings. Jeremiah lived during the reign of Josiah and wrote about the historical incidents under examination. Scholars used to believe that Jeremiah was a full-grown man when he first received the prophetic utterance in 627, but more recent scholarship holds this prophetic call was probably more like Samuel's, so he was only a boy of twelve or thirteen when he received the call. Nonetheless, he certainly would have been a fully mature man for the last ten years of Josiah's reign. Most of the references to Josiah within Jeremiah are cursory in nature, where he is often described as the father of Jehioakim (Jer 35:1) or Zedekiah (Jer 27:1). Jeremiah's

---

[30] A. B. Lloyd, "The Late Period, 664–323 BC," in *Ancient Egypt: A Social History*, by B. G. Trigger, B. J. Kemp, D. O'Connor, and A. B. Lloyd (Cambridge, UK: Cambridge University Press, 1983), 284: "The half century of Psammetichus I's reign clearly achieved such success in the resurgence of the country that his son Necho II (619–595) was able to commit a high proportion of his resources and energies to a policy of expansion abroad."

[31] Malamat, "Twilight of Judah," 125.

[32] Miller and Hayes, *History of Ancient Israel and Judah*, 461.

only substantive remarks about Josiah are at 22:15, when he is condemning Jehoiakim: "Did not your father eat and drink and do justice and righteousness?" One can infer from these remarks a certain amount of respect for Josiah, but one does not see the perfect ruler of Judah, as he is described by DH (2 Kgs 23:25). Jeremiah's failure to describe Josiah as a reformer stands in clear contrast to descriptions of Josiah in Kings and Chronicles. This failure to describe Josiah as a reformer is hardly surprising when one considers that Jeremiah condemns the temple in chapter 7, the lack of covenant fidelity in chapter 11, and those who are wise in the Torah in chapter 8. In the Anchor Bible Dictionary article on Josiah, one critic has argued that "Josiah's motives for cultic reform were not purely religious, and it is likely that even in his lifetime its *limited* effect on the people was perceptible. . . . This Jeremiah saw, and his cool appraisal of Josiah furnishes a corrective to the enthusiasm of the Deuteronomic Historian."[33] It is notable that Jeremiah does not mention the death of Josiah. Jeremiah had an intense dislike of Israel's political involvement with Egypt, as can be seen from his oracle against Egypt in chapter 46. One wonders why in his antipathy for Egypt he would fail to mention that Egypt killed this just and righteous king. One would also think that he would not hesitate to mention the Egyptian hand in the death of Josiah's father, Amon, which Malamat posits. It is left to the later sources to flesh out Josiah.

Biblical scholars often see Jeremiah as participating in the Josianic reforms. Steven McKenzie seems to affirm Norbert Lohfink's understanding that the "broad-based and short-lived renewal movement that took place under Josiah had a form of Deuteronomy as its charter and produced an incipient Deuteronomistic History. Both were supplemented in the exile, when Jeremiah was also written."[34] Jeremiah has even been described as a propagandist on behalf of Josiah.[35] Although parts of Jeremiah seem sympathetic to Josiah and the Deuteronomistic

---

[33] R. Althann, "Josiah," in *The Anchor Bible Dictionary*, ed. David Noel Freedman (New York: Doubleday, 1992), 4:1017.

[34] Steven L. McKenzie, "The Still Elusive Deuteronomists," in *Congress Volume: Helsinki 2010*, ed. Martti Nissinen, Supplements to *Vetus Testamentum* 148 (Leiden/Boston: Brill, 2012), 402.

[35] Norbert Lohfink, "The Cult Reform of Josiah of Judah: 2 Kings 22–23 as a Source for the History of Israel," in *Ancient Israelite Religion: Essays in Honor of Frank Moore Cross*, ed. Patrick D. Miller (Philadelphia: Fortress Press, 1987), 469: "The

reform, Robert Kugler will argue, "[I]t is just as easily explained by positing the conversion of Jeremiah's disciples to a deuteronomic outlook."[36] Although Jeremiah's enemies give voice to disillusionment with Josiah in Jeremiah 44:17-18,[37] we cannot assume that Jeremiah agreed with Josiah's opinions. Na'aman discusses the possibility that only a small core of the material even existed at the time of Josiah's life. The stories and incidents around the life of Josiah were built up at a later stage, such as the finding of the Book of the Law. The figure that Jeremiah knew may be very different from the later figure that DH so carefully constructed. I think that is the safer assumption based on the lack of unequivocal evidence[38] in the book of Jeremiah. If we compare Josiah with Hezekiah, we see numerous sources (Isaiah, 2 Kings, and 2 Chronicles) attesting to their relationship. We do not see this same relationship between Jeremiah and Josiah. Josiah has a clear prophet that he turned to: Huldah. The writers and editors of Kings and Chronicles seem inclined to connect the major prophets with kings, and we must ask why they do not make the same connection between Josiah and Jeremiah as they do between Hezekiah and Isaiah.

3. Josiah in His Ancient Near Eastern Environment

The reforms attributed to Josiah are far from anomalous. Josiah follows a long line of ancient Near Eastern monarchs who made major religious reforms such as Akhenaten in Egypt, Muwatalli II and Tudhaliya IV in Hatti, Nebuchadnezzar and Sennacherib in Assyria, and Nabonidus in Babylon.[39] Perhaps the most instructive of these reformers for our purposes is Tudhaliya IV. Nadav Na'aman's article points

---

young Jeremiah also appears to have been active as a propagandist for a pilgrimage to Jerusalem, springing from joy over new salvation to be wrought by Jerusalem."

[36] Robert Kugler, "The Deuteronomists and the Writings," in *Those Elusive Deuteronomists: The Phenomenon of Pan-Deuteronomism*, ed. Linda S. Schearing and Steven L. McKenzie, Journal for the Study of the Old Testament Supplement Series 268 (Sheffield, UK: Sheffield Academic Press, 1999), 144.

[37] Na'aman, "The King Leading Cult Reforms in His Kingdom," 166.

[38] Norbert Lohfink, "Der Junge Jeremia Als Propagandist Und Poet: Zum Grundstock Von Jer 30–31," in *Le Livre De Jérémie: Le Prophète Et Son Milieu, Les Oracles Et Leur Transmission*, ed. Pierre Bogaert (Leuven: Leuven University Press, 1997), 358–59. Lohfink points to important themes of Josiah that Jeremiah echoes, but I don't think that these themes are unequivocal.

[39] Na'aman, "The King Leading Cult Reforms in His Kingdom," 141.

to a situation in Hatti with clear parallels to Judah and the possible motive for the Deuteronomistic reforms after its devastating defeats at the hands of the Assyrians and Babylonians: "It seems, therefore, that the ruler was driven to carry out the reform by a profound remorse arising from the sins of his ancestors, perhaps also by his devastating defeat at the hands of the Assyrians."[40] Similar dynamics characterize this period of Judean history. The expansion of Babylonian power has destabilized Palestine, and Egypt now plays a menacing new role. Josiah either chooses new policies or is forced by necessity to implement new policies. The religious reforms also display a remorse for the sins of the past (2 Kgs 22:11) but may well be influenced by the realpolitik of newly found Babylonian power.

E. The Role of Historiography

I have noted the difficulty of historical narrative repeatedly throughout this book. The material on Hezekiah, Manasseh, and Josiah underscores the need to recognize the fragmentary and contested nature of certain parts of the Bible. We see a different hermeneutic in the work of the Chronicler and DH, producing different portrayals of these figures. At times, these portrayals are radically different, as in the case of Manasseh. These differences force us to consider the politics of the times that produced these texts. While we cannot be sure as to either the exact dates of Kings and Chronicles or how many redactions of them we have, there is a general scholarly consensus that both Kings and Chronicles were influenced by the fall of Jerusalem. Each is based in a theology and theodicy that account for this loss. DH ultimately seems to be pessimistic; Chronicles seems more hopeful.

New Historicism offer us some tools for understanding these differences. As opposed to earlier views of historiography that viewed the past as retrievable, "New Historicism, with its postmodern connections, manifests an underlying skepticism about knowledge of the past."[41] This builds on the earlier discussion in chapter 5 of Hayden White's *invented and found* aspects of historical narrative. The material on Josiah brings this into sharp relief. When we look at the dependence of Kings on the view of kingship found in Deuteronomy 17:14-20,

---

[40] Ibid., 150.
[41] Gina Hens-Piazza, *The New Historicism* (Minneapolis: Fortress Press, 2002), 26.

we can question our objective knowledge of the past. The Chronicler does not seem to be restricted by Deuteronomy 17:14-20 and views the life of Josiah in a different way. The discovery of the "Book of the Law" plays a much bigger role for DH, but the literary nature of this discovery can lead us to skepticism regarding our actual knowledge of the past. "New Historicism trains its view upon the processes of production and consumption of texts."[42] Na'aman has offered powerful evidence as to the production of a text like the discovery of the Book of the Law across the ancient Near East. New Historicism will push us to sideline the distinctions between biblical literature and history in order to see the importance of both the Chronicler and DH. The attempt to privilege one over the other plays into contemporary politics, but it is a result of ancient politics.

Chronicles displays the cracks, the underside, and the signs of disarray latent in Kings. New Historicism opts for these types of considerations.[43] The figure of Josiah appears almost impossible to understand fully. Whereas archaeology was able to help us understand parts of the material culture influenced by Hezekiah, archaeology is of little help here. The two texts concerning Josiah leave this reader cautious of saying too much about Josiah. He may be like Cromwell as some would have it, but even Cromwell is a very different figure for the Irish than the English. There are certain figures who do not allow us to push much beyond the cracks, underside, and fissures.

Conclusion

The books of Chronicles and Kings portray Josiah as a great king, but the portrayal of Josiah in Kings is part of a much larger narrative arc. This narrative arc of Josiah as the perfect king and the greatest king in the history of Israel and Judah fails to consider Chronicles. This failure to recognize a literary pattern within Kings has led to overly historical representations of Kings, especially by Egyptologists. Josiah is a carefully constructed figure; contemporaries like Jeremiah may have understood him as very different from the person he is ultimately presented as in both Kings, Chronicles, and much contemporary biblical scholarship.

---

[42] Ibid., 6.
[43] Ibid., 39.

Conclusion

As we have tried to come to an understanding of kingship, I have frequently noted the domineering position of DH in this debate. A quick survey of biblical studies' authoritative histories of Israel will highlight how so much of the history is based on DH's understanding of it. I have tried to take the book of Chronicles into account more than is customary, but Chronicles is heavily influenced by DH. The Chronicler chooses to tell the story differently, but we have seen how the Chronicler shares many of the biases of DH. What has emerged powerfully throughout the book is how both DH and the Chronicler are involved in a reconceptualization and recontextualization of kingship. I chose to examine the Royal Psalms in order to think about the original concept and contextualization of kingship.

This book has focused on five of David's successors: two from the North (Jeroboam and Ahab) and three from the South (Hezekiah, Manasseh, and Josiah). While David both ruled the United Kingdom of the North and the South and handed this kingdom on to his successor Solomon, none of his successors were able to accomplish this feat as it quickly divided upon the death of Solomon. David is mentioned a number of times in the book of the Psalms, but his successors are never mentioned there; nonetheless, I believe the Royal Psalms give us important insights into his successors. Most scholars would agree that the stories found in the books of Kings and Chronicles are relatively late, most written hundreds of years after Jeroboam and Ahab. Many are also probably written after the reigns of Hezekiah, Manasseh, and Josiah. They should not be thought of as contemporaneous with them; rather, many pericopes are highly influenced by the fall of Jerusalem and try to explain its fall in some way. Although the psalms are not without Deuteronomistic influence, they offer access to a different and more positive outlook on kingship. The Deuteronomistic influence is not so much in the content of the psalms but in their placement within the book of Psalms. The hopes for the king are still very instructive and quite different than Chronicles and, especially, the book of Kings.

A. Reconceptualization and Recontextualization

The reconceptualization and recontextualization of kingship accentuate much of our knowledge of biblical kingship. We have seen how many stress the role of Deuteronomy 17:14-20 in this reconceptualization of kingship. Deuteronomy 17:14-20 puts strong limitations around the role of king. The vocabulary of Deuteronomy 17:14-20 reappears in many of the important passages about the kings under study in both the books of Kings and Chronicles. It is generally understood that Deuteronomy 17:14-20 was written after the fall of Jerusalem; hence, it offers a program for a utopian future rather than a reflection of the actual concerns and restraints imposed on the kings under consideration. This utopia is projected on the biblical heroes of Moses and Joshua. They become the models for kingship in the Bible. This allows the writers of Kings and Chronicles to set a very high bar for holiness, which generally seems to be beyond the realm of actual kings. Chronicles will allow King David to approach this realm, but the books of Samuel present an inferior King David struggling with family problems and the control of his own libido. We never see these difficulties with Moses or Joshua.

The psalms generally celebrate kingship in a full-throated manner. They have a distinct set of royal psalms that display the full measure of great possibilities present within a king. While foreign kingship is not considered within the psalms, most scholars would see them reflecting the exalted status of the king within the ancient Near East. Some scholars see these psalms recontextualized as different concerns dominate the book of Psalms than kingship. While the Royal Psalms may have existed prior to the other psalms, issues like *Torah* and refuge come to have a much more central role within the psalms. Some scholars even speculate that *Torah* is meant to control kingship and is exalted above kingship. *Torah* comes first, and kingship comes second. The reality of a king being governed by law is hard to imagine in any of the countries outside Israel and is even harder to imagine in light of the Royal Psalms. Be that as it may, there are only a few royal psalms and dozens of other psalms that may serve to recontextualize these royal psalms.

B. Beyond Reconceptualization and Recontextualization

Deuteronomy 17, Joshua 24, and 1 Samuel 8 and 12 all offer us the reconceptualization of kingship. We find within these texts both highly idealized models of leadership for ancient Israel as well as similar vocabulary and interests. Rather than something to be celebrated, kingship is something to be limited and controlled. Israel accepts kingship within these texts, but it is almost a regret or a concession to sinful reality. While an acknowledgment of the king as God's anointed will appear in 1 Samuel, this is not present in Deuteronomy 17:14-20. I have agreed with those who see this current of thought as distant from the actual perspective on the king by his contemporaries. The reconceptualization is on account of the fall of Jerusalem. A scribal class seems to have emerged that viewed kingship in a considerably more negative manner because of the catastrophic collapse of Israel.

I have argued that we must weigh this negative reconceptualization against the positive evidence for kingship garnered by the social sciences. The nations around Israel had kings. Many scholars have speculated that the nation-states of the ancient Near East needed a king when they transitioned from tribal societies to nations. Kingship was just a natural part of this evolutionary process. The social sciences offer strong evidence of this pattern in Egypt and Mesopotamia. Although the Bible will focus on King David and his successors in the south of Israel in Hebron and Jerusalem, the material culture points to the north of Israel as the part of Israel that first transitions to kingship. Shechem is often referred to as nature's capital of Israel. King Omri and his successors, including Ahab, set up their capital just north of Shechem in Samaria. These are the first kings to be found definitively in the archaeological record, as we see the Assyrians battling with them and assessing them tribute. These Omride kings were acknowledged and recognized by the small nation-states and the large superpowers around Israel. The social sciences yield this evidence of the importance of kingship.

We also turned to narrative criticism of the stories themselves to highlight the importance of kingship. While DH's heroes are often prophets pitted against the king, the nature of the story itself points to the centrality of kingship. Contemporary biblical scholars may gravitate toward the figure of a prophet, but they may be telling us more about themselves than the text. An isolated reading of the Bible will focus on DH's desacralization of kingship, but a broader reading of the Bible moves us back to the centrality of the king. The text itself points to the king as central and the other characters as helpers or opponents. Later scribes may elevate these characters, but the king comes to the fore of the text in spite of opponents or helpers according to narrative criticism.

The positive evidence for kingship emanates most strongly from the Royal Psalms. Although there has been a lot of speculation about them and their presence within putative royal rituals or ceremonies, they undoubtedly offer a positive view of kingship. They also speak to the shared attitudes toward kingship across the ancient Near East. The shared attitudes revolve around the importance of the autumn New Year's Festival that seems to have been commonly celebrated in many of the nations of the ancient Near East. The theme of renewal is closely associated with this feast, and it is tied to kingship. We find many of the royal psalms stress the deity's role in the enthronement of the king. This also serves to reinforce the basic legitimation of the king as the deity is so prominent in these events. Although this may not have been as common in other parts of the ancient Near East, abasement is part of the Royal Psalms. Unlike a country like Egypt, there is no mistaking the king for a god. As we have considered the negative material in Deuteronomy 17:14-20 and 1 Samuel 8 and 12, we can see how this represents a minority position across the ancient Near East, where very little negativity toward kingship is found. It may be sounder to see Israel as having more in common with the other countries of the ancient Near East than to understand the negativity of DH as representing common opinion in ancient Israel rather than the interests of a small scribal class trying to explain catastrophes long after the time of many of the kings.

C. Jeroboam

Jeroboam provides an interesting case study, as the Chronicler has far less interest in him than DH does. He is a troubling figure in both accounts, but his troubles seem limited to his times in Chronicles, whereas he is included across the arc of monarchic history in the Deuteronomistic History. Jeroboam shares many of the more troubling features of King David in the Deuteronomistic History. He fights with his predecessor, he flees from his predecessor, he is commissioned by a prophet, he loses a child, and he moves the capital. We get a much more abbreviated view of Jeroboam in the book of Chronicles. There is plenty of negative material about him there, but it is presented a little differently and does not have the same long-term impact. David does not have nearly as many negative qualities in Chronicles as in the books of Samuel and Kings. Interestingly, some of the negative qualities associated with David in Samuel become associated with Jeroboam in Chronicles, as we hear of him attracting a group of troubled people around him who are in debt.

A lot of ambiguity exists in the presentation of Jeroboam in Kings. We see how the Greek version can be much more positive than the Hebrew version. Most of this ambiguity is no longer present in Chronicles; yet, the importance of Jeroboam also seems to be diminished.

King David may be the most helpful figure for understanding Jeroboam. They both seem to be classic Weberian charismatic figures who are respected more for what they can do rather than what they say. David leads a band of mercenaries before he eventually reemerges within the kingdom of Israel. Jeroboam leads a group of rebellious northerners who seem to resent their powerful southern overlords. The book of Samuel can be seen as an apology for these wayward parts of David's life. The books of Chronicles seems to include very little of these wayward episodes. The accounts of Jeroboam have no apology for him. There are many helpful comparisons with David, but he always remains an outsider.

Archaeology suggests that the books of Samuel and Chronicles do not quite relate the reality of the northern kingdom of Israel. Jeroboam is easily portrayed as idolatrous, but there was probably a lack of centralization during this time period that the texts simply cannot capture. Most of the stories about Jeroboam seem to have been written centuries after his death and perhaps have a different king in mind. An aniconic tradition never seems to have existed in the North, so Jeroboam's idolatrous ways could easily be the result of a misunderstanding. The Deuteronomistic program appears to come well after the time of Jeroboam, but he was turned into a useful minatory figure for both Chronicles and the Deuteronomistic History.

D. Ahab

Chronicles takes far less interest in Ahab than does Kings. His father, Omri, founded what would appear to be the most successful dynasty in the northern kingdom of Israel. Israel has been referred to as the House of Omri at this time period, but it is Ahab who is the first figure from Israel or Judah to truly appear in the archaeological record. He was an important part of the anti-Assyrian alliances of his time. Judah and Moab both seem to be vassal states under Israel during parts of his reign. Like Solomon, he marries outside of Israel and Judah.

Kings makes him a much more complicated figure than Chronicles. He interacts with many more prophets. Both Kings and Chronicles will have him interact with Micaiah ben-Imlah, but only Kings will present the interactions with Elijah. This will be a pattern that we will continue to see in Kings. We appear to have a level of interactions with the king that often expresses Deuteronomistic concerns in a bolder fashion than Chronicles. Elijah is a figure quite similar to Moses; he confronts foreign enemies and retreats to Mount Horeb after his difficulties. The book of Kings describes an Ahab who becomes the greatest threat to Israel as he has worship in the wrong places, with the wrong symbols, and most dangerously, with the wrong gods. Jeroboam accomplished the first two, but only Ahab has all three. The book of Kings ultimately seems to have concerns of theodicy at the heart of its description of Ahab. It wants to explain the fall of Israel in 722 and ultimately the fall of Jerusalem (ca. 587).

Chronicles moves in a different direction with a different theodicy. Ahab is closely associated with Jehoshaphat in Chronicles, as the Chronicler is much more interested in the Southern kings than the Northern kings. While Ahab will be condemned in Chronicles as well, Jehoshaphat has the opportunity for repentance and restoration after his sinful dealings with Ahab. The Chronicler is much more interested in the restoration of right relationship with God than in explaining the sufferings of Israel and Judah.

Although Ahab becomes an enormous threat to Yahwistic religion, close attention to the text will provide a more ambiguous picture of Ahab. He is not all bad. He will repent in Kings in a manner that will foreshadow later kings like Manasseh in Chronicles. He will die in a manner reminiscent of Josiah. The expectations of the Royal Psalms must be taken into account when we consider Ahab. Glimmers of light shine through a very negative portrait. The negativity of the portrait intensifies when the Deuteronomistic overlay is added, but the original concept and context of the king cannot be forgotten.

E. Hezekiah

Hezekiah is the first of the kings to receive nearly equal treatment from DH and the Chronicler. He is depicted in a positive manner by both writers, but we begin to see important differences in the writers in how they choose to depict him. The archaeological record accentuates Hezekiah's centralizing tendencies. Although some scholars downplay these tendencies, there seems to have been a shift from official cult sanctuaries throughout the Judean countryside in Beersheba, Arad, and Lachish to just an official sanctuary in Jerusalem. The book of

Deuteronomy wants more reforms than just this centralization and does not fully celebrate Hezekiah. The Chronicler seems to hold a different view and describes Hezekiah as the greatest king.

One of the chief differences is how the two books depict Hezekiah's interactions with fellow Israelites. The book of Kings limits Hezekiah primarily to Isaiah. We see Isaiah depicted as an equal to the king and his spiritual leader. The book of Chronicles focuses much more on Hezekiah with the people and depicts Hezekiah as a spiritual leader who does not seem dependent on the prophets. Hezekiah prays directly to Yahweh, with the prophet as an intermediary. Hezekiah embodies the Chronicler's spiritual imperative of joy—a word we rarely find in the Deuteronomistic History but used repeatedly in Chronicles and especially in the account of Passover.

The book of Chronicles revels in Hezekiah's status as a builder. This does not seem as important to DH, but it connects Hezekiah to accomplishments such as Hezekiah's Tunnel that are part of the archaeological record. Hezekiah exercises a charismatic leadership that is seen in the ability of Jerusalem to survive the Assyrian onslaught when other great cities and centers like Samaria are falling. Hezekiah is also associated with a lot of building around Jerusalem that seals his elevated status as a builder. Finally, Hezekiah has to use discernment, as there seems to be a great fluidity of leadership between Egypt and Mesopotamia. He manages to negotiate this balance carefully without alienating either side. He would seem to be a tolerant leader who avoided the extremes of not paying tribute to Assyria in order for Jerusalem to survive and turning to Egypt as a savior. He seems to have accurately diagnosed the shift in power to the East and the weakened state of Egypt and its Nubian overlords.

F. Manasseh

Manasseh is initially characterized by both Chronicles and Kings as an evil ruler. Kings depicts him as falling into many of the same sins as Ahab before him, yet these errors are unrelenting for Manasseh in Kings, whereas there is, in Kings, some repentance for Ahab. Manasseh just goes from bad to worse in Kings, and there is no improvement. He is the archvillain in Kings, which makes him the perfect setup for Josiah. The contrast could not be starker.

Manasseh may be the most confusing figure in the Bible. Although Chronicles will also describe him (initially) in the most negative of terms, here he will undergo an extraordinary conversion experience. Manasseh highlights the different theologies present in the two books. He turns his life around in Chronicles and seemingly serves as a witness to all of Israel and Judah that real change is possible.

Manasseh shares a number of key traits with Hezekiah in the book of Chronicles. They are both builders. As Hezekiah did not need Isaiah to pray for him in Chronicles, Manasseh is also presented as praying directly to God (2 Chr 33:12-13). Manasseh is much more connected with the people than with prophets. Ultimately Manasseh governs over Judah during a time of prosperity, where some of the most productive cash crops in the entire ancient Near East are produced. The echoes of the Royal Psalms should be heard before he is too quickly dismissed.

G. Josiah

Negativity toward kingship is found in the Bible, but Jewish and much Christian tradition has chosen to elevate kingship. The kings are far from perfect, yet was there another viable way for Israel to maintain some independence? The elevation of Josiah suggests that there was not. Josiah fulfills the ideals of Deuteronomy 17:14-20. He lives during a very difficult time, but he is portrayed as being unwilling to sacrifice his ideals. The pious character of Josiah ends up controlling our notions of kingship in a way much more powerful than other key institutions like prophecy and priesthood. Deuteronomy 34:10 tells us there has never been a prophet like Moses, and Deuteronomy 18:15-22 tells us the qualities of a prophet; yet, these parts of Deuteronomy do not control what it means to be a prophet like Deuteronomy 17:14-20 controls what it means to be a king. There is an idealism to the portrayal that has left scholars struggling to understand who Josiah truly is.

The discovery of the Book of the Law stands out as a central and controlling pericope in the Josiah narrative. This pericope connects Josiah to a number of similar stories across the ancient Near East. Recent scholarship has come to see this pericope as more of an invented tradition than a found tradition. This also serves as an important contrast with Hezekiah. The archaeological record consistently confirms important elements of his reign, such as the centralization of worship in Jerusalem or his fame as the builder of a tunnel that allowed Jerusalem to endure Sennacherib's siege. The archaeological record is far more neutral when it comes to Josiah. Some small elements of reformation can be seen (at best), but some would deny even this.

Ultimately, Josiah may be best understood within the narrative arc of Jeroboam at the beginning and Manasseh directly preceding him. Both Jeroboam and Josiah have a prophet associated with the foundational element of their rise to profound leadership according to Kings, but Josiah never wavers, whereas Jeroboam quickly goes astray. Jeroboam inaugurates worship at the wrong place with the wrong symbols. We will see Ahab add the wrong deity into this mix, but Ahab repents. Manasseh also seems to get involved with the wrong deity as he is accused of child sacrifice and erecting altars to Baal (2 Kgs 21:3). Manasseh does not repent. It is then left to Josiah to overcome all these sins in Kings, and he is more than up to it. Archaeology and Chronicles will give us a different understanding about Josiah, but this is largely a minority report only developed in the last few years.

Final Thoughts

The examination of various kings offers a more nuanced vision than the book of Kings, as suggested by the Psalms, Chronicles, Sirach, and the many prophets who interacted with them. Much energy has gone into understanding the reconceptualization and recontextualization of kingship, but Psalms and Chronicles put us in touch with a powerful vision. The Deuteronomistic History lends itself to the cynicism of this age when it comes to politicians, but it is important to realize that this is not the only vision in the Bible—nor is it the original vision; it is, however, an important vision. DH has high ideals for kingship, but Chronicles wants to leaven these ideals with joy, repentance, and restoration.

Archaeology and literary theory suggest that we must not be naïve about the role theology and ideology play in the various depictions of kingship. All this may leave us with a more ambiguous picture of kingship than we started with, but it also allows us to avoid being the captives of ideology. The picture of kingship created by text and context, as well as history and literature, distances itself from the polarities of text alone. Is Manasseh evil incarnate or not? Did Hezekiah or Josiah reinstitute Passover? How positively did the people feel about Ahab and Jeroboam during their reigns? We cannot get easy answers to these questions, but a fuller vision, aided by archaeology, narrative theory, the Deuteronomistic History, Chronicles, and the Psalms, suggests that we may have to be much more open to nuanced characters rather than angels and monsters.

Bibliography

Ahlström, Gösta W. *The History of Ancient Palestine*. Edited by Diana V. Edelman. Minneapolis: Fortress Press, 1993.
Althann, R. "Josiah." In *The Anchor Bible Dictionary*, edited by David Noel Freedman, 4:1014. New York: Doubleday, 1992.
André, G. "Kashap." In *Theological Dictionary of the Old Testament*, edited by G. Johannes Botterweck, Helmer Ringgren, and Heinz-Josef Fabry, 7:360–66. Translated by David E. Green. Grand Rapids, MI: Eerdmans, 1995.
Assmann, Jan. *Religion and Cultural Memory: Ten Studies*. Translated by Rodney Livingstone. Stanford, CA: Stanford University Press, 2006.
Aubin, Henry. *The Rescue of Jerusalem: The Alliance between Hebrews and Africans in 701 BC*. New York: Soho Press, 2002.
Auld, A. Graeme. *I & II Samuel: A Commentary*. The Old Testament Library. Louisville, KY: Westminster John Knox Press, 2011.
———. *Kings without Privilege: David and Moses in the Story of the Bible's Kings*. Edinburgh: T & T Clark, 1994.
Baines, John, and Norman Yoffee. "Order, Legitimacy, and Wealth in Ancient Egypt and Mesopotamia." In Feinman and Marcus, *Archaic States*, 199–260.
Bal, Mieke. *Narratology: Introduction to the Theory of Narrative*. 3rd ed. Translated by Christine van Boheemen. Toronto: University of Toronto Press, 2009.
Ben Zvi, Ehud. "Who Wrote the Speech of Rabshakeh and When?" *Journal of Biblical Literature* 109 (1990): 79–92.
Benz, Brendan. "The Varieties of Sociopolitical Experience in the Late Bronze Age Levant and the Rise of Early Israel." PhD diss., New York University, 2012.
Berlejung, Angelika. "The Assyrians in the West." In Nissinen, *Congress Volume: Helsinki 2010*, 21–59.
Best, Stephen, and Sharon Marcus. "Surface Reading: An Introduction." *Representations* 108, no. 1 (Fall 2009): 1–21.
Boer, Roland T. "Utopian Politics in 2 Chronicles 10–13." In *The Chronicler as Author: Studies in Text and Texture*. Edited by M. Patrick Graham and Steven McKenzie. Journal for the Study of the Old Testament Supplement Series 263. Sheffield, UK: Sheffield Academic Press, 1999.
Brewer, Douglas J., and Emily Teeter. *Egypt and the Egyptians*. Cambridge/New York: Cambridge University Press, 2007.

Clifford, Richard J. *Psalms 1–72*. Abingdon Old Testament Commentaries. Nashville, TN: Abingdon Press, 2002.

Cogan, Mordechai. *1 Kings: A New Translation with Introduction and Commentary*. Anchor Bible, vol. 10. New York: Doubleday, 2001.

———. "Into Exile: From the Assyrian Conquest of Israel to the Fall of Babylon." In *The Oxford History of the Biblical World*, edited by Michael D. Coogan, 242–75. Oxford/New York: Oxford University Press, 1998.

Dever, William G. *What Did the Biblical Writers Know, and When Did They Know It? What Archaeology Can Tell Us about the Reality of Ancient Israel*. Grand Rapids, MI: Eerdmans, 2001.

Dietrich, Walter. *The Early Monarchy in Israel: The Tenth Century B.C.E.* Atlanta: Society of Biblical Literature, 2007.

Dirks, Nicholas B. "Is Vice Versa? Historical Anthropologies and Anthropological Histories." In *The Historic Turn in the Human Sciences*. Edited by Terrence McDonald. Ann Arbor, MI: University of Michigan Press, 1996.

Eaton, J. H. *Kingship and the Psalms*. Studies in Biblical Theology: 2nd Series. London: SCM Press, 1976.

Edelman, Diana. "Hezekiah's Alleged Cultic Centralization." *Journal for the Study of the Old Testament* 32, no. 4 (2008): 395–434.

Endres, John C. "The Spiritual Vision of Chronicles: Wholehearted, Joy-Filled Worship of God." *Catholic Biblical Quarterly* 69, no. 1 (2007): 1–21.

———. *Temple, Monarchy and Word of God*. Message of Biblical Spirituality, vol. 2. Wilmington, DE: Michael Glazier, 1988.

Faust, Avraham. *Israel's Ethnogenesis: Settlement, Interaction, Expansion and Resistance*. London: Equinox, 2006.

Feinman, Gary M., and Joyce Marcus, eds. *Archaic States*. School of American Research Advanced Seminar Series. Santa Fe, NM: School of American Research Press, 1998.

Finkelstein, Israel. *The Forgotten Kingdom: The Archaeology and History of Northern Israel*. Ancient Near East Monographs. Atlanta: Society of Biblical Literature, 2013.

Finkelstein, Israel, and Neil Asher Silberman. *The Bible Unearthed: Archaeology's New Vision of Ancient Israel and the Origin of Its Sacred Texts*. New York/London: Free Press, 2001.

Flannery, Kent V., and Joyce Marcus. *The Creation of Inequality: How Our Prehistoric Ancestors Set the Stage for Monarchy, Slavery, and Empire*. Cambridge, MA: Harvard University Press, 2012.

Fleming, Daniel. *The Legacy of Israel in Judah's Bible: History, Politics, and the Reinscribing of Tradition*. New York: Cambridge University Press, 2012.

Franklin, N. "Samaria: From the Bedrock to the Omride Palace." *Levant* 36 (2004): 189–202.

Giddens, Anthony. *The Constitution of Society: Outline of the Theory of Structuration*. Berkeley: University of California Press, 1984.

Grabbe, Lester L., ed. *Ahab Agonistes: The Rise and Fall of the Omri Dynasty*. The Library of Hebrew Bible/Old Testament Studies, vol. 421. London/New York: T & T Clark, 2007.

———, ed. *Good Kings and Bad Kings: The Kingdom of Judah in the Seventh Century BCE*. The Library of Hebrew Bible/Old Testament Studies, vol. 393. London/New York, T & T Clark, 2005.

———. "Omri and Son, Incorporated: The Business of History." In Nissinen, *Congress Volume: Helsinki 2010*, 61–83.

———. "Reflections on the Discussion." In Grabbe, *Ahab Agonistes*, 331–41.

———. "Reflections on the Discussion." In Grabbe, *Good Kings and Bad Kings*, 339–50.

Grant, Jamie A. *The King as Exemplar: The Function of Deuteronomy's Kingship Law in the Shaping of the Book of Psalms*. Society of Biblical Literature Academia Biblica. Atlanta: Society of Biblical Literature, 2004.

Green, Barbara. *King Saul's Asking*. Interfaces. Collegeville, MN: Liturgical Press, 2003.

Grottanelli, Cristiano. *Kings and Prophets: Monarchic Power, Inspired Leadership, and Sacred Text in Biblical Narrative*. New York/Oxford: Oxford University Press, 1999.

Halpern, Baruch. *The Constitution of the Monarchy in Israel*. Harvard Semitic Monographs 25. Chico, CA: Scholars Press, 1981.

———. *David's Secret Demons: Messiah, Murderer, Traitor, King*. The Bible in Its World Series. Grand Rapids, MI: Eerdmans, 2001.

———. "Levitic Participation in the Reform Cult of Jeroboam I." *Journal of Biblical Literature* 95, no. 1 (1976): 31.

———. "Sybil, or the Two Nations? Archaism, Kinship, Alienation, and the Elite Redefinition of Traditional Culture in Judah in the 8th–7th Centuries B.C.E." In *The Study of the Ancient Near East in the Twenty-First Century: The William Foxwell Albright Centennial Conference*, edited by Jerrold S. Cooper and Glenn M. Schwartz, 291–338. Winona Lake, IN: Eisenbrauns, 1996.

Hamilton, Mark W. *The Body Royal: The Social Poetics of Kingship in Ancient Israel*. Biblical Interpretation Series. Leiden/Boston: Brill, 2005.

Hens-Piazza, Gina. *1–2 Kings*. Abingdon Old Testament Commentaries. Nashville, TN: Abingdon Press, 2006.

———. *The New Historicism*. Minneapolis: Fortress Press, 2002.

Hobbs, T. R. *2 Kings*. Word Biblical Commentary. Waco, TX: Word Books, 1985.

Hooker, Paul K., and John H. Hayes. "The Year of Josiah's Death: 609 or 610 BCE?" In *The Land that I Will Show You: Essays on the History and Archaeology of the Ancient Near East in Honor of J. Maxwell Miller*, edited by J. Andrew Dearman and M. Patrick Graham, 96–103. Journal for the Study of the Old Testament Supplement Series 343. Sheffield, UK: Sheffield University Press, 2001.

Hutton, Jeremy Michael. *The Transjordanian Palimpsest: The Overwritten Texts of Personal Exile and Transformation in the Deuteronomistic History*. Berlin/New York: Walter de Gruyter, 2009.

Iggers, Georg G. *Historiography in the Twentieth Century: From Scientific Objectivity to the Postmodern Challenge*. Hanover, NH: Wesleyan University Press, 1997.

Janowski, Bernd. *Arguing with God: A Theological Anthropology of the Psalms*. Translated by Armin Siedlecki. Louisville, KY: Westminster John Knox Press, 2013.

Japhet, Sara. *I & II Chronicles: A Commentary*. The Old Testament Library. Louisville, KY: Westminster/John Knox Press, 1993.

———. *The Ideology of the Book of Chronicles and Its Place in Biblical Thought*. Winona Lake, IN: Eisenbrauns, 2009.

Jobling, David. *1 Samuel*. Berit Olam. Collegeville, MN: Liturgical Press, 1998.

Joseph, Alison L. *Portrait of the Kings: The Davidic Prototype in Deuteronomistic Poetics*. Minneapolis: Fortress Press, 2015.

Kalimi, Isaac. *The Reshaping of Ancient Israelite History in Chronicles*. Winona Lake, IN: Eisenbrauns, 2005.

Keel, Othmar, and Christoph Uehlinger. *Gods, Goddesses, and Images of God in Ancient Israel*. Translated by T. Trapp. Minneapolis: Fortress Press, 1998.

Kelly, Brian E. "'Retribution' Revisited: Covenant, Grace and Restoration." In *The Chronicler as Theologian: Essays in Honor of Ralph W. Klein*. Edited by M. Patrick Graham, Steven McKenzie, and Gary Knoppers. Journal for the Study of the Old Testament Supplement Series 371. London/New York: T & T Clark, 2003.

Klein, Ralph W. *2 Chronicles: A Commentary*. Hermeneia. Minneapolis: Fortress Press, 2012.

Knauf, Ernst. "The Glorious Days of Manasseh." In Grabbe, *Good Kings and Bad Kings*, 164–88.

Knoppers, Gary N. *Jews and Samaritans: The Origins and History of Their Early Relations*. New York: Oxford University Press, 2013.

———. "The Relationship of the Deuteronomistic History to Chronicles: Was the Chronicler a Deuteronomist?" In Nissinen, *Congress Volume: Helsinki 2010*, 307–41.

———. *Two Nations under God: The Deuteronomistic History of Solomon and the Dual Monarchies*. Vol. 2, *The Reign of Jeroboam, the Fall of Israel, and the Reign of Josiah*. Harvard Semitic Monographs 53. Atlanta: Scholars Press, 1994.

Kraus, Hans-Joachim. *Theology of the Psalms*. Translated by Keith R. Crim. Minneapolis: Augsburg, 1986.

Kugler, Robert. "The Deuteronomists and the Writings." In *Those Elusive Deuteronomists: The Phenomenon of Pan-Deuteronomism*, edited by Linda S. Schearing and Steven L. McKenzie, 127–44. Journal for the Study of the Old Testament Supplement Series 268. Sheffield, UK: Sheffield Academic Press, 1999.

Lasine, Stuart. *Knowing Kings: Knowledge, Power, and Narcissism in the Hebrew Bible*. Semeia Studies. Atlanta: Society of Biblical Literature, 2001.

———. "Manasseh as Villain and Scapegoat." In *The New Literary Criticism and the Hebrew Bible*, edited by J. Cheryl Exum and David J. A. Clines, 163–83.

Journal for the Study of the Old Testament Supplement Series 143. Sheffield, UK: JSOT Press, 1993.

Leuchter, Mark. "Closing Remarks." In *Soundings in Kings: Perspectives and Methods in Contemporary Scholarship*. Edited by Mark Leuchter and Klaus-Peter Adam. Minneapolis: Fortress Press, 2010.

———. "Jeroboam the Ephratite." *Journal of Biblical Literature* 125, no. 1 (Spring 2006): 51–72.

Levenson, Jon. *Sinai and Zion: An Entry into the Jewish Bible*. San Francisco: Harper & Row, 1987).

Levinson, Bernard M. "The Reconceptualization of Kingship in Deuteronomy and the Deuteronomistic History's Transformation of Torah." *Vetus Testamentum* 51, no. 4 (October 2001): 511–34.

Lloyd, Alan. "The Late Period (664–332 BC)." In *The Oxford History of Ancient Egypt*. Edited by Ian Shaw. Oxford/New York: Oxford University Press, 2000.

Liverani, Mario. *Israel's History and the History of Israel*. London: Equinox, 2005.

Lohfink, Norbert. "The Cult Reform of Josiah of Judah: 2 Kings 22–23 as a Source for the History of Israel." In *Ancient Israelite Religion: Essays in Honor of Frank Moore Cross*, edited by Patrick D. Miller, 459–65. Philadelphia: Fortress Press, 1987.

———. "Der Junge Jeremia Als Propagandist Und Poet: Zum Grundstock Von Jer 30–31." In *Le Livre de Jérémie: Le Prophète et Son Milieu, Les Oracles et Leur Transmission*, edited by Pierre Bogaert, 351–68. Leuven: Leuven University Press/Uitgeverij Peeters, 1997.

Long, Burke O. *1 Kings: With an Introduction to Historical Literature*. Forms of the Old Testament Literature. Vol. 9. Grand Rapids, MI: Eerdmans, 1984.

———. *2 Kings*. Forms of the Old Testament Literature. Vol. 10. Grand Rapids, MI: Eerdmans, 1991.

Malamat, Abraham. "The Twilight of Judah: In the Egyptian-Babylonian Maelstrom." In *Congress Volume: Edinburgh 1974*. Supplements to *Vetus Testamentum* 28, 123–45. Leiden: Brill, 1975.

Mann, Thomas W. *Deuteronomy*. Westminster Bible Companion. Louisville, KY: Westminster John Knox Press, 1995.

McCann, J. Clinton. *A Theological Introduction to the Book of Psalms: The Psalms as Torah*. Nashville, TN: Abingdon Press, 1993.

McCarter, P. Kyle. *I Samuel: A New Translation*. Anchor Bible, vol. 8. Garden City, NY: Doubleday, 1980.

McKenzie, Steven L. *1–2 Chronicles*. Abingdon Old Testament Commentaries. Nashville, TN: Abingdon Press, 2004.

———. "The Still Elusive Deuteronomists." In Nissinen, *Congress Volume: Helsinki 2010*, 401–8.

Mendenhall, George E. "The Monarchy." *Interpretation* 29, no. 2 (1975): 155–70.

Millar, William R. *Priesthood in Ancient Israel*. St. Louis, MO: Chalice Press, 2001.

Miller, James Maxwell, and John Haralson Hayes. *A History of Ancient Israel and Judah*. Louisville, KY: Westminster John Knox Press, 2006.

Miller, Patrick D. *The Religion of Ancient Israel*. Louisville, KY: Westminster John Knox Press, 2000.

Moore, Megan Bishop, and Brad E. Kelle. *Biblical History and Israel's Past: The Changing Study of the Bible and History*. Grand Rapids, MI: Eerdmans, 2011.

Moreno Garcia, Juan Carlos. "The Study of Ancient Egyptian Administration." In *Ancient Egyptian Administration*, edited by Juan Carlos Moreno Garcia, 1–17. Leiden/Boston: Brill, 2013.

Mykytiuk, Lawrence J. *Identifying Biblical Persons in Northwest Semitic Inscriptions of 1200–539 B.C.E.* Atlanta: Society of Biblical Literature, 2004.

Na'aman, Nadav. "The 'Discovered Book' and the Legitimation of Josiah's Reform." *Journal of Biblical Literature* 130, no. 1 (Spring 2011): 47–62.

———. "Israel, Edom and Egypt in the 10th Century B.C.E." *Tel Aviv* 19 (1992): 71–93.

———. "The King Leading Cult Reforms in His Kingdom: Josiah and Other Kings in the Ancient Near East." *Zeitschrift für Altorientalische und Biblische Rechtsgeschichte* 12 (2006): 131–68.

———. "The Kingdom of Judah under Josiah." *Tel Aviv* 18 (1991): 3–71.

Nihan, Christophe. "Rewriting Kingship in Samuel: 1 Samuel 8 and 12 and the Law of the King (Deuteronomy 17)." *Hebrew Bible and Ancient Israel* 2, no. 3 (2013): 315–50.

Nissinen, Martti, ed. *Congress Volume: Helsinki 2010*. Supplements to *Vetus Testamentum* 148. Leiden/Boston: Brill, 2012.

Olivier, J. P. J. "In Search of a Capital for the Northern Kingdom." *Journal of Northwest Semitic Languages* 11 (1983):117–32.

Pope, Jeremy. "Beyond the Broken Reed: Kushite Intervention and the Limits of L'histoire Événementielle." In *Sennacherib at the Gates of Jerusalem: Story, History and Historiography*, edited by Isaac Kalimi and Seth Richardson, 105–60. Culture and History of the Ancient Near East. Leider: Brill, 2014.

Porter, Anne. "From Kin to Class and Back Again! Changing Paradigms of the Early Polity." In *The Development of Pre-State Communities in the Ancient Near East: Studies in Honour of Edgar Peltenburg*, edited by Diane Bolger and Louise C. Maguire, 72–78. Oxford/Oakville, CT: Oxbow Books, 2010.

Pruin, Datmar. "What Is in a Text?—Searching for Jezebel." In Grabbe, *Ahab Agonistes*, 209–29.

Rainey, Anson F., and R. Steven Notley. *The Sacred Bridge: Carta's Atlas of the Biblical World*. Jerusalem: Carta, 2006.

Redford, Donald B. *Egypt, Canaan, and Israel in Ancient Times*. Princeton, NJ: Princeton University Press, 1992.

Ringgren, H. "Nûd̲." In *Theological Dictionary of the Old Testament*, edited by G. Johannes Botterweck, Helmer Ringgren, and Heinz-Josef Fabry, 9:271–72. Translated by David E. Green. Grand Rapids, MI: Eerdmans, 1999.

Rogerson, John. *Chronicle of the Old Testament Kings: The Reign-by-Reign Record of the Rulers of Ancient Israel*. London: Thames and Hudson, 1999.

———. *A Theology of the Old Testament: Cultural Memory, Communication, and Being Human*. Minneapolis: Fortress Press, 2010.

Römer, Thomas. "The Case of the Book of Kings." In *Deuteronomy–Kings as Emerging Authoritative Books: A Conversation*. Edited by Diana V. Edelman. Ancient Near East Monographs, 1. Online resource, 2014. https://www.sbl-site.org/assets/pdfs/pubs/9781589837409_OA.pdf.

———. *The So-Called Deuteronomistic History: A Sociological, Historical, and Literary Introduction*. London/New York: T & T Clark, 2005.

Rooke, Deborah W. *Zadok's Heirs: The Role and Development of the High Priesthood in Ancient Israel*. Oxford/New York: Oxford University Press, 2000.

Schenker, Adrian. "Jeroboam and the Division of the Kingdom in the Ancient Septuagint: LXX 3 Kingdoms 12.24 A-Z, MT 1 Kings 11–12; 14 and the Deuteronomistic History." In *Israel Constructs Its History: Deuteronomistic Historiography in Recent Research*. Edited by Albert de Pury, Thomas Römer, and Jean-Daniel Macchi. Sheffield, UK: Sheffield Academic Press, 2000.

Schipper, Bernd Ulrich. *Israel Und Ägypten in Der Königszeit: Die Kulturellen Kontakte Von Salomo Bis Zum Fall Jerusalems*. Orbis Biblicus Et Orientalis 170. Freiburg, Schweiz/Göttingen: Universitätsverlag/Vandenhoeck & Ruprecht, 1999.

Schneider, Tammi. "Ahab." In *New Interpreter's Dictionary of the Bible*, edited by Katharine D. Sakenfeld, 1:81–82. Nashville, TN: Abingdon Press, 2009.

Snijders, L. A. "Sûr." In *Theological Dictionary of the Old Testament*, edited by G. Johannes Botterweck, Helmer Ringgren, and Heinz-Josef Fabry, 10:199–207. Translated by David E. Green and Douglas W. Stott. Grand Rapids, MI: Eerdmans, 1999.

Spalinger, Anthony. "The Year 712 B.C. and Its Implications for Egyptian History." *Journal of the American Research Center in Egypt* 10 (1973): 95–101.

———. "Egypt and Babylonia: A Survey (c. 620 B.C.–550 B.C.)." *Studien zur Altägyptischen Kultur* 5 (1977): 228–44.

Spencer, Neal. "Priests and Temples: Pharaonic." In *A Companion to Ancient Egypt*. Edited by Alan Lloyd. Blackwell Companions to the Ancient World. Malden, MA: Wiley-Blackwell, 2010.

Spiegel, Gabrielle M. "History, Historicism, and the Social Logic of the Text in the Middle Ages." *Speculum* 65 (January 1990): 59–86.

Starbuck, Scott R. A. *Court Oracles in the Psalms: The So-Called Royal Psalms in Their Ancient Near Eastern Context*. Society of Biblical Literature Dissertation Series. Atlanta: Scholars Press, 1999.

Stavrakopoulou, Francesca. "The Blackballing of Manasseh." In Grabbe, *Good Kings and Bad Kings*, 248–63.

———. *King Manasseh and Child Sacrifice: Biblical Distortions of Historical Realities*. Beihefte Zur Zeitschrift FüR Die Alttestamentliche Wissenschaft. Berlin/New York: Walter de Gruyter, 2004.

Stern, Ephraim, and Amihay Mazar. *Archaeology of the Land of the Bible*. Vol. 2, *The Assyrian, Babylonian, and Persian Periods, 732–332 BCE*. Anchor Bible Reference Library. New York: Doubleday, 2001.

Stott, Katherine. "Finding the Lost Book of the Law: Re-Reading the Story of 'The Book of the Law' (Deuteronomy–2 Kings) in Light of Classical Literature." *Journal for the Study of the Old Testament* 30, no. 2 (December 2005): 153–69.

Sweeney, Marvin A. *I & II Kings: A Commentary*. The Old Testament Library. Louisville, KY: Westminster John Knox Press, 2007.

———. *King Josiah of Judah: The Lost Messiah of Israel*. Oxford/New York: Oxford University Press, 2001.

———. "King Manasseh of Judah and the Problem of Theodicy in the Deuteronomistic History." In Grabbe, *Good Kings and Bad Kings*, 264–78.

Suriano, Matthew J. "The Apology of Hazael: A Literary and Historical Analysis of the Tel Dan Inscription." *Journal of Near Eastern Studies* 66 (2007): 163–76.

———. *The Politics of Dead Kings: Dynastic Ancestors in the Book of Kings and Ancient Israel*. Forschungen Zum Alten Testament 2. Vol. 48. Tübingen: Mohr Siebeck, 2010.

Tappy, Ron E. "Samaria." In *New Interpreter's Dictionary of the Bible*, edited by Katharine D. Sakenfeld, 5:61–71. Nashville, TN: Abingdon Press, 2009.

Thomas, Benjamin D. *Hezekiah and the Compositional History of the Book of Kings*. Forschungen Zum Alten Testament 2. Tübingen: Mohr Siebeck, 2014.

Throntveit, Mark A. "The Relationship of Hezekiah to David and Solomon in the Books of Chronicles." In *The Chronicler as Theologian: Essays in Honor of Ralph W. Klein*. Edited by M. Patrick Graham, Steven L. McKenzie, and Gary N. Knoppers. The Library of Hebrew Bible/Old Testament Studies. London/New York: T & T Clark, 2003.

Tigay, Jeffrey H. *Deuteronomy = [Devarim]: The Traditional Hebrew Text with the New JPS Translation*. The JPS Torah Commentary. Philadelphia: Jewish Publication Society, 1996.

Van Winkle, D. W. "1 Kings XII 25–XIII 34: Jeroboam's Cultic Innovations and the Man of God from Judah." *Vetus Testamentum* 46, no. 1 (1996): 101–14.

Walsh, Jerome T. *1 Kings*. Berit Olam. Collegeville, MN: Liturgical Press, 1996.

———. *Ahab: The Construction of a King*. Interfaces. Collegeville, MN: Liturgical Press, 2006.

———. *Old Testament Narrative: A Guide to Interpretation*. Louisville, KY: Westminster John Knox Press, 2009.

———. "The Rab Šāqēh between Rhetoric and Redaction." *Journal of Biblical Literature* 130, no. 2 (Summer 2011): 263–79.

———. *Style and Structure in Biblical Hebrew Narrative*. Collegeville, MN: Liturgical Press, 2001.

Weinfeld, Moshe. *Deuteronomy 1–11: A New Translation with Introduction and Commentary*. The Anchor Bible, vol. 5. New York: Doubleday, 1991.

White, Hayden V. "The Historical Text as Literary Artifact." In *Tropics of Discourse: Essays in Cultural Criticism*. Baltimore: Johns Hopkins University Press, 1978.

Whitelam, Keith W. *The Just King: Monarchical Judicial Authority in Ancient Israel*. Journal for the Study of the Old Testament Supplement Series. Sheffield, UK: JSOT Press, 1979.

———. "King and Kingship." In *The Anchor Bible Dictionary*, edited by David Noel Freedman, 4:40–48. New York: Doubleday, 1992.

Williamson, H. G. M. "The Death of Josiah and the Continuing Development of the Deuteronomistic History." *Vetus Testamentum* 32, no. 2 (1982): 242–48.

Wilson, Gerald Henry. *The Editing of the Hebrew Psalter*. Dissertation Series / Society of Biblical Literature. Chico, CA: Scholars Press, 1985.

Yoffee, Norman. *Myths of the Archaic State: Evolution of the Earliest Cities, States and Civilizations*. Cambridge/New York: Cambridge University Press, 2005.

Young, Robb Andrew. *Hezekiah in History and Tradition*. Supplements to *Vetus Testamentum*. Leiden/Boston: Brill, 2012.

Zevit, Ziony. "The Textual and Social Embeddedness of Israelite Family Religion: Who Were the Players? Where Were the Stages?" In *Family and Household Religion: Toward a Synthesis of Old Testament Studies, Archaeology, Epigraphy, and Cultural Studies*, edited by Rainer Albertz, Beth Alpert Nakhai, Saul M. Olyan, and Rüdiger Schmitt, 287–314. Winona Lakes, IN: Eisenbrauns, 2014.

Scripture Index

Genesis
1:26-28	x–xi
2:13	38
13	69
23:19	69
32:22-32	43
35:1-2	43

Exodus
7:22	107

Numbers
12:1	100
32:41	46

Deuteronomy
3:14	46
12:3	131
16	6, 131
17	2, 4–7, 10, 12, 14, 31, 55, 110, 113, 144
17:9	113
17:12	113
17:14-20	6, 10, 18, 32–34, 96, 103, 141–42, 144–46, 150
17:15-20	131
17:20	108
18:15-22	150
20	6
34:10	103, 150

Joshua
5:10-12	127
8:30-35	131
17:13	42
21:21	46
22:13	46
22:30-32	46
24	2–4, 144
24:33	46

Judges
1:28	42
8:24-28	40
9	1
10:1-2	68
17–18	22, 40

1 Samuel
2:12	45
2:15-17	46
2:22-25	46
4:3	43
5:5	51
8	2, 4, 7, 10, 12, 14, 33, 144, 146
8:1-18	111
8:7-8	4
8:11-17	7
8:22	7
10:9	8
10:11	8
10:18-19	4
12	2, 4, 7–8, 10, 12, 14, 33, 144, 146
12:1	7
12:3	7
12:17	4
16:8	43
16:13	8
18:7	8
22:2	59
23:14-15	41
25	70
31:12	79

2 Samuel
4:5-7	52
6:2	43
6:6	112
7:8	52
7:10	109
11:1-13	45
12:14	49
12:31	42
20:24	42
20:26	46
24	45

1 Kings
1:40	86
3:1	112
4:8	46
5:27	42
9:6-9	110

162   David's Successors

11	45, 53, 55, 64	16:11-13	44	22:1-6	74
11–12	49	16:23	51	22:4	73
11:26	22	16:24	80	22:5-28	75
11:28	42–43	16:27	8	22:15	74
11:29-39	44, 57	16:29–22:40	62	22:29	75
11:30	23	16:30	64	22:30	30
11:31-39	52, 73	16:31	60	22:34-37	30
11:40	17, 42, 53–54, 116	16:33	64	22:37-38	75
		17:1	72, 76	22:39	24
11:41	55	17–19	77		
12–13	22	18	76–77	**2 Kings**	
12:2	41, 58	19:8	76	1:3	69
12:16	23, 49	20	64, 78–79	3:3	60
12:18	54	20:2	78	9	63
12:20	58	20:4	78	9:6-10	44
12:21	54	20:7	78	10:29	47, 60
12:25	51, 68	20:11	78	10:31	60
12:25–13:34	60	20:13	78	13:2	60
12:26-33	22, 40	20:21	78	13:11	60
12:28	47	20:22	78	14:24	60
13	50, 68–69, 78–79, 123–24, 126	20:28	78–79	15:5	60
		20:31	78	15:8	60
		20:32	78	15:24	60
13–14	64	20:35-36	79	15:28	60
13:2	44, 60, 123	20:40	78	15:31	8
13:6	111	20:41	78	17:4	100
13:24	79	20:42	79	17:7-20	110
13:32	68	20:43	78	17:22	60
13:37	79	21	24, 64, 66, 69–71, 73, 76–78	18	86
14	45, 73			18–20	10
14:2-18	53			18:2	84
14:7-18	44	21:1	69	18:3	84, 112, 123
14:8	54	21:7	70	18:4	25, 84, 94, 123
14:10	47	21:15	70	18:5	84
14:12	49	21:21-24	44	18:9-12	85
14:17	51, 68	21:7	27	18:13-37	86
14:25	17, 52, 80	21:17	72	18:14-16	83
14:25-28	128	21:20	78	18:19-25	101–2
15:6	59	21:23	72	18:22-24	101–2
15:21	51	21:27	78	18:21	98, 128
15:30	42	22	66, 73–74, 77–78	18:22	25, 86
16	65, 69			18:26	86
16:1-4	44, 66	22:1-4	75	19–20	87

Reference	Page	Reference	Page	Reference	Page
19:2	87	22:3	125	12:4	58
19:5-35	11	22:5	125	12:6	128
19:6	88	22:8	125	13	59–60
19:6-7	87	22:11	125, 141	13:1	58
19:9	17	22:14	125	13:7	59
19:9-37	115	22:19	111	13:20	59
19:15-20	87	23	135	17:2	112
19:16	88	23:2-3	127	18	65–66
19:9	97	23:3	125	19	66
19:20	87–88	23:4-15	132	19:1-3	66
19:21-34	88	23:4-20	25, 126	19:5-6	113
19:35	100	23:4	126	19:5	112
20:1	10, 89	23:5	126	19:7	66
20:1-3	11	23:10	107	19:8	66, 113
20:1-11	89	23:15	124	20:1-30	66
20:7	89	23:16-20	123	20:14	66
20:9	89	23:16	123	20:15-17	66
20:11	89	23:17	126	20:20	67
20:13	90	23:21	127	20:30	67
20:14	15	23:22	127	20:37	65
20:17-18	90	23:24	30	22	63
20:20	90	23:25	11, 28, 122, 139	24:30	125
21	106			28:3	107
21:3	25, 107, 151	23:29	127, 133	29	85–86
21:3-4	28	24:2	115	29:1	84
21:3-5	114	24:19	115	29:2	84, 123
21:6	117	25:6	115	29:3-4	85
21:7	28, 107	25:22	39	29:34	85
21:8	109			29:36	85
21:9	109	**1 Chronicles**		30:1-18	127
21:10-16	120	13:2	59	30:1	127
21:10	109	22:9	67	31:1	123
21:11-17	112	25:15	87	31:21	24, 83
21:11	116			32	86
21:13	109, 112, 114–15	**2 Chronicles**		32:1-19	86, 101
				32:1	112
21:17	112	9:29	55, 57	32:3	86
21:23	133	10	59	32:5	86, 112
22	115	10–13	58	32:6	86
22–23	11	10–36	67	32:10-19	88
22:1	123	10:2	58	32:11-12	86
22:2	123	10:15	57	32:18	88
22:3-8	124	12:3	116	32:20	87–88

32:21	96, 100	**Nehemiah**		132:5	114
32:24	89	9:10	39	132:11	38
32:24-26	89			132:13-14	114
32:25	89	**Psalms**		141	9
32:27-30	90	2	9, 32–34, 36–38, 113	144	39
32:31	90			144:1-10	34, 36
32:32	87	2:2	32	144:10-11	39
32:33	90	2:6	32		
33:2	115	2:6-9	37	**Ecclesiastes**	
33:3	105, 107, 112	2:7	38	1:1	12
33:7	107	18	34, 36		
33:10	110–11, 113	20	9, 34, 36	**Sirach**	
33:11	111, 115, 117	21	9, 34, 36	48:17	101
33:12-13	150	24	37	48:18	101
33:14-16	112	29	37	49:2	123
33:14	113–14, 117	45	9, 34, 36, 113		
33:16	114	46	37	**Isaiah**	
33:17	110, 116	47	7, 37	19	98
33:18	112	47:8	37	36–39	10
33:19	112	48	37	37:21-36	11
33:21	114	72	9, 34, 36	38:1-3	11
34:1	123	74	7		
34:2	123	89	7, 9, 36, 39	**Jeremiah**	
34:3	123	89:48-52	38	7	11, 139
34:4	123, 125	93	7, 37	7:18	116
34:5	123–24	93:1	37	8	11, 139
34:6	125, 132	95	37	11	11, 139
34:8	124	96	7, 9, 37	15:4	115–16
34:10	125	96:10	37	22:15	11, 139
34:15	125	97	7, 9, 37	26:21	12
34:19	125	97:1	37	27:1	11, 138
34:22	125	98	7, 9, 37	29:22	12
34:30-32	127	99	7, 9, 37	35:1	11, 138
34:32	125	99:1	37	36–45	128
35:18	127	101	9, 34, 36	36:31	39
35:20	128	110	36–38, 110	43	50
35:21	128	110:1	38	44:17-18	139
35:23	127, 134	110:2	38	44:17-25	116
35:24	127	110:3	38	46	11, 98, 139
35:25	128	110:4	38	46:3	134
		110:7	38	**Lamentations**	
Ezra		132	9, 34, 36–38, 114	2:8	112
4:4	39			4:20	12

Ezekiel		**Micah**		**Zephaniah**	
29–32	98	3:11	95	1:1	100
Hosea		**Nahum**			
12:2	100	3:8-10	97		

Author and Subject Index

Abijah, 50, 58–59, 66, 84
Abraham, 69, 135, 137, 156
Adoram, 42, 52, 54
adversaries, 12, 24, 72, 97
advisors, 39, 86–87
Ahab, vii, x, 12–13, 21, 23–24, 27, 30, 62–82, 91, 103–7, 109–10, 112, 115, 118, 143, 145, 147–49, 151, 154, 157–59
Ahaz, 92, 107, 126
Ahaziah, 13, 23, 65, 69
Ahijah, 23, 43, 45, 49, 52–53, 55, 57–59, 64, 73, 76
Ahlström, Gösta, 29, 75–76, 129, 152
alliance, 33, 53, 65–66, 70–71, 82, 85, 99, 113, 126–28, 135
altars, 25, 86, 114, 123–24, 126, 151
American, 21, 23, 28, 99, 153, 158
Ammon, 66, 111, 118
Amon, 118, 133, 137, 139
ANE, 4, 6, 32, 40, 42, 52–53, 115, 122, 130, 140, 158–59
aniconic, 43, 45, 47, 60, 147
annals, 8, 24, 96, 100
anointed, 7, 9, 12, 32–33, 37, 145
antisovereign, 106–7
apology, 40–41, 52–53, 60, 147
apostasy, 48, 60, 64, 104
Arad, 84, 95, 131, 148
archaeology, 13, 59, 62, 65, 80–82, 94, 113, 117–18, 129, 134, 136, 142, 147, 151, 153–54, 159–60
archaic, 21, 24–25, 31, 152–53, 160

archaism, 29, 129, 154
Asher, 13, 118, 153
Asherah, 28, 66, 77–78, 81, 84, 105, 107–8, 123, 126, 131
Assmann, Jan, 49–50, 152
Assyria, 2, 13, 26, 30, 72, 75, 83, 86–87, 96–100, 102, 111, 115, 118, 121, 127, 140, 149
Assyrian, 11, 13, 25, 28, 62, 68, 80–83, 88, 95, 97–100, 111, 115, 121–22, 134, 138, 141, 145, 147, 149, 152–53, 159
attendants, 8, 12, 52, 126, 137
attitudes, 15, 34, 36, 68, 146
Aubin, Henry, 98, 100, 152

Baal, 48, 65, 71, 76–78, 81, 105, 107, 151
Baasha, 51, 66, 68, 77
Babylon, 88, 90, 109, 111, 115, 117, 140, 153
Babylonia, 13, 111, 136, 158
Babylonian, 97, 132, 134, 136–37, 141, 156, 159
Bathsheba, 45, 55, 71
Beersheba, 84, 95, 131, 148
Bethel, 22, 26, 40, 43, 45–49, 51, 60, 64–65, 68, 81, 93, 124, 136
boundaries, 15, 36
Bronze Age, 2, 19, 47–48, 152
builder, 13, 85–86, 90, 94, 101, 114, 149–50
bull, 47–48, 59, 64

campaign, 28, 88, 117, 136
Canaan, 2, 135, 157
Canaanite, 42, 65, 70
capital cities, 23–24, 26, 28, 41, 43, 50–51, 53, 60–61, 65, 68–69, 72, 80, 96, 98, 145–46, 157
centralization, 19–20, 25–27, 30, 39, 81–82, 84, 92, 94–96, 116, 136, 147, 149–50, 153
Chronicler, 16, 24, 26–27, 54–60, 63, 65–67, 77, 81–82, 85–87, 89–90, 96, 101, 105, 107–9, 112, 114–15, 117, 120–21, 125–28, 141–43, 146, 148–49, 152, 155, 159
Chronicles, x, 1, 5–6, 9–11, 15–16, 18, 31, 33–34, 45, 49, 54–60, 63–67, 77, 83–95, 100–117, 119–32, 134, 136–44, 146–53, 155–56, 159
cities, 21, 43, 50–51, 60–61, 63, 94, 112–13, 124, 132, 149, 160
complexity, 15, 21, 23, 27, 46, 50, 56
concept, x, 42, 53, 82, 131, 143, 148
conceptualization, 5, 9–10, 34, 50
Constitution, 2, 20, 35, 153–54
context, x, 32, 34, 41, 48, 52, 69, 99, 115, 148, 151
contexts, 41, 48, 143
conversion, x, 78, 104, 140, 150
corvée, 23, 41–43
countries, x, 144, 146
covenant, 2, 11, 38, 43, 67, 108, 125, 127, 131, 134, 139, 155
creation, 23, 47, 73, 85, 93–94, 153
cult, 11, 25, 30, 40, 43, 48, 81, 93, 95–96, 101, 108, 126, 129–30, 132, 136, 139–40, 148, 154, 156–57
cultic, 22, 33–34, 40, 48, 51, 84, 96, 136, 139
cultural, 14, 36, 41, 44, 50, 91, 113, 152, 158, 160

culture, 2–3, 13, 21, 29, 50, 57, 65, 99, 103, 120, 129, 131–32, 136, 142, 145, 154, 157

Damascus, 71, 75, 82
Dan, 22, 26, 40, 43, 45–46, 49, 51–52, 60, 64–65, 68, 80–81, 93, 159
Daniel, 27, 54, 76, 153, 158
David, x, 2–10, 12, 14, 16, 18, 20, 22–24, 26–28, 30, 32–34, 36, 38–56, 58–62, 64, 66–70, 72–74, 76, 78, 80, 82, 84, 86, 88, 90, 92, 94, 96, 98, 100, 102, 104–10, 112, 114, 116, 118, 120, 124, 126, 128, 130–32, 134, 136, 138–40, 142–48, 150, 152, 154–60
Deborah, 47, 70, 158
decentralization, 19–20, 22–23, 27, 39
deity, 65, 82, 107, 114, 146, 151
democracies, 1–2, 74
Deuteronomistic, 3–5, 8–9, 14, 16, 25–30, 32, 40, 44–45, 48–51, 54–55, 59, 61, 64, 81, 96, 101–2, 104–6, 108–9, 115, 118, 121, 124, 126–27, 134, 139, 141, 143, 146–49, 151, 154–56, 158–60
Deuteronomy, 2, 4–10, 12–14, 18, 31–34, 55, 81, 83, 95–96, 103, 105, 108, 110–11, 113, 130–31, 139, 141–42, 144–46, 149–50, 154, 156–59
DH, 3–5, 11–12, 16, 25–28, 30, 44, 46, 50, 54–56, 81–82, 102, 106, 110, 121, 125, 128, 139–43, 145–46, 148–49, 151
Dietrich, Walter, 22, 27, 44, 65, 104, 153–54, 158
disparity, 77, 84, 95, 119, 132
divine, x, 7, 28, 35, 52, 67, 87
domestic, 52–53, 71, 138
dominant, 4, 26, 40, 47, 75, 77, 80, 89–90, 95, 113–14, 133, 144

dynasty, 2, 17, 54, 62–63, 65, 67–71, 77, 80–81, 99, 133–34, 137, 147, 154

economic, 20, 24–26, 28, 99, 110
Edelman, Diana, 8, 29, 75, 83, 92, 95, 136, 152–53, 158
Egypt, 6, 10–11, 13–14, 17, 19–20, 25, 28, 35–36, 39, 42, 50, 53–54, 58, 92–93, 96–100, 102, 111, 116–17, 128, 130, 133–42, 145–46, 149, 152, 156–58
Elijah, 24, 44, 63, 67, 70–73, 75–78, 87, 148
Elisha, 71–72, 75–76, 87
elite, 28–29, 43, 100, 129, 154
empire, 2, 23, 88, 117–18, 136, 153
Endres, John 55, 120, 153
enemies, 13, 37–39, 49–50, 71, 77, 113, 117, 128, 140, 148
enthronement, 7, 35–38, 146
envoys, 90, 97, 100–102
Ephraim, 51, 100, 124, 132, 134, 159
epigraphic, 29, 122, 138
evil, 64–65, 73, 76–77, 95, 103–4, 106, 108, 112, 115, 126, 149, 151
exile, 41, 44, 50, 88, 109, 116, 118, 132, 139, 153–54
Exodus, 47, 50, 107
Ezekiel, 10, 98, 128
Ezra, 39, 116–17

famous, 24–25, 49, 63, 90, 96
festival, 35–38, 85, 146
Finkelstein, Israel, 13, 80–81, 118, 153
foreign, 6, 30–31, 39, 42, 53–54, 60, 65, 69–70, 72, 81–82, 98, 105–6, 110, 112–14, 116–18, 133, 138, 144, 148
Foucault, Michel, 5, 14

genealogies, 92–93

Genesis, x–xi, 37–38, 51, 69
Gilead, 72, 75–76, 79
goddesses, 48, 107, 155
gods, 47–48, 81, 94, 105, 110, 112, 148, 155
governance, 39, 66, 68–71, 74, 76, 78, 82
Grabbe, Lester, 26–28, 71, 73, 80–81, 116, 118, 154–55, 157–59
Greek, 40, 47, 91, 100, 120, 134, 147
Greeks, 93, 134, 138

Hadad, 42, 75, 128
Halpern, Baruch, 2, 29, 35, 43, 45, 128–29, 154
Hebrew, 4, 6, 12, 15, 26, 32–33, 40, 47, 49, 51, 64, 69, 71, 92, 104, 106, 110–11, 116, 133–34, 138, 147, 154–55, 157, 159–60
Hebron, 45, 50, 69, 145
Hens-Piazza, Gina, 51, 141, 154
hermeneutic, x, 9, 141
hero, 12, 24–25, 28, 40, 60, 75, 86, 96, 120, 144–45
Hezekiah, vii, x, 3, 10–11, 13, 21, 24–31, 55, 72, 78, 83–99, 101–3, 105–6, 112, 114–16, 118, 121–23, 126–28, 131–32, 136, 140–43, 148–51, 153, 159–60
Hilkiah, 30, 125–26
historian, 3, 29, 56, 76, 86, 91–93, 100, 102, 134, 139
historical, 3, 12, 15–16, 22, 26–30, 35, 46, 52, 56–57, 60, 62–63, 65, 72–75, 85–86, 91–93, 100, 104, 108, 115, 118–22, 132–34, 138, 141–42
historiography, 3, 8, 17, 29, 54, 83, 91–92, 95, 99, 129, 141, 155, 157–58
holiness, 32, 63, 144
Huldah, 76, 125, 140
Hutton, Jeremy 44, 48, 99, 154, 157

Author and Subject Index   169

ideology, 2, 4, 12–13, 16, 24, 29, 54, 56, 66–67, 92, 95, 103–6, 108, 112, 118–19, 123, 132, 151
idolatry, 28, 47, 59, 61, 67, 70, 72–73, 81, 94, 106–7, 109, 114, 116, 123, 126, 129, 147
indigenous, 2–3, 17, 45, 100
inhabitants, 67, 89–90, 109–10, 125
inscription, 29, 52, 72, 82, 100, 122, 159
institution, xi, 2, 6, 9–10, 12–13, 19, 23, 32–34, 42, 44, 67, 112–13, 150
interpretation, 1–2, 5, 15, 33, 35, 47, 50, 86, 92, 113, 119, 154, 156, 159
Isaac, 56, 99, 155, 157
Isaiah, 5, 10–12, 76, 83, 86–90, 94–96, 98, 101–2, 106, 115, 128, 140, 149–50
Israel, ix–xi, 2–6, 8–14, 17–24, 26–29, 32–37, 41, 43, 45, 47–51, 53–54, 58–59, 62, 65, 68–70, 72–74, 76–82, 85, 88, 91–95, 97–100, 104, 106, 109–13, 116–18, 120, 122, 124, 128, 131–32, 134–39, 142–48, 150, 152–60
Israelites, 2, 4, 7, 10–11, 34, 42, 51, 53, 56, 65, 69–72, 75–77, 80, 84, 113, 125, 139, 149 155–56, 160

Japhet, Sara, 57, 66, 85, 155
Jebusite, 45–46, 93
Jehoiakim, 11–12, 134, 139
Jehoshaphat, 3, 63, 65–67, 73–75, 148
Jehu, 63, 66, 68, 71, 80, 105
Jeremiah, 5, 10–12, 30–31, 39, 50, 98, 104, 107, 115–16, 128, 134, 138–40, 142
Jeroboam, vii, x, 13, 21–23, 40–55, 57–62, 64–65, 68, 72–73, 75–79, 81, 91–93, 97, 104–6, 111, 118, 121, 124, 126, 131, 143, 146–48, 151, 154–56, 158–59
Jerusalem, 2–3, 11–14, 22, 25–28, 35, 37–39, 43, 45–48, 51, 53, 58, 60, 67, 69, 81–82, 84, 88–90, 93–96, 98–101, 106–10, 112–18, 122, 124, 126, 128–30, 134, 136–37, 140–41, 143–45, 148–50, 152, 157
Jewish, 6, 93, 132, 136, 150, 156, 159
Jezebel, vii, 62–63, 65, 69–72, 76, 80, 157
Jezreel, 69–70, 72, 98, 137
Joseph, Alison, 40, 64, 105, 107–8, 123–24, 131, 155
Joshua, 2–4, 42, 44, 51, 127, 131, 144
Josiah, vii, x, 6, 8, 11, 13, 21, 24–25, 27–31, 44, 50, 60, 65, 72, 75, 78, 83–84, 92, 96, 104–7, 111, 118, 121–43, 148–52, 154–57, 159–60
Judah, ix–x, 8, 11–13, 19–31, 34–37, 58–60, 66, 68–69, 73–74, 76, 82, 84, 86, 90–91, 94–98, 109–12, 114–18, 121, 124, 126, 129, 132–34, 136–39, 141–42, 147–48, 150, 153–54, 156–57, 159
Judean, 2, 26, 29, 53–54, 120, 138, 141, 148

Kalimi, Isaac, 56–57, 99, 155, 157
kingdom, 4, 13, 17, 19, 22–23, 26–27, 30–31, 34, 40, 46–48, 51, 54, 58–59, 66, 68–69, 80–82, 85, 95, 97–100, 111, 116–17, 124, 130, 132–34, 136, 140, 143, 147
Kings, the book of, 8, 11, 17, 22–25, 28, 30, 39–40, 42–44, 46–47, 49, 51–52, 54–55, 60, 62, 64–66, 68, 73, 76, 78–80, 83–90, 100–101, 107, 114–15, 117, 123–27, 139, 141, 151

kingship, x–xi, 1, 3–10, 12–14, 12–21, 23, 25, 27, 29, 31–35, 37–40, 42, 52–53, 57–60, 62–64, 67–68, 70, 83, 89, 93, 105, 107–8, 110–11, 113–14, 122, 141, 143–46, 150–51
kinship, 20–21, 29, 129, 154
Klein, Ralph, 55, 65, 67, 85, 155, 159
Knauf, Ernst, 26, 116, 155
Knoppers, Gary, 47, 67, 104, 108, 155, 159
Kraus, Hans, 9–10, 36, 38, 155
Kushite, 99–101, 133, 157

Lachish, 84, 96, 131, 148
Lamentations, 5, 12, 112, 128
Lasine, Stuart, 106–7, 111, 155
leader, ix, 3, 8, 25, 41–42, 51, 58, 72–73, 76, 95, 99, 106, 149
leadership, 19, 22, 26, 43, 51–52, 64, 70–71, 73, 87, 119, 144, 149, 151
legitimacy, 25, 28, 47, 69, 110, 112, 130, 152
Leuchter, Mark, 48, 57, 156
Levant, 19, 26, 53, 75, 80, 88, 91, 99–100, 102, 118, 135, 152–53
Levinson, Bernard, 4–6, 105, 156
Levites, 22, 43, 46–47, 60, 66, 85, 125, 127
literary, 1, 14–16, 26, 40–41, 50, 52, 56–57, 62, 72–73, 75, 91, 102, 106, 129, 132, 142, 151
Liverani, Mario, 23–24, 29, 129, 136, 156
Lohfink, Norbert, 11, 139–40, 156
loyalty, 76, 79, 97
LXX, 48–50, 54, 158

Malamat, Abraham, 135, 137–39, 156
Manasseh, vii, x, 6, 9, 13, 25–30, 46, 72, 77, 83, 85, 93, 103–7, 109–22, 124, 126, 132–33, 141, 143, 148–51, 155, 158–59
McKenzie, Steven, 55–56, 58, 67, 87, 139–40, 152, 155–57, 159
Mediterranean, 17, 93, 120, 134, 136, 138
Megiddo, 75, 80, 135, 137
Megilloth, 5, 12
memories, 14, 41, 44
Mendenhall, George, 2–3, 34–35, 156
mercenary, 53–54, 134, 138, 147
Mesopotamia, 6, 10, 17, 21, 25, 28, 31, 35–36, 39, 91, 97, 111, 145, 149, 152
Messiah, 28, 45, 132, 154, 159
Micaiah ben Imlah, 63, 66–67, 73–78, 87, 147
Moab, 66, 73, 111, 118, 147
monarchy, 2–3, 6, 17, 21–23, 27, 32, 34–35, 41, 55, 65, 95, 105, 123–24, 128, 131
Moses, 2–3, 28, 40, 46, 70, 76, 84, 100, 103, 131, 144, 148, 150, 152

Na'aman, Nadav, 30, 129–30, 140, 157
Naboth, 24, 63, 66, 70–72, 74, 77
narrative, 3, 15–16, 18–19, 27–28, 31, 36, 39–41, 48–49, 50, 58, 60, 64–65, 72–73, 76, 79, 84, 90–92, 94, 101, 103–5, 107–10, 112, 114, 119–20, 123, 126, 130–31, 141–42, 145, 150–51
narratives, 15–16, 19, 39, 41, 79, 84, 91–92, 103, 105, 107–9, 112, 119–20, 130
narrator, 42, 53, 64–65, 68–70, 74–75, 78–79, 84, 104, 106
Nathan, 45, 49, 52, 55, 72
nations, xi, 4, 10, 12, 29, 36–37, 104, 129, 145–46, 154–55
Necho, 127–28, 133–34, 136–38

Author and Subject Index   171

Nehemiah, 39, 116–17
Nehushtan, 25, 84, 94
Nihan, Christophe, 4, 7, 110, 157
Norbert, 11, 139–40, 156
Nubian, 17, 97, 149

Omri, vii, 13, 23, 27, 53, 62, 65, 68–69, 71, 73, 80–81, 118, 145, 147, 154
Omride, 13, 23–24, 27, 51, 62–63, 65, 69–71, 77, 80–81, 145, 153
oracle, 11, 32–33, 37–38, 56, 78, 87–90, 98, 112, 125, 128, 139, 140, 156, 158

palace, 23, 69, 80, 90, 93, 153
Palestine, 29–30, 75–76, 134, 136, 141, 152
Passover, 26, 83, 85, 127, 131–32, 134, 149, 151
Penuel, 43, 51, 68
Persian, 97, 117, 134, 159
Pharaoh, 39, 49–50, 52, 54, 100, 107, 127–28
Philistine, 52–53, 99
Phoenician(s), 70–71, 82
piety, 1, 31, 82, 84, 96, 130, 150
Poetics, 5, 40, 64, 105, 113, 119, 124, 140, 154–56
polities, 13, 19–27, 30–31, 39, 97, 157
postexilic, 29, 34, 106, 120
prayer, 6, 67, 87, 89, 94, 112
predecessors, 1–2, 28, 52, 62, 71, 85, 129, 146
preexilic, 33, 105–6
priests, 13, 30, 41, 45–47, 66, 85, 93, 101, 123, 125–26, 129
privilege, 15, 40, 49, 119, 142
propaganda, x, 11, 47–48, 98, 139–40
prophet, 5, 7–8, 10–11, 13, 16, 23, 31, 39, 45, 53, 55–57, 58–59, 63–64, 66–67, 71–74, 76–79, 81–83, 85–87, 89–90, 94, 96, 101, 103–4, 106–7, 109, 116, 119–20, 125–28, 140, 145–46, 149–51
prosperity, 26, 81, 103, 117–18, 150
psalms, iv, x, 1–3, 5–7, 9–10, 13–14, 17–18, 31–39, 55, 57, 60, 67, 82, 113–14, 119–21, 131, 143–44, 146, 148, 150–51, 153–56, 158
Psammetichus, 133–34, 136–38

Rabshakeh, 25, 86–87, 101–2, 152
rebellion, 53, 58–59, 99–100, 118, 147
reconceptualization, 4, 6–8, 12, 14, 17, 32, 34, 105, 107–8, 131, 143–45, 151, 156
recontextualization, 32, 34, 107, 143–44, 151
redaction, 16, 32, 44, 49, 56, 102, 106, 141
Redford, Donald, 99, 135, 137, 157
reforms, 11, 25, 28–30, 43, 81, 83–84, 96, 101, 106, 122–27, 129–41, 149
refuge, 50, 99–100, 109, 128, 144
Rehoboam, 42, 49, 52–54, 58–59, 64, 66–68, 76, 78, 128
reinscribing, 27, 76, 153
religious, 2, 20, 22, 25–28, 35, 41, 43, 45–48, 51, 65, 76–78, 79, 81, 83–87, 95–96, 103–4, 110, 116, 122, 126, 134, 136–37, 139–41
repentance, 67, 77, 103, 115, 120, 148–49, 151
resources, 21, 24, 46, 68, 74, 95, 138
restoration, 67, 84–85, 94, 120–21, 132, 148, 151
righteous, 11, 84–85, 123–24, 139
Ringgren, Helmer, 107–9, 152, 157–58
rituals, ix, 34, 36–37, 146
Rogerson, John 14, 41, 44, 62, 158

172 *David's Successors*

roles, 13, 16, 67, 70, 87, 98, 101, 105, 110, 125
Römer, Thomas, 8, 26–27, 54, 83, 158
royal, x, 2–3, 5, 11, 17–18, 23–24, 27, 32–39, 52, 54–55, 57, 60, 67, 80, 82, 93, 108, 113, 121, 131, 143–44, 146, 148, 150
ruler, 6, 9, 11, 13, 62, 81–83, 113–14, 133, 139, 141, 149

sacral, 4–9, 12, 31, 33, 55, 120
sacred, 10, 13–14, 95, 118–19, 137, 153–54, 157
Saite, 133, 135, 137
salvation, 11, 88, 140
Samaria, 23–27, 53, 65, 68–69, 72, 78, 80, 82, 93–94, 98, 115, 118, 145, 149, 153, 159
sanctuaries, 22, 26, 45–48, 51, 68, 95, 148
Saul, 4–6, 8, 41, 43, 45, 52–54, 62, 79, 154
scapegoat, 71, 106–7, 155
Scripture, 11, 14, 23, 32
secular, 6–7, 9, 23
Semitic, 2, 29, 35, 51, 104, 154–55, 157
Sennacherib, 24, 86–88, 97, 99–102, 140, 150, 157
servants, 88–89, 109, 133
Shechem, 43, 46, 51, 58, 60, 64, 68, 145
Shiloh, 43, 45–47, 51, 60–61
Shishak, 17, 52, 80, 116, 128
shrines, 22, 43, 45–47, 59, 84, 86, 94–95, 105, 110, 112, 114, 116, 123–24
Sirach, x, 101–2, 122–23, 151
societies, 2–3, 18, 20, 23–24, 145
sociological, 26, 40–42
soldiers, 82, 100, 111
Solomon, x, 2, 12, 22–23, 27–28, 42, 44–46, 49, 53–56, 62, 65, 67, 72, 76, 104–5, 112, 114, 128, 143, 147, 155, 159
sons, 7, 38, 45–46, 71, 90, 111, 133
sovereign, 4, 35, 38
Spalinger, Anthony, 99, 135–38, 158
speeches, ix, 56, 59, 66, 87, 101, 106
spiritual, 38, 120, 149
Starbuck, Scott, 32–34, 158
status, 4–5, 9, 22, 24, 43, 46, 89–90, 93, 118, 144, 149
Stavrakopoulou, Francesca, 27, 104, 115, 118–19, 158
Stott, Katherine, 108, 129–30, 158–59
strength, 11, 25, 41, 53, 77, 84
success, xi, 27, 31, 66, 78, 113, 118, 133, 138
successful, 27, 73, 103, 113, 118, 147
succession, 2, 11, 52, 93, 97, 133
superpowers, 35, 39, 97, 145
Sweeney, Marvin, 10, 28, 70, 94, 100, 118, 132, 159
symbol, 20, 23, 47, 53, 64–65, 82, 95, 119, 148, 151
Syria, 74, 75, 136
systems, 20–21, 24

Taharqo/Tirhakah, 17, 97–98, 100–101
temple, 11, 23, 28–29, 41, 45, 53, 55, 65, 80, 83–85, 91, 93–94, 96, 103, 114, 123–26, 129, 132, 139
theodicy, 11, 115, 118, 120, 141, 148
theological, 9–10, 31–32, 35, 40, 54, 57, 94, 103, 107–9, 122, 129, 133, 135
theology, 9, 13–14, 16, 32, 35–36, 38, 41, 44, 114, 118–19, 130, 132, 141, 150–51
Tirzah, 43, 51, 68, 93
Torah, 4, 6, 11, 28, 32, 50, 105, 108, 110, 123, 125–26, 136, 139, 144, 156, 159

tradition, 2, 20–21, 24–25, 27, 30–31, 43–45, 48, 60–61, 69, 73, 75–76, 97, 106, 111, 131, 114, 147, 150
Transjordanian, 43–44, 66, 154
translation, 6–7, 11, 23, 28, 32, 79, 153, 156, 159
tribal, 6, 20–22, 24, 26–27, 72, 116, 145
tribes, 20, 22, 26–28, 43, 54, 72
tunnel, 26, 90, 96, 102, 122, 131, 149–50

unity, 21, 31, 43, 55, 86
utopian, 58, 105–6, 144

valor, 41, 43–44, 52, 60, 75
victory, 39, 66, 78, 100
vision(s), x, 6–7, 10, 35, 55, 64, 107, 117, 120, 151
vital, 14, 17, 53, 71, 90, 113, 120

women, 45, 69–71

words, 15, 19, 23, 30, 32–33, 55, 57, 66, 77, 88, 112, 125
worship, 10, 25, 47–48, 51, 55, 57, 59, 64, 77, 81–82, 84–86, 106, 116, 120, 134, 148, 150–51
writer, 13, 16, 18, 22, 49, 92–93, 95, 105, 109, 117, 126–27, 129, 135–36, 140, 144, 148
writings, 36, 39, 133, 140

Yahweh, 4, 7, 9, 29, 33, 37, 77, 86–89, 109–11, 113–14, 123, 126, 128, 136, 149
Yahwistic, 76, 81–82, 148
YHWH, 2, 28, 30, 50, 70, 79
Yoffee, Norman, 21, 24–25, 28, 31, 152, 160
Young, Robb Andrew, 24–25, 97, 131, 160

Zadok, 45–47, 158
Zechariah, 84, 134
Zedekiah, 11–12, 115, 138
Zephaniah, 100, 126, 134

www.ingramcontent.com/pod-product-compliance
Lightning Source LLC
Chambersburg PA
CBHW051945290426
44110CB00015B/2120